Greece
&
Turkey

Greece
&
Turkey

Economic and Geopolitical Perspectives

Nicholas V. Gianaris

New York
Westport, Connecticut
London

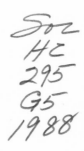

Library of Congress Cataloging-in-Publication Data

Gianaris, Nicholas V.
    Greece and Turkey : economic and geopolitical perspectives /
Nicholas V. Gianaris.
        p.   cm.
    Bibliography: p.
    Includes index.
    ISBN 0–275–93025–4 (alk. paper)
    1. Greece—Economic conditions—1974– 2. Turkey—Economic
conditions—1960–   3. Greece—Foreign economic relations.
4. Turkey—Foreign economic relations.   I. Title.

HC295.G5   1988
330.9495′076—dc19   88–2396

Library of Congress Catalog Card Number: 88–2396
ISBN: 0–275–93025–4

First published in 1988

Praeger Publishers, One Madison Avenue, New York, NY 10010
A division of Greenwood Press, Inc.

Printed in the United States of America

The paper used in this book complies with the Permanent
Paper Standard issued by the National Information Standards
Organization (Z39.48–1984).

10   9   8   7   6   5   4   3   2   1

To Magda, Bill, and Mike

Contents

Tables and Illustrations

TABLES

ILLUSTRATIONS

Preface

Greece and Turkey are located at the crossroads of Europe, Africa, and Asia and constitute a natural bridge between eastern Europe and the Middle East. For political, military, and nationalistic reasons, the two countries have been frequently in conflict in the past and still view each other with suspicion. However, from an economic point of view, good relations between these two neighboring countries could increase trade and investments, reduce military spending in favor of domestic development, and improve sociocultural conditions. There is need for closer economic and cultural cooperation between them. It should be recognized, though, that there are many deep-seated ethnic, political, and social elements involved that make it impossible to concentrate on economic analysis without regard to the noneconomic issues. It takes the courage and wisdom of men like Eleutherios Venizelos and Kemal Ataturk, the 1930s leaders of Greece and Turkey, respectively, to subdue the differences and bring peace and friendship to these two nations.

The main problems facing Greece and Turkey now are: inflation, unemployment, urban concentration, a bureaucratic public sector, large budget and trade deficits, and huge foreign debts. To reduce unemployment, increase productivity, suppress inflation, improve income distribution, and mitigate budget and foreign trade deficits, fiscal and monetary tools as well as investment incentives are currently urged by both nations.

To improve economic efficiency, both nations have introduced or are considering the introduction of employee sharing in enterprise revenue and decision making. Although they need rapid industrialization, the services and housing sectors have been given more importance, to the neglect of manufacturing and, to some extent, agricultural sectors. Transportation, a key sector in the region, deserves high priority so that commodities can be easily transferred to the marketplaces of Europe and the Middle East. Intraregional and international tourism is expected to play its traditional beneficial role in both countries, particularly in the Aegean Islands of Greece and the seashores of Turkey.

The antiquated and complicated tax system of these two nations needs substantial change and reform not only for providing government revenue but also for distributional and countercyclical reasons. Comparatively speaking, it is expected that higher proportions of income will be taxed by the government and a shift from indirect to direct taxes will occur in the foreseeable future. Moreover, the present gradual transfer of inefficient public enterprises to the private sector will enhance the government budgets and reduce their deficits, the main causes of inflation and external borrowing.

Although trade between these countries is presently limited, a closer cooperation on economic and political matters would increase transactions in supplementary products and services, especially in transportation and tourism. Greece's membership in the European Economic Community (EEC) provides good opportunities for expansion of Turkey's trade to the Common Market of Europe. This membership is expected to be a prelude to the advancement of Turkey from an associated to a full member of the Community. In addition to long-term economic advantages, democratic institutions of both countries will be advanced as a result.

Greece and Turkey, as less economically developed and more agriculturally based countries, will face problems of adjustment to the EEC conditions for some years to come but, in the long run, investment, tourism, trade, financial, and other services would improve.

The purpose of this book is to examine the main characteristics of the economies of Greece and Turkey and to review developmental trends toward closer cooperation between them, as well as with other groups of countries, particularly the EEC, the other neighboring Balkan nations, and CMEA (Council for Mutual Economic Aid) or COMECON nations. The comparative analysis of these two countries with different economic structures and sociocultural conditions remains a challenge to researchers and students of economic policy and international relations.

After an overview in chapter 1, a brief historical review is presented in chapters 2 and 3 and an analysis of economic and sociopolitical conditions is made. Emphasis is given to the recent economic and sociopolitical life of the peoples in these two nations with a hope for cooperation in the future. To make this study clearer and more practical, ample statistical data are presented in tabular and graphical forms. Chapters 4, 5, 6, and 7 deal with natural and human resources and their productivity, the sectoral and regional development, and related fiscal and monetary policies. Chapters 8, 9, and 10 examine the foreign sector, from the viewpoint of trade and investment, relations with the EEC and other countries, and future expectations for economic cooperation.

I would like to express my gratitude to Professors Ernest Block, George Giannaris, George Karatza, Anna Mannion, James Martin, William McGrew, Victoria Litson, Gus Papoulia, Adamandia Polis, Harry Psomiades, John Roche, Dominick Salvatore, John Shine, and Amin Zeiwel for their stimulating comments. My thanks to Nicholas Notias, Mike Stratis, Mario Karonis, and Josephine Leyton for their assistance and typing services.

Greece

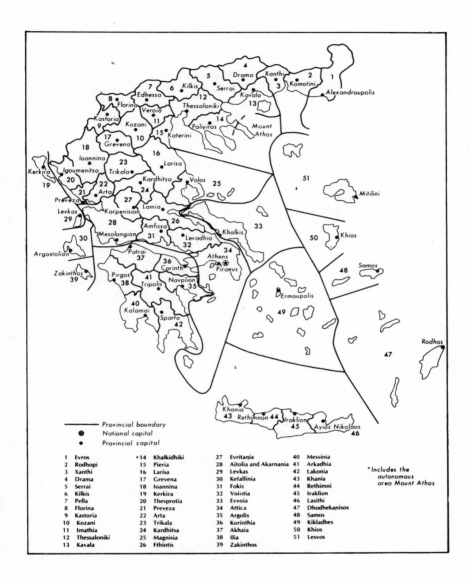

	Provincial boundary					
	National capital					
	Provincial capital					

1	Evros	•14	Khalkidhiki	27	Evritania	40	Messinia
2	Rodhopi	15	Pieria	28	Aitolia and Akarnania	41	Arkadhia
3	Xanthi	16	Larisa	29	Levkas	42	Lakonia
4	Drama	17	Grevena	30	Kefallinia	43	Khania
5	Serrai	18	Ioannina	31	Fokis	44	Rethimni
6	Kilkis	19	Kerkira	32	Voiotia	45	Iraklion
7	Pella	20	Thesprotia	33	Evvoia	46	Lasithi
8	Florina	21	Preveza	34	Attica	47	Dhodhekanisos
9	Kastoria	22	Arta	35	Argolis	48	Samos
10	Kozani	23	Trikala	36	Korinthia	49	Kikladhes
11	Imathia	24	Kardhitsa	37	Akhaia	50	Khios
12	Thessaloniki	25	Magnisia	38	Ilia	51	Lesvos
13	Kavala	26	Fthiotis	39	Zakinthos		

*Includes the
autonomous
area Mount Athos

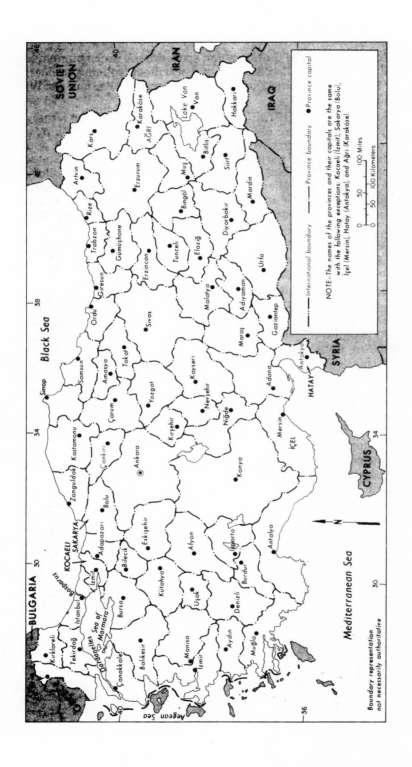

Turkey

Reprinted by permission from Richard F. Nyrop, ed., *Turkey: A Country Study*, Third Edition, Washington, D.C.:
The American University, 1980, p. xviii.

Greece
&
Turkey

I

BACKGROUND

Part I emphasizes the importance of historical events in shaping socioeconomic relations between the peoples of Greece and Turkey. After a brief review of the turbulent history of these two neighboring (and frequently in conflict) nations, concentration is placed on trends of posible economic and political cooperation.

From an economic and geographical point of view, the Achaean, the Dorian, the Thracian, and the Ionian Hellenic races played a vital role in the historical developments of Greece and Western Turkey, while the Hittites, the Hurrians, the Armenians, and the Kurds affected Eastern Asia Minor, in ancient times. During the Byzantine and Ottoman periods, both Greece and Anatolia remained, more or less, feudalistic without impressive cultural and economic achievements. Constantinople (Istanbul), though, and, to a lesser extent, Salonika became major trade and financial centers, facilitating transactions between Europe, Asia, and Africa. The strategic position of the area has attracted the involvement of the great powers in the economic and sociopolitical affairs of Greece and Turkey.

Since the liberation of Greece from the Turks and during the turbulent years between World Wars I and II and thereafter, socioeconomic and political relations between the two nations remained at a very low level, mainly because of the belligerent conditions that prevailed in the area. In the very recent history serious hatred and conflicts emanated from the expansionary policies of Turkey over Cyprus and the Aegean Sea.

Admittedly, the following historical review is very brief and largely selective, but it was considered necessary for a better understanding of the recent socioeconomic and geopolitical relations and the complexities of these two strategically important countries.

1

Introduction

A BRIEF RETROSPECT

Greece and Turkey are located in an area where Greek, Roman, and Oriental cultures collided and colluded. Geographically, Greece and part of Turkey are located at the southern part of the Balkan Peninsula, southeast of the Alps. At times, Turkey is included in Balkan studies and at other times it is excluded as an Asian or Middle Eastern country. Because both countries are located at the crossroads of three continents (Europe, Asia, and Africa), they beckoned to invaders who were involved in promoting their own interests. Their location at a strategic region attracted continuous involvement of the great powers in their economic and political affairs throughout history.

Although the Illyrians and the light-haired and gray-eyed Thracians were probably the first inhabitants of the southern and southeastern part of the Balkan Peninsula, the Hellenes (Greeks) were the first to leave a record of themselves and their neighbors. The Minoans (Cretans), third millennium B.C., the Achaeans (Mycenaeans), and later the Athenians were the main inhabitants of the eastern Mediterranean in ancient times. The Achaeans, Alpine people who had migrated from central Europe, were descendants of Achaeus, grandson of Hellen, the legendary ancestor of the Hellenes—a branch of the Indo-European race to which Romans, Germans, Slavs, and other Europeans belong. Later (eleventh century B.C.), the Dorians, related to the Achaeans, conquered Greece and parts of Asia Minor. From the sixth century B.C. on, the Athenian civilization flourished in the area.

Asia Minor or Anatolia, which was invaded by the Turks in the eleventh century, has a recorded history that dates to the Hittites in the second millennium B.C. The Indo-European Hittites were flanked by the Hurrians who had crossed the Caucasus earlier (third millennium B.C.) and built a kingdom southeast of Anatolia. Related to the Hurrians were the rules of Urartu in the Lake-Van region close to the Ararat mountain. After the fall of Urartu, the Armenians arrived (before the sixth century B.C.) and established a kingdom stretching from the

Black Sea to the Caspian Sea. Also, the Kurds, descendants of the Medes who migrated from the Eurasian region (second millenium B.C.), settled in eastern Anatolia. In the western part of Anatolia the Thracians (third millennium B.C.), the Ionian Greeks (twelfth century B.C.), the Phrygians (eighth century B.C.), and the Lydians (seventh century B.C.) were in control. Thereafter, and before the coming of the Turks (eleventh century), the Hellenistic, the Roman, and the Byzantine civilizations flourished in Anatolia.

During the Roman and Byzantine periods, the economy of the area remained primarily agricultural and pastoral. When the Turkish conquerors came from Mongolia in 1071 and later, the Ottoman Empire was established. The sultans ruled the area and all the other Balkan lands from Constantinople, the previous capital of Byzantium, in an autocratic fashion. During the more than 400 years of the Ottoman occupation of Greece and the other neighboring countries, economic and cultural stagnation largely prevailed.

Since the liberation of Greece from the Turks in the 1820s, the economic relations of these two nations have been and still are affected mainly by political and military conditions in the region. The whole Balkan area has been influenced by ethnic conflicts and territorial parcelization known as "Balkanization." The saying, which originated in Western Europe, was that "peace in the West would prevail only when the Balkans are sunk."

Toward the end of the nineteenth and the beginning of the twentieth centuries, the industrial revolution in Western Europe brought the need of new resources. Backward Balkan countries, including Greece and Turkey, offered opportunities for good investment returns. In the early 1890s, German and other European companies built railways, including the line from Haidar Pasha, opposite to Constantinople, to Angora and as far south as Baghdad. With the help of French and Italian technicians, the Corinth Canal, the impressive Diakofto-Kalavryta Tooth Train, and other railroads were built in Greece toward the end of the nineteenth century. To pay for imports, both countries exported tobacco, grapes, and other agricultural products, especially to Germany, Britain, and Austria. Industrial development, though, remained in the embryonic stage, but shipping kept its traditional importance for Greece.

During the years between World Wars I and II, Greece's relations with Turkey remained at very low levels mainly because of the belligerent conditions that prevailed in the area. After the Greco-Turkish war of 1921–1922, the influx of some 1.5 million refugees from Asia Minor, when added to the 5.5 million population of Greece, proved to be beneficial to the Greek economy, although serious housing and employment problems appeared. Rug and textile industries, pottery, and shipping were rapidly developed by the skilled labor of the refugees.

The policy of conciliation and friendship, which was pursued by the Greek leader Eleutherios Venizelos and Kemal Ataturk (1928–1933), as well as other leaders in the Balkan Peninsula, stimulated economic development in the area. Also, Alexander Papanastassiou, a prime minister of Greece, together with other Balkan politicians, made geniune efforts toward a closer economic and political cooperation among the Balkan nations in the early 1930s. As a result, a number of conferences were held for further collaboration in tariffs, credit, protection of agricultural products, tourism, and foreign trade. Similar conferences of the Balkan countries, including Greece and Turkey, were organized recently (the most important one in 1976) but with limited results. Another important Balkan conference for better cooperation, in which Albania participated, was held in Belgrade in February 1988.

INFLATION, UNEMPLOYMENT, AND DISTRIBUTIONAL PROBLEMS

The main problems of the economies of Greece and Turkey are those of inflation and unemployment. As these economies waver between the Scylla of unemployment and the Charybdis of inflation, policymakers in these countries may turn away from relying on the market mechanism and adopt control measures that lead to more government, despite the fact that this may result in more bureaucracy and less efficiency.

Severe unemployment and underemployment in Greece and Turkey forced many young people to emigrate to other countries, particularly to West Germany, in the 1950s, 1960s, and early 1970s. Domestic migration from the countryside to the cities was also intensified and created urban problems, especially in Athens and Salonika in Greece and to a lesser extent in Istanbul and Ankara in Turkey. In Greece, where per capita income is about $3,400, repatriation of immigrants and decentralization from the cities back to the countryside started slowly in recent years. In Turkey though, where per capita income is only about $1,100 and population growth is high (more than double that of Greece), pressures of emigration and urbanization continue and will present serious economic problems in the years to come.

In spite of the decentralization measures taken, regional inequalities persist in both countries. Thus, per capita income in the less developed areas of Epirus, the islands of eastern Aegean Sea, and Thrace in Greece is about half of that of the Athens-Piraeus area, as are the number of vehicles and telephones per 1,000 persons. Similar inequalities can be observed in Turkey especially between the poor eastern and the more developed western regions. As in other developing nations, inequality in Turkey is relatively high, as 10 percent of the population absorbs 41 percent of national income.

Low efficiency in state-owned concerns is forcing the governments of Greece and Turkey to resort to a system of privatization, in which a number of public enterprises are sold back to the public. Such state-owned firms may be sold totally or partially to the general public, private companies or banks, and to their own employees. An effective way to encourage small investors and employees to buy shares of these government-controlled enterprises is to offer fiscal and monetary incentives. They may include tax concessions, low-interest loans, and other benefits. Also, there may be a preference given to small investors and employees over large companies and foreign investors. For example, the demands of company employees and small investors may be satisfied first. Moreover, certain percentages of shares may be allotted to different investment groups.

Such a split of ownership, which is a form of what Joseph Schumpeter called "people's capitalism," is implemented in Britain, France, and other nations. For example, in France some 65 companies and banks are in the process of being transferred to private ownership through sales of shares to the employees, the general public, and foreign investors. Similar schemes may be used in Greece and Turkey to stimulate incentives, increase productivity, and reduce unemployment.

The introduction of employee participation in decision making and partial or total ownership of the enterprises in which they work can reduce inflation and improve income distribution. This measure is used in other countries such as the United States, where more than 6,000 enterprises with more than 8 million employees are under Employee Stock Ownership Plans (ESOPs). Also, some 309,000 U.S. companies use the profit sharing system, while EEC new transnational firms are required to have labor participation in decision making. Another technique is the Japanese system of paying the workers about a third of average wages and giving the rest at three-month intervals according to the revenue of the enterprise. Such forms of co-management and revenue or profit sharing could reduce strikes, increase productivity, limit inflationary government subsidies to problematic enterprises, and reduce the large budget deficits of Greece and Turkey.

A number of manufacturing firms in Turkey and especially in Greece encounter financial difficulties because they cannot service their debt obligations. Managerial shortcomings and inefficient marketing techniques, to promote products at home and abroad, may be considered responsible for these difficulties. Moreover, many products are under official price control, and in many instances they cannot cover their costs from increased wages, raw material prices, and high interest rates.

Commercial banks, which are, more or less, controlled by the government, continue to finance such inefficient or "problematic" firms without requesting or enforcing improvement in organization, innovation, and competitiveness at home and abroad. The main reasons are that abandoning such moribund firms financially can lead to bankruptcy, the loss of the money already lent to these firms, and to higher unemployment. As a result, the unorthodox and dangerous practice of short-term loans to such weak firms continues, short-term lending is rolled over to long-term financing, debts pile up, and the inflationary pressures are permanently looming behind the economies of Greece and Turkey.

Greece and Turkey are rich in mineral resources. Large amounts of minerals, such as bauxite, lignite, and aluminum, are exported in the form of raw materials, primarily to other EEC countries, while a good deal of finished metal products are imported from these countries. It would be proper, then, for Greece and Turkey to utilize fiscal and monetary policy incentives to develop their metal industries even by using protective tariffs for a transitional period. Such a policy would help domestic employment and improve the balance of trade by reducing imports of metal products, the raw materials of which are produced in these countries. Moreover, more value added taxes would be levied from the multistage process of manufacturing these products domestically.

Greek and Turkish enterprises are largely family owned and small in size and as such are unable to apply modern technology of mass production. On the other hand, labor cost in Greece and Turkey is far less than that of the EEC. This gives a comparative advantage to these small industries. It would seem that such small enterprises need to merge into larger ones to be able to implement capital-intensive production techniques and advanced managerial know-how so that they can be efficient and competitive in domestic and foreign markets.

Tourism, already a flourishing sector, would not only keep its importance but would expand further, mainly because of the excellent climate and archaeological remains. It may be expected that this sector would continue to play a vital role in covering a large part of Greece's and Turkey's balance-of-trade deficit, which is about $6 billion annually for each country.

Loose taxing/spending policies and the conflict over Cyprus significantly contribute to operating budget deficits and trade deficits as well as to rising prices and interest rates. To reduce economic growth, for purposes of moderating inflation, would mean higher unemployment and perhaps lower real per capita income for Greece and more so for Turkey.

FOREIGN TRADE AND DEBT PROBLEMS

A common problem for Greece and Turkey is the sizeable deficit in the balance of foreign trade. More revenue from exports of goods and services is required to pay for growing imports; the value of the currency is under pressure of devaluation; and the credit position deteriorates. However, the geographical location of the countries in relation to markets of Europe and the Middle East makes them important for trade and investment opportunities. Both countries have introduced laws that encourage foreign investments, so that new technology can be acquired and hard currency can be earned.

Modest fiscal and monetary policies may be designed to spur growth, control inflation, and improve the balance of payments. However, in the effort to reduce trade deficits, care should be taken to avoid reduction of such imports as machinery and raw materials needed for further development. Moreover, distributional and regional investment policies should not discourage technological innovations and long-run growth to the extent of severely impairing the international trade position of these countries.

Both countries have close trade relationships with Western European nations. Greece, like Odysseus in Homer's epic, returned to her European home after a long period of uncertainty and historical disturbances. The accession of Greece to the European Economic Commuity (EEC) in January 1981 and the association of Turkey since 1964 are challenges to their economies. From an industrial point of view, Turkey and, more so, Greece face problems of European competition. However, in agriculture, tourism, shipping and trade services, expectations are favorable if modernization and better organization are implemented.

Policies to reduce economic growth and moderate imports and price rises may make exports more competitive because of declining inflation. As a result of such policies, projections are that even if the deficits of the balance of payments are eliminated, debt-servicing expenses would increase because of the previous debt obligations already undertaken. It is expected, therefore, that interest and amortization (domestic and foreign) would rise for both countries in the near future.

However, real debt would be substantially lower if inflation in creditors' currencies, mainly the dollar, occurs. Thus, a 5 percent annual inflation in such currencies would reduce real debt to less than half in ten years, while a 10 percent annual inflation would reduce it by more than 50 percent in only five years.

Because of poor coordination in the 1980s between fiscal and foreign trade policy, Turkey became a country with a large external debt (more than $25 billion). The policy of liberalization of the economy and the emphasis on the free market forces of supply and demand led to an increase of imports and high trade deficits. And this in spite of the favorable trade conditions with the Islamic nations of the Middle East and, to some extent, the EEC countries. In order to reduce budget and trade deficits, the government has imposed high taxes on imported luxury products and gasoline. As a result, the price of gasoline remains high, despite the fact that petroleum prices were reduced drastically.

Recently, Turkish exports to the Persian Gulf countries and to Islamic countries in general fell significantly, while imports increased. If high trade deficits continue, the Turkish government may approach the International Monetary Fund (IMF) for a new standby agreement to shore up a deteriorating balance of payments, as it did in the late 1970s. To mitigate the problem, the government is expected to provide credit facilities and subsidies to the flagging export sector, so that excessive trade deficits can be avoided. Likewise, Greece faces high trade deficits and problems of debt servicing.

There is serious skepticism in Western Europe regarding the impact on the EEC of the eventual acceptance of Turkey's petition for admission. The rapid population growth and the high rates of unemployment and underemployment would present severe problems in the EEC countries with already high unemployment. Another problem would be the millions of Turkish peasant farmers and millions of tons of produce expected to be brought under the Community subsidies umbrella. The high cost of subsidizing and storing grain stocks, which absorbs three-quarters of the total Community budget, is expected to rise substantially. Without Turkey, EEC unsaleable grain stocks total currently 17 million tons and are expected to rise in a few years to 80 million. At present, the farm-subsidy program costs about $25 billion a year. With Turkey, the Common

Agricultural Policy (CAP) of the EEC, already in serious difficulties, would be in jeopardy.

From a political point of view, full membership of Turkey in the EEC would bring a large number of delegates, more than 100, to the European Parliament. This number would increase year after year with the rapidly growing Turkish population. When the Turkish population reaches 70 to 80 million in the near future, Turkey with some 150 members would control more than one-fourth of the total seats of the EEC Parliament. Moreover, all the problems of Turkey, with so many troubled neighboring countries, would become, to some extent, problems for the European Defense Community that may gradually supplant NATO. Other difficulties the EEC would encounter with Turkey's admission are the Turkish problems regarding human rights, the Cyprus conflict, and the Kurdish and Armenian issues.

2

A Historical Perspective

ANCIENT TIMES

From the times of the Minoan (Cretan) and the Homeric civilizations (about 3400–750 B.C.) to the Athenian Golden Age (fifth century B.C.), the Greeks were distinguished by their maritime and commercial activities along the shores of the eastern Mediterranean.[1]

The first Greek culture flourished on Crete, a Mediterranean island south of the Balkan Peninsula. Gradually the Cretan (Minoan) culture, radiating over the neighboring areas, influenced the Achaeans, who came in successive waves from the Alps and central Europe. The Achaeans, with Mycenae (in Peloponnesus) as their center, adopted the Cretan culture and developed their own civilization, which in turn spread to Asia Minor and to other Mediterranean lands. They developed into a powerful maritime nation, and by 1400 B.C. had overrun Crete. Around 1230 B.C., they started the long Trojan expedition in Asia Minor (recounted by Homer in his *Iliad* and *Odyssey*). Using the abduction of Helen of Sparta as a pretext, allied Greek city-states (including the Minoans) under Agememnon of Mycenae undertook the Trojan expedition for imperialistic political and economic reasons. Their foe was Troy, a city-state allied with the dynasty of the Hittites, which prevailed in Asia Minor at that time. Heavy rains of volcanic ash (about 1450 and 1200 B.C.) and prolonged wars marked the end of the Minoan and Mycenaean dynasties.

Other people, such as the Ionians and the Aeolians, who probably originated in the northern Greek mainland, were driven south. After the successful siege of Troy by the Mycenaeans, an amalgam of Achaeans, Ionians, and Aeolians settled in the coastlands of Asia Minor, now part of Anatolia Turkey. Smyrna and Miletus became great cultural and commercial cities after the eleventh and tenth centuries B.C., respectively. Later, these cities, together with others on mainland Greece and the islands, established many colonies primarily along the coasts of Spain and Italy and other Mediterranean lands. In these colonies, which remained in close touch with the mother country, craftsmanship, art, and commerce were developed. However, the people of mainland Greece remained primarily agricultural and pastoral.

During the eleventh century B.C. the Dorians, from the same Hellenic race as the Achaeans, appeared. They were considered to be the descendants of Dorus, the son of Hellen. Under pressure from the Thracians and Illyrian barbarians, they infiltrated and finally colonized central Greece, the Aegean islands, southwestern Asia Minor, Sicily, and Crete, gradually destroying the civilizations of the Minoans and the Mycenaeans. From the sixth to the third century B.C., Athens had become an important economic and cultural center. The appearance of silver and iron coins facilitated transactions and improved trade not only among the city-states, but also between Greece and other Mediterranean lands from the Middle East to Gibraltar (the Pillars of Hercules).[2] Moreover, economic and political unions or confederacies, such as the Achaean League during the sixth and third centuries B.C., similar to the present European Economic Communities (EEC and COMECON), were established to formulate common economic and foreign policy on coinage, tariffs, and the removal of trade barriers.

With the establishment of political democracy in Athens came the development of public finance. The constitution of Solon (594 B.C.) abolished bondage and gave people a share in the government. However, together with the people's right came their obligation to pay taxes in proportion to their incomes, derived primarily from landed property. Although there are disagreements as to the time this tax system was first introduced, economic historians agree that it dealt with a progressive taxation, similar to that of our times. Plato also seemed to support it in his *Laws* as a fair and simple system. It provided for four tax classes: The lowest class (*thetes*) who paid no taxes; the next class (*zeugites*), with an estimated 13.3 percent income tax; the class of *knights*, with a 20 percent income tax; and the richest class (*pentacosiomedimni*), with a 24 percent income tax.[3] However, when a number of people became fully occupied in governmental services, public expenditures grew rapidly and reserves suffered. Moreover, the use of public funds for welfare payments increased the proportion of idle persons, reduced production, and demoralized the citizens. These symptoms can also be observed today in countries with expensive social programs.

Wider improvements of commercial activities and crafts took place when Philip II, emperor of Macedonia, and his son Alexander the Great unified the Greek city-states (338 B.C.). Alexander, a student of Aristotle, marched through the Middle East to Persia and still farther eastward, where a number of colonies were established and the culture and trade or *emporium* were extended. This Greco-Macedonian state survived until the Romans conquered Greece along with the other neighboring areas during the second century B.C. The main commodities exported by the Greek cities at that time were metals, pottery products, textiles, and similar goods.

Anatolia in Ancient Times

Turkey was known to ancient geographers by the Greek word *Anatolia* (the rising of the sun) and in Turkish as *Anadolu*. Around the seventh and sixth millennia B.C., Anatolia was inhabited by prehistoric people known as the Hatti. Their language was known as Hattic. Around 2500 to 2000 B.C. tribes from the north and the east, known as Hittites, coming by way of the Caucasus, settled in Anatolia and northern Syria and Mesopotamia and superimposed their Indo-European speech on the indigenous Hattic. They were noted for their working of iron and the use of eight languages found in numberous clay tables in Hattusas (present-day Bagozköy).

After the second millennium B.C., Anatolia or Asia Minor, primarily its central and eastern part, was under the Hittites. The city of Hattusas, east of present-day Ankara, was their capital. The Hittites adopted the deities and even their name from the indigenous Hatti people whom they conquered. After 1200 B.C. the Hittite Empire collapsed when the Phrygians from western Anatolia rebelled and burned Hattusas.[4] Later, Assyrians and the emerging Aegean powers, primarily the Greek Dorians, conquered the area.

On the northwestern section of Anatolia were the lands of Troy (close to the Dardanelles or Hellespont). From the third millennium B.C. the Thracians controlled the area of Troy and levied tolls on traffic across the Dardanelles. The region was settled about 1900 B.C. by newcomers related to the early Greeks. From that time to 1200 B.C. the Aegean coast of Anatolia was largely affected by the Minoan-Mycenaean civilization. In about 1300 B.C. an earthquake devastated the city of Troy, while around 1200 B.C. the city was sacked and burned by the expedition force of Mycenae and other Greek city-states under Agamemnon, as Homer's *Iliad* indicates. Later, the site was known as the Greek Ilion and Roman Ilium.

In western and southwestern Anatolia, Ionian Greek settlers appeared (1200–900 B.C.). In this region the Phrygians had a strong state between 750 to 300 B.C., with Gordium their capital and Midas as their fabled king (725–675 B.C.). Later, Lydian kings, such as Croesus (560–546 B.C.), controlled the area. The city-state of Lydia, Lycia, and Caria flourished briefly as part of the Ionian Greek civilization.[5] In Lydia the first coins appeared during the sixth century B.C. In 546 B.C. the Persian king Cyrus defeated the Lydians, and Anatolia became part of the Persian Empire of the Achaemenid dynasty for two centuries.

In the eastern part of Anatolia were the Armenians, stretching from the Black Sea to the Caspian, and the less organized Kurds who migrated from the Eurasian steppes in the second millennium B.C. to the southeastern part of Anatolia, as described by Xenophon (400 B.C.) and other writers and ethnographers. The Armenians (after 600 B.C.) were settled in the area for good, mainly south of the Caucasus mountains. They had come earlier from the east and had merged with the Hittites of the region. They preserved a distinct Indo-European language and were to endure in the region as a separate ethnic group.

In 334 B.C., Alexander the Great crossed the Hellespont, defeated the Persians at the nearby Granicus River, and, cutting the Gordian knot, advanced into Asia and incorporated Anatolia into his empire. After his death (325 B.C.), Anatolia was divided among a number of small kingdoms. During the third century B.C., Gallic peoples from Europe settled in central Anatolia, an area known as Gallatia during the Roman times.

ROMAN CONQUEST AND BYZANTIUM

Roman Period

The Romans first conquered Macedonia, coming from the Adriatic coast, and then southern Greece and Asia Minor, during the second century B.C. Under the Roman rule, Greece (named Achaea), except Macedonia, suffered a steady economic decline. The main contributions of the Romans to the economies of the conquered lands were the development of a well-organized transportation network, the security of life and property, and the establishment of an efficient apparatus of public administration. Under these conditions, a large number of trade centers with theaters and numerous local industries developed.

Although the Latin language was spread throughout the area, Greek culture influenced the Roman rulers and administrators, particularly the upper classes, to the extent that many scholars call this era the Greco-Roman period. Educated Romans sent their children to Athens to study and shipped home much Greek sculpture. Salonika became an administrative and trade center of the Roman and the successor Byzantine empires. Its advantageous location at the crossroads of the Balkans made it an important commercial city. People and products moved from Adriatica to Byzantium and vice versa mainly through Egnatia Street (still used in Salonika). The objective of Roman road builders was to connect the east with the west and facilitate trade, primarily through Byzantium (later named Constantinople) and Salonika. Also, the Aegean islands, particularly Delos and Rhodos, were used by the Roman armies and merchants as way stations for the transport of merchandise and slaves from the Middle East.[6] Prosperous markets were developed on the Adriatic coast, where thousands of slaves from the Balkan and other countries were sold to Italy and Sicily at relatively high prices, because of the variety of their skills.

Ephesus, a masterpiece of urban planning and Hellenistic architecture, was annexed to the Roman Empire in 133 B.C. It became the capital of the rich Roman province of Asia. An extraordinary cosmopolitan city with its monumental Temple of Artemis, it was a major port and commercial center both before and after the Romans came. Situated on the southwest coast of Turkey, near Smyrna, it was known for its outstanding theater, where Mark Antony greeted Cleopatra, and the famous Library of Celsus.

The excellent administration of justice, the good roads, the comforts of the towns, with their theaters and baths, and the granting of Roman citizenship to all free men of the empire in 212 facilitated travel and enhanced the economic and cultural development of the region. As a result, the Romans managed to bring together the diverse Balkan and other Mediterranean peoples and keep them under their control for centuries. However, a number of invaders, mainly of German and Slavic origin, started to move toward the south and gradually weakened the Roman military and administrative apparatus in the area.

Byzantine Period

The Byzantine Empire existed for some eleven hundred years and extended over parts of Europe, Asia, and northern Africa. From that point of view, knowledge of Byzantine economic history requires extensive research and volumes of publications. Here, an attempt is made to present a short review of the main features of Byzantine economics, with emphasis on agriculture and public administration.

When the eastern section of the Roman Empire separated from Rome itself, cultural and commercial activities moved largely to Constantinople, which became the capital of the Eastern Roman or Byzantine Empire (326 A.D.).[7] The emperors of Byzantium introduced a common (Hellenic) language and stimulated trade by reducing taxes and making administrative reforms. Silk production, pottery, jewelry, and shipping were the main industries that flourished in Constantinople, which became an international trade center. Constantinople remained for some ten centuries the economic and political heart of the Byzantine Empire and the center of the Greek Orthodox religion and intellectual life. However, the spread of Christianity changed the ancient Greek culture, caused the closing of ancient Greek temples, and ended the Olympic Games after the fourth century.

The geographical position of the Balkan Peninsula, with its mountainous area and the protection given by the Danube to the north, enhanced the prospects for the survival of Byzantium. As a result, the reputation of Constantinople as a commercial and industrial center was furthered. In addition to jewelry, pottery, and shipping, textiles and weaponry were its main industries. Nevertheless, attacks from the north continued against the Byzantine Empire. During the fourth century hordes of Slavs crossed the Danube and pushed the native Illyrians and Thracians southward. The influx of the Slavs into the Balkan Peninsula began as a gradual infiltration. Although other peoples crossed the area, they did not settle as the Slavs did.

During the millennium of Byzantium, Constantinople and Salonika kept their commercial importance and became vital ports in the Mediterranean. After the eleventh century, the empire and its capital city began a slow process of decline. However, a number of scholars fled or were summoned to western Europe, carrying with them Greek philosophy and culture, "the seeds" of which "grew into some of the finest flowers of the Renaissance."[8] Crete came under the Arabs for over one hundred years around the ninth century and Candia, now Herakleion, became an important commercial port during that period.

In 1204 Venice occupied Crete, a "rich and lovely island," as Homer called it, strategically located amidst the dark blue sea, almost equidistant from Europe, Asia, and Africa. Crete, which remained for over four centuries under Venetian rule, developed a prosperous commerce, as did other islands and coastlands, where old Venetian fortresses can be seen today. Also, Franks, anxious to enjoy the sun, climate, and pleasant way of life of the area, established their feudal system in various locations, particularly in Achaea and Athens, as did the Genoese along the Anatolian coast and on various Aegean islands in the thirteenth century.

Fiscal and monetary policies of the Byzantine Empire were used not so much in support of trade but primarily to supply the state's needs for revenue, to pay the army and administrative personnel mainly in the capital city, as well as to pay bribes for keeping enemy powers in check.[9] Such policies proved to be effective in providing stability and serving the empire well across so many centuries.

However, because of the pressures from the north, the west, and especially the east, the economy of Byzantium experienced a continuous decline. Commercially minded Venetians, who were better organized in shipping and foreign trade, managed to settle in a number of ports and other strategic areas around the Balkan Peninsula. With the Crusaders they captured Constantinople in 1204 and annexed many islands and coastal areas where they established a feudal system. Although they fled from Constantinople in 1261 under pressure from Michael VIII Palaeologus, the Nicaean emperor, they continued to drain the financial resources of Byzantium by collecting customs revenues and controlling banking activities. Being relieved of imperial taxes, the Venetians could undersell the Greek and other merchants in the lucrative Balkan and Mediterranean markets. Moreover, the Genoese, another commercial people, competed with the Venetians for the possession of the Golden Horn and the lucrative trade of the Black Sea.

Within domains under their control, the emperors debased the currencies, increased taxes, spent lavishly on luxurious living, and pawned their crown jewels with Venetian financiers. This economic behavior, on top of social, religious, and military weaknesses, paved the way for the collapse of the empire.[10] However, the spread of Byzantine religious concepts and educational and legal ideas throughout the Balkan countries influenced all the peoples of the peninsula's interior, who until then had been considered barbarians.

With the increase on imperial expenses, the weight of taxation became greater. The main levies were land and hearth taxes. The latter may have been payable by every head of household while the former seems to have included taxes on arable and pasture land, vineyards, and mountain land. Local administrators, at times, resorted to the use of labor services in road construction, shipbuilding, and similar public works, instead of levying provincial taxes.

Economic mismanagement, high taxes, currency debasement, and the luxurious living of the Byzantine rulers led the empire to the point of bankruptcy.

Moreover, internal strife and external invasions, mainly by Mongols from the east, brought about the final collapse and the occupation of the empire by the Seljuk Turks. Conquest by the Latins from the west and the Turks from the east made the Byzantine Empire look like a slender and miserable body upon which rested an enormous head.

From a sociopolitical point of view, the attitudes of the modern people in the area, to a large extent, stem from that time. The importance of the Church, the centralized bureaucratic state, the dominance of personalities in politics, and the primacy of politics over economics in policy discussions are mostly the heritage of the Byzantine and Ottoman mentality.

THE OTTOMAN EMPIRE

The Ottoman Turks gradually advanced from the Central Asian steppes to the Anatolian plateau. Toward the close of the thirteenth Christian century, flying before the face of the Mongols, the nomadic stock-breeding invaders passed from the basin of the Oxus and Jaxartes, on the northeastern marches of Islam, to their new settlements.

The Turks, who originally moved out of Mongolia, advanced in a slow and "oriental" fashion and in waves conquered most of Asia Minor. The occupation of the area was marked by the defeat of the Byzantine emperor Romanus IV in Armenia in 1071. The conquering Turks called the area Anatolia, from the Greek word *anatolé* (sunrise; figuratively "the east"), a name used by the Byzantines.

The Islamic Ottoman Empire grew up very alien and hostile to the contemporary Christian communities that had sprung from the soil of the West during the Greco-Roman civilization. To extract a livelihood, these nomadic herdsmen kept constantly on the move in search of pasture at different seasons with their cattle and other animals (dogs, camels, horses) that assisted them.[11]

In 1345, John Cantacugenus, a Byzantine official, invited the Ottomans to support his bid for the throne. In 1349, the Ottomans were invited again to help save Salonika from the Serbs (under Stephen Dushan). Thus the Ottomans, further strengthened by additional troops, began to settle down in eastern Thrace (Gallipoli). From 1354 onward they began pushing westward to the rich lands of Thrace, Macedonia, Thessaly, and the rest of Greece and the Balkans. Eventually they captured Adrianople (1360) and Salonika (1430).

Constantinople fell on May 29, 1453, Athens three years later, and the Peloponnesus in 1460. Chios and many other Aegean islands, which were occupied by the Genoese for three centuries, fell also to the Ottomans in 1566.

The forceful recruitment of infant Christian males converted to Islam (*janissaries*) helped establish and sustain Ottoman rule in the area for four centuries. Nevertheless, from time to time Venetian fleets gained control of many coastal areas and islands, including the Ionian Islands (1386–1797) and the Peloponnesus (1687–1718).[12]

For purposes of maintaining the gulf between the Eastern (Orthodox) and

Western (Catholic) churches and precluding any combined Christian resistance to Ottoman rule, the Turks practiced religious tolerance and permitted exemptions from taxation and expropriation of church properties, like the Byzantines before them. This helped preserve and promote the rapid growth of monasteries, which acquired large estates, even outside Greece (metochia), from the donations of the heavily taxed peasants. The transfer of the accumulated properties of the monasteries to the tillers or the government presented and still presents serious problems in Greece's agricultural economics.

From an economic and social point of view, the feudal system of Western Europe prevailed, to a large extent, in Greece, Asia Minor, and other Balkan areas during the Ottoman period. Aristocrat landlords and Turkish chiefs (pashas and agas) lived luxuriously while the masses lived in poverty. Between them was the class consisting of a few well-to-do local people who retained and enlarged their privileges and their large properties, sometimes through collaboration with the Turkish rulers.

Following their usual practice, the Turkish newcomers distributed conquered lands (*ziamets* or smaller *timars*) to their warriors and collaborators (mainly the *spahis*), while the Greek and other Balkan peoples (the *rayahs*) were subjected to heavy taxation and economic exploitation. Rich lands were confiscated by the Turkish chiefs, who transformed them into their own estates (*chifliks*) and cultivated them in a feudalistic manner.[13]

From an economic and social point of view, the feudal system of Western Europe prevailed, to a large extent, in Greece, Asia Minor, and other Balkan areas during the Ottoman period. Aristocrat landlords and Turkish chiefs (pashas and agas) lived luxuriously while the masses lived in poverty. Between them was the class consisting of a few well-to-do local people who retained and enlarged their privileges and their large properties, sometimes through collaboration with the Turkish rulers.

During the Ottoman years, a limited number of new manufacturing units were created primarily with European capital and know-how. To pay for imports from Europe, exports of cotton and thread from areas under the Ottomans increased, while export tariffs declined from 5 to around 1 percent of the value of exports. European markets dictated, to a large extent, the pattern of production for cotton, silk, and othe raw materials.

Trade and industry were conducted primarily by Greek merchants and to a limited extent by Armenians, Jews,and Vlachian traders and artisans. In order to promote the economy, the sultans renewed the privileges that Venice enjoyed under Byzantium and even wanted to repopulate occupied areas with mainly merchants and seafaring Greeks. A number of cultural and commercial centers, such as those of Salonika, Athens, Smyrna, and Ioannina, developed, and the Greek language gradually spread throughout the Balkan areas, especially in the ports of the Black Sea. Transportation and trade were further expanded when Greek ships were permitted to fly the Russian flag (Russo-Turkish Treaty of Tassy, 1792). Handicraft industries and production cooperatives were also created. An outstanding example was the Ambelakia enterprise in Thessaly (1795), which manufactured textile products and sold them primarily to central Europe. Another example was that of shipping cooperatives, with seamen, captains, and carpenters, who pooled their resources and shared proportionally in revenue.[14]

Bursa also was an important center of silk and textile industries in the Near East. It used to compete with other nations, mainly Persia, in local and European markets. Salonika was another center of production and exports of primarily wooden products.

However, the tax form of stamp duties on cloth and price fluctuations in European markets led, in many instances, to instability and stagnation of the textile industries. Moreover, the use of hand-operated looms and other primitive Ottoman technology, compared to more efficient steam-powered machines in Europe, increased production cost and squeezed profits in these industries. Bursa and other cloth centers, though, continued to specialize in producing the raw materials demanded by the hungry industries of Europe, mainly those of France, England, and Holland.

The capitation tax was the major personal tax (*harach* in Turkish), which each adult Christian male was required to pay. It was computed for the whole village, regardless if the number of taxpayers was reduced as people fled to the mountain areas to escape oppression and heavy taxation. In mountain communities, such as Arcadia and Roumely, where people found asylum from Ottoman oppression, one could meet precipices "where a few men with stones might destroy armies."

Another major land tax was the tithe (*dhekati* in Greek, *usr* in Turkish), varying from one-tenth to one-half of the produce. Also, a tax paid by the Christian subjects was that in lieu of military service, as well as an irregular impost (*avariz*) which varied in purpose and amount. There were cases, as in Epirus, for example, in 1867, in which taxes and all kinds of charges under the Turkish rule amounted to 67 percent of the farm proceeds.[15] Such large payments and other charges were very difficult to meet; even the mythological giant Cyclops would be distressed.

Although the establishment of a common Ottoman system put an end to internal strife in the occupied areas and perhaps brought some economic development, this was accomplished with some sacrifice of the liberty of the people and their cultural improvement. For four centuries, the Greek and other Balkan peoples were subjected to ruthless exploitation. But, "far worse than the material injuries were the spiritual wounds, the traces of which it will require generations of educational effort and moral reconstruction to obliterate."[16] Under the laws of Islam, polygamy was permitted and harems (where women were treated as inferior beings) were common. The sultan and his family ruled the empire for the benefit of Moslems, who monopolized the professions and exploited their Christian subjects in the occupied principalities and vassal states.

GREECE'S STRUGGLE FOR INDEPENDENCE

In Greece and all of the other areas occupied by the Ottomans, economic exploitation, export tariffs, and the bureaucratic centralism discouraged rapid expansion and modernization. Large fertile areas that had become prosperous during the Byzantine period and the Frankish and Venetian occupations were left idle after the Ottomans captured them.

Heavy taxation and oppression practiced by Moslems and janissaries and the border wars helped the Greek *rayahs* to rise and to start a long and difficult war of liberation. Moreover, separate authorities, independent of the sultan, were created primarily by Ali Pasha in Epirus and Albania during the early 1800s. About that time the Greeks of the Morea and archipelago, influenced by the promise of support from Empress Catherine of Russia, rose up against their Ottoman masters. Although the revolts of the *rayahs* in Morea and other Balkan areas were put down with massacres, the stubbornness of the Greek *klefts* and Serbian *heyduks*, supported by popular ballad literature praising them, gave new impetus to the struggle against the Turkish rule.

Toward the end of the eighteenth century, a number of teachers were sent to Western Europe by rich merchants, shipowners, and a few Phanariots (high clergy and Greek elite) to revive studies of the Greek past. These teachers became interested in bringing the French Revolution's principles of liberty and equality to Greece. One of them, Rhigas Pheraios (Valentinlis), composed revolutionary battle hymns to encourage the Greek *rayahs* (semi-slave subjects) to participate in the struggle for liberation from the Turks. For this reason he was captured and executed in 1798.

During Ottoman rule, a number of the educated Greeks (Phanariots) served as administrators and even dragomans of the Porte (the sultan's regime in Constantinople). They became rich and powerful under the Turks and, as a result, they opposed the rebellion of the *rayahs*. They remained a group apart, hated by many Greeks struggling for their freedom. High priests of the Orthodox Church, with some exceptions, were criticized for their exhortation to resignation and acquiescence in Ottoman rule and the prevailing authority.[17] This attitude retarded intellectual progress and discouraged efforts at political liberation. However, local priests helped preserve the Greek language and heritage in secret night schools and sparked resistance in the villages.

In 1814, a secret revolutionary society, known as the Philike Hetairia or "Friendly Society," was formed at Odessa by three Greek merchants (Nicholas Skouphas, Athanasios Tsakalof, and Panagiotes Anagnostopoulos). The society approached Alexander Hypselantes, a major-general in the Russian army, to be the commander of the movement. He accepted the position on June 27, 1820. On March 6, 1821, he crossed the Russian-Turkish borders in Pruth and liberated Jassy. However, his "sacred battalion" was annihilated on June 19.

In the meantime, the revolution broke out in Morea and "on April 2 [old calendar] the revolt became general; on that day the Greeks besieged the Turks in Kalavryta."[18] They attacked after Germanos, Metropolitan of Patras, raised the sacred banner in the nearby monastery of Hagía Lávra on March 21, 1821. Official confirmation dates the outbreak from March 25 to coincide with the holiday of "Evangelismos."

Thereafter, the *klefts* of Morea started their struggle for liberation, gradually wiping out the regional Turkish garrisons. Under Theodore Kolokotrones, an experienced and clever leader (born of *kleft* parents and a former officer in the British army in the Ionian Islands), the Greeks managed to besiege and take Kalamata, Tripolis, Navarino, and other towns of Morea. The fighting quickly spread to Sterea Hellas, Thessaly, Epirus, and the islands, despite massacres on the island of Chios (by Sultan Mahmud II), in Missolonghi, and in Morea (by Imbrahim Pasha with his Turkish-Egyptian forces). With the help of the philhellenic societies in Europe and the romantic supporters of the Greek liberation struggle, such as Lord Byron, the Greeks achieved their independence. The pressure by the Russians against the Ottomans in the Caucasus and in Balkania, and the help of the European fleet at Navarino in 1827, were additional factors affecting the progress of liberation in Greece and the establishment of a free Greek state with its borders at Thessaly, the Arta-Volos line.

Greek merchants and mariners living abroad, as well as other philhellenic societies and governments in Europe and elsewhere, helped the revolutionary *rayahs* to liberate their lands and establish a free state that included the Peloponnesus (Morea), Sterea Hellas, and part of Thessaly (by 1828). Greek independence was established by the Treaty of Adrianople in 1829 and the London Convention of 1832. After liberation, land distribution was slow and highly unequal, as *kodjabashis* and other powerful persons acquired title to large and rich estates. Only one out of six peasants had land of his own, and litigations and violence among them were frequent in the postliberation years.

Toward the end of the Ottoman Empire, the influence of the industrial revolution in Western Europe was felt in the Balkans, particularly in Greece and Yugoslavia. As a result of Europeanization, the administrative structure of the Porte changed, the units of janissaries were dissolved in 1826, and the bureaucratic centralism of the Ottoman Empire started to change. Even high-ranking administrators and army generals suggested that "Either we follow the European trend, or we have to return to Asia."

The newly liberated people of Balkania were by and large uneducated and not anxious to establish their own governments and manage their own economic affairs. Thus, during the struggle for liberation and afterward, the Greek ex-*rayahs* appeared as courageous individualists with characteristics similar to those of their ancestors. However, the violent and fatal quarrels among the Greek *klefts* and among the sea captains over personal or territorial interests (similar to the ones among the ancient city-states) reappeared. With the economic and educational improvement of the newly created Greek state came the mystic fervor to expand the state to engulf the Greek "brothers" of Crete, Thessaly, Epirus, Macedonia, and the coast of Asia Minor. A socioeconomic survey of that period would reveal the painful transformation of nineteenth-century Greece from an Asian to a European society, which was closer to the Hellenic civilization.

The Ottoman law, derived from the Koran's scriptures, determined that sovereignty over property could pertain only to God and was exercised on his behalf by the Moslem spiritual and military leaders. As a result, the ownership and taxation rights remained with the Ottoman state, religious institutions, or Moslem lords. The Ottoman rulers siphoned off agricultural surplus from the provinces, through taxes, and not much incentive for farm improvements was left.

During the war of independence the country was ruined physically and its economy was in shambles. International treaties after liberation placed former Ottoman holdings in the legal possession of the Greek government, declaring them as "national estates." One of the difficult problems of that period was the transfer of the property ownership from the Ottoman owners and the Greek government to the tillers. In practice, some Turkish rules had to be used, especially on matters of land holding and taxation.

NOTES

1. Further valuable information is provided in George Botsford and Charles Robinson, Jr., *Hellenic History*, 5th ed., rev. Donald Kagan (London: Macmillan, 1971), chaps. 1–3; C. Strarr, *The Economic and Social Growth of Early Greece: 800–500* B.C. (New York: Oxford University Press, 1977); and S. Todd Lowry, "Recent Literature on Ancient Greek Economic Thought," *Journal of Economic Literature* 17 (March 1979): 65–86.

2. Terrot Glover, *The Challenge of the Greeks and Other Essays* (New York: Macmillan, 1942), 78; C. Stanley, *Roots of the Tree* (London: Oxford University Press, 1936), 24; and Norman Angell, *The Story of Money* (New York: F. A. Stokes, 1929), chap. 4.

3. Augustus Boeckh, *The Public Economy of Athens* (New York: Arno Press, 1976), 494–510; Andreas Andreades, *A History of Public Finance in Greece* (Cambridge: Harvard University Press, 1933), 330–350; Nicholas Gianaris, *Greece and Yugoslavia: An Economic Comparison* (New York: Praeger, 1984), 10–12.

4. C. W. Ceram, (pseud. for Marek, Kurt), *The Secret of the Hittites: The Discovery of an Ancient Empire* (New York: Alfred A. Knopf, 1956); Richard F. Nyrop, ed., *Turkey: A Country Study* (Washington, D.C.: The American University, 1980), chap. 1.

5. M. J. Cook, *Greeks in Ionia and the East* (London: Thames and Hudson, 1962).

6. Emperor Augustus, Julius Caesar's adopted son and heir (first century B.C.), selected Aphrodisias, a site in southwest Turkey with Aphrodite's temple and other monuments, as his city, granting it autonomy and tax-free status. More details in Kenan Erim, *Aphrodisias* (New York: Facts on File, 1986). Also Jules Toutain, *The Economic Life of the Ancient World* (New York: A. Knopf, 1930), 232; and John E. Day, *An Economic History of Athens under Roman Domination* (New York: Arno Press, 1973), chap. 7.

7. The Dorians of Megara (a city west of Athens) had established colonies in the Dardanelles during the seventh century B.C. and had given the name *Byzantium* to the city later known as Constantinople.

8. Jane Carey and Andrew Carey, *The Web of Modern Greek Politics* (New York: Columbia University Press, 1968), 35.

9. Land products provided about 80 percent and trade 20 percent of the imperial revenue. Michael Hendy, *Studies in the Byzantine Monetary Economy, c. 300–1450* (London: Cambridge University Press, 1985), chap. 3.

10. For more on economic and administrative problems of Byzantium, see Robert Wolff, *The Balkans in Our Time* (New York: W. W. Norton, 1967), chap. 4.

11. Claude Cahen, *Pre-Ottoman Turkey* (New York: Tabbinger, 1968), 318–35; and William Davis, *A Short History of the Near East* (New York: Macmillan, 1937).

12. A serious attack by the Venetians took place in 1687 when they bombarded and partially damaged the Parthenon, which was used as a powder magazine by the Moslems.

13. Under the timar system, "Ottoman onslaught . . . destroyed peasant villages and generally disrupted settlement in the grain-growing lowlands." John Lampe and Martin Jackson, *Balkan Economic History, 1550–1950* (Bloomington: Indiana University Press, 1982), 33.

14. Leften S. Stavrianos, *The Balkans since 1453* (New York: Holt, Rinehart and Winston, 1958), 276, 298–99.

15. More on taxation under the Ottoman rule in William McGrew, *Land and Revolution in Modern Greece, 1800–1881* (Kent, Ohio: Kent State University Press, 1985), chap. 2; and Leften Stavrianos, *The Ottoman Empire: Was It the Sick Man of Europe?* (New York: Holt, Rinehart and Winston, 1959), 49.

16. Ferdinand Schevill, *The History of the Balkan Peninsula*, rev. ed. (New York: Harcourt, Brace, 1933), 10; and George W. Hoffman, *The Balkans in Transition* (New York: D. Van Nostrand, 1963), chap. 3.

17. Nicholas Kaltchas, *Introduction to the Constitutional History of Modern Greece* (New York: Columbia University Press, 1940), 11. A broader review in Justin McCarthy, *The Arab World, Turkey, and the Balkans (1878–1914)* (Boston: G. K. Hall, 1982).

18. William Miller, *The Ottoman Empire and Its Successors, 1801–1927* (New York: Octagon Books, 1966), 71–72. Also Nicholas Gianaris, *The Province of Kalavryta: A Historical and Socioeconomic Review* (New York: National Herald, 1983), 35.

3

The Establishment of Modern
Greece and Turkey

GROWTH OF MODERN GREECE

After liberation, Greece, a small infant nation (about one-third of its present size) began a slow and painful process of rehabilitation and development. After Athens became the capital of the nation in 1833, replacing Nauplion, the city became a magnet of people and wealth, as it had been in ancient times, while inhabitants of the poor islands and other parts of Greece emigrated to other lands.

In the countryside, many estates belonged to the Turks. Land distribution was slow and highly unequal. The primates and other powerful persons helped themselves first, acquiring title to large and rich Turkish estates. Land appropriations through legal recognition of squatters' rights and title gains (if land was cultivated continuously for a period varying from one to fifteen years) helped land distribution somewhat but gave rise to frequent litigation and violence among the peasants. The struggle for independence and nationhood distracted the infant nation from economic development. The area of the new nation was small, as was its population (some 753,000 people). It included central Greece, below the Arta-Volos line in Thessaly, the Peloponnesus, and the Cyclades Islands in the Aegean Sea.

The first republic was established in 1827. Ioannis Capodistrias, an educated cosmopolitan who had served as Russia's secretary of state, became the president of the republic (1827–1831). After his assassination the protecting powers, primarily Britain, selected Prince Otto of Bavaria, a Roman Catholic, to be king of Greece without consulting the Greeks. During the thirty years of his reign, King Otto introduced an autocratic system of centralized administration which, ever since, has resulted in a slow-moving bureaucracy. He also imported his own artisans and a brewer, Fuchs (Fix), whose firm remained active up to the recent past in Athens. In 1862 Otto was deposed by a revolt ignited by students and middle-class intellectuals. After Otto's deposition, King George I from the Danish Glückseberg family was brought to Greece's throne, primarily with the support of the British. By that time, the population had doubled, as had the shipping industry, while foreign trade had more than quadrupled.

Due to occupancy and inheritance of land without legal proofs, usurpation and squatting were widespread. Traditional occupants had mostly been share-croppers on lands that the Turks controlled during the Ottoman period. The Greek-Bavarian regime of King Otto (1833–1862) refused to recognize the cultivators as owners and obliged them to pay heavy usufruct taxes as tenants. To end many property disputes between the state and its citizens, important land distribution laws were enacted in 1835, 1855, 1864, and 1871.

Greece, as a weak and poor agricultural nation, resorted to foreign borrowing in order to finance its growing government expenditures. The revolutionary governments of 1824 and 1825 issued bonds that were sold abroad. In 1832, the large Rothschild loan, guaranteed by the three major powers (Britain, France, Russia), was received for servicing prior debts, the indemnity to Turkey, and administrative and military expenses. Such expenses were largely increased after 1833, when Otto recruited paid foreign soldiers and civil servants, mainly Germans. Military expenditures alone absorbed from 40 to 100 percent of annual revenues from 1833 through 1841 and about one-third thereafter.[1] More loans to service the debt and to cover budget deficits continued to flow and the country faced serious problems of payments.

From a political and economic point of view, directly or indirectly, Greece was controlled by foreign powers. Thus, President Capodistrias had to submit to the allied representatives at the Poros Conference in 1828 statistics concerning frontiers, tribute, and indemnity for lands, including large estates that belonged to the Turks (*chifliks*). British, Russian, and German rivalry for regional influence played an important role in the formation and development of the new Greek state and its financing.

At the time the new Greek nation was established, all the fertile plains of Thessaly and Macedonia remained in Ottoman control. However, in the hills and plains of Attica and Boeotia and the coastlands of Peloponnesus, the farms produced cereals, olives, grapes, and other fruits as in ancient times. The typical Greek peasant was engaged in subsistence farming. Agricultural techniques were poor. Rudimentary tools and wooden plows were still in use. Grain was mostly imported from Trieste, Alexandria, and the Black Sea ports. Taxes in the form of tithes on threshing floors were heavy and unjust, and collection was time consuming. Grain had to remain piled up for months awaiting the tax collector's inspection. Animal husbandry was neglected, agricultural credit was limited, and interest ranged from 20 to 24 percent on mortgage loans and from 36 to 50 percent on personal loans.[2] Grapes and later tobacco were exported primarily to Britain, Austria, and Germany. Industrial development remained in the embryonic stage. However, shipping kept its traditional importance. A limited number of small, labor-intensive enterprises were developed in the Piraeus-Athens area, Syra, and Patras.

Foreign Influence and Political Changes

Greece acquired the Ionian islands from Britain (1864). The rest of Thessaly (1881), as well as Macedonia, the rest of Epirus, Crete, and a number of Aegean Islands were acquired from Turkey (1913), while Western Thrace was acquired from Bulgaria (1918). By that time, agricultural production and exports, especially currants and tobacco, were significantly increased. However, more than 2,200 *chifliks* of low productivity still existed in the country at that time (818 in Macedonia, 584 in Thessaly, and 410 in Epirus).

With the new acquisitions, Greece's production capacity increased significantly. Production of grain, cotton, and tobacco in Thessaly, Macedonia, and Thrace improved domestic economic conditions and helped increase exports. The city of Kavala became an important port for tobacco exports. However, much of Epirus, with rugged mountains, eroded lands, and limited means of transportation, remained an economic liability to Greece.

As a result of the Greek expedition in Asia Minor (in 1919) and the disaster thereafter (autumn 1922), a massive population exchange took place. Some 1,500,000 Greeks left Asia Minor, where their ancestors had lived for possibly thirty centuries, for Greece, and 400,000 Turks left Greece for Turkey. Although there were serious housing and employment problems at the beginning, in the long run the progressive and industrious refugees proved to be a great asset to the Greek economy, especially in the rug industry, new textiles, pottery, copper ware, and shipping.

The policy of conciliation and friendship pursued by Eleutherios Venizelos, prime minister of Greece, and Kemal Ataturk, president of Turkey, as well as other leaders of the Balkan countries, resulted in the stimulation of trade and development in the area. Genuine efforts to achieve closer economic cooperation among the Balkan nations were made after 1924, primarily by Alexander Papanastassiou, a premier of Greece, and Nicolas Titulescu, foreign minister of Romania. In a number of conferences among the Balkan states, including Greece and Turkey, emphasis was given to further collaboration in tariffs, tourism, and credit.

On October 28, 1940, in the second year of World War II, Mussolini's Italy launched an attack against Greece from Albania. The poorly equipped Greek troops managed to push the invading Italians back to Albania, probably because, as Napoleon's dictum goes, "in war the proportion of moral to material factors is as three to one." However, Greek troops, fighting on so many fronts, were unable to resist the well-equipped armored units of Adolf Hitler, which on April 6, 1941 penetrated far into the country.

Under occupation by Germany, Italy, and Bulgaria (in Macedonia and western Thrace), Greece suffered heavy losses. During the first year of occupation the Germans printed inflationary money and drained the country of needed resources,[3] while imports dropped significantly because of the Allied blockade.

Some 450,000 people died of starvation alone, primarily in Athens. Adults and children suffered from malnutrition, malaria, and tuberculosis. Factories were destroyed, transportation and communications throughout the country almost disappeared, and about three-quarters of the country's large commercial fleet was sunk. Civilian massacres were carried out by the Nazis throughout Greece. At Kalavryta alone, a town near Patras, 1,300 unarmed persons were gunned down on December 13, 1943.

In April 1942, ELAS (the National Popular Liberation Army), the military arm of EAM (the National Liberation Front), started offensive activities against the Germans. EPON (the United All-Greece Youth Organization) was also formed to train and provide recreation for young boys and girls. Another minor resistance group of some importance was EDES (the Greek National Democratic League), organized by Colonel Napoleon Zervas mainly in Epirus.

As a result of the Moscow Conference in October 1944, Winston Churchill and Josef Stalin agreed that Britain would "have ninety percent of the say in Greece, and go fifty-fifty in Yugoslavia."[4] On December 3, 1944, clashes between ELAS and the police (mostly German collaborators) started in Athens, and clashes between ELAS and the British, already in Athens, went on until February 1945. The Yalta Conference in February 1945, with Churchill, Franklin Roosevelt, and Stalin, accepted the arrangement of the Moscow Conference. However, Churchill decided to crush EAM-ELAS, which had been gradually infiltrated and dominated by the Communists, and finally to restore King George II. Before the people could lift their heads above World War II's starvation and tragedy, mutual hatred between left-wing and right-wing groups flared up into a serious civil war that persisted until 1949.

Britain terminated all aid to Greece in March 1947 and soon thereafter all of its troops were withdrawn. Thus British political and economic tutelage in Greece, which prevailed for more than a century, came to an end. On May 22, 1947, $300 million in aid was initially appropriated by the United States (under the Truman Doctrine), most of which went for the Greek army and the expenditures of largely corrupt public administrations. American experts were assigned to administer the program and to supervise related policies.

With the Truman Doctrine, American aid, favoring mainly military needs at the neglect of other economic considerations such as inflation and unemployment, began flowing into Greece and Turkey. As Walter Lippman remarked, these two countries had been selected "not because they are especially in need of relief, not because they are shining examples of democracy . . . but because they are the strategic gateway to the Black Sea and the heart of the Soviet Union."[5]

Greece and Turkey became members of NATO (the North Atlantic Treaty Organization) in 1952. United States advisers exercised control on weaponry and had great influence on important decisions through the palace and the Greek army command, not only on military but also on political and economic matters. American military and economic aid to Greece amounted to about $100 million per year.

From an economic point of view, the reforms of 1953 by Spyros Markezinis (the minister of coordination) which included devaluation of the drachma (from 15 to 30 drachmas per U.S. dollar), improvement in public administration, and incentives to attract foreign investments (Law 2687/1953) somewhat improved domestic and foreign trade conditions. With political and fiscal stability in the late 1950s, money deposits increased, exports improved, and the wheels of industry began moving rapidly.

Furthermore, increasing numbers of tourists from Europe and America came to enjoy the sun-drenched haven and Homer's "wine-dark" sea of Greece. However, unemployment and underemployment remained high, and the gap in per capita income between the city and the countryside increased. Government subsidies on wheat, tobacco, and other crops did not accomplish much. Instead, together with large military expenditures, they increased budgetary deficits. Moreover, the growth of imports over exports had detrimental effects on the balance of payments and the debt accumulation.

Total United States aid to Greece in 1947–1966 amounted to $3,749 million, about half of which ($1,854 million) was military assistance and half economic aid. The largest part of the aid ($3,411 million) consisted of grants, and the rest ($338 million) of loans. Technical assistance was terminated in 1962 and major economic aid was ended in 1964. Only military assistance under the auspices of NATO continued thereafer. U.S. present aid is about $350 million annually.

GRECO-TURKISH WAR AND ITS AFTERMATH

The assassination of the heir to the Hapsburg (Austrian-Hungarian) throne, Archduke Francis Ferdinand, on June 28, 1914 at Sarajevo, the capital of Bosnia (now part of Yugoslavia), was used as a reason for the outbreak of World War I. However, other factors such as nationalistic and imperialistic expansions were in the background of the ignition of this bloody war that engulfed Greece and Turkey as well. These two nations had already been enemies in serious fighting during the Balkan Wars, 1912–1913.

Turkey joined the Central Powers on November 2, 1914, and German warships entered the straits of the Dardanelles. Winston Churchill, the First Lord of the British Admiralty, persuaded the cabinet and the Allies to send an expedition to take Constantinople and the straits. On April 25, 1915, Allied forces, mainly British, landed on the Gallipoli beaches but were badly defeated by the Turkish and the Central Powers troops.

On March 18, 1915, the Constantinople Agreement among Britain, France, and Russia promised Russia Constantinople, the Dardanelles, part of eastern Anatolia and Inbros and Tenedos, among other areas. But the Bolsheviks renounced all claims to Turkish territories in 1917. Greece entered World War I on the side of the Allies in 1917.

In July 1918 Sultan Mehmet V died and his brother, known as Mehmet VI, succeeded him. His policy was to remain sultan, no matter how much of his territory might be taken by the Allies (British, French, Russians, and later Italians and Greeks). On November 13, 1918, Allied vessels, including the Greek ship *Averoff*, anchored at Istanbul, where French troops were disembarked on February 8, 1919.

For purposes of fighting the Bolsheviks in Russia, Greece sent 45,000 soldiers to join the other Allied forces, but they were defeated and returned home.

On May 6, 1919, Woodrow Wilson, the president of the United States, advanced a proposition to the Council of Four (Britain, France, Italy, and the United States) to unite the Smyrna district and the Dodecanese with Greece. On May 15, Greek forces landed in Smyrna, under the cover of British, French, and U.S. vessels. This was the beginning of the terrible Greco-Turkish drama of 1919–1922. With the blessings of Lloyd George, Greek troops fanned out of the Smyrna zone on June 22 and occupied large territories, enclosing Bursa, the Panderma railway, and Ushak.

On August 10, 1920, the Constantinople government signed the Treaty of Sèvres, under which Greece was to receive eastern Thrace and the islands of Inbros and Tenedos, while Smyrna and its hinterland were to be administered by Greece for five years.[6] Thereafter, a plebiscite would decide the future status of the region. Also, an autonomous Kurdish state and an independent Armenia were to be created.

Venizelos, who survived an assassination attempt in Paris on August 10, returned to Athens to organize the November 14 national elections. However, people were tired of some ten years of war and put him out of office. His Liberal party won only 118 of 369 parliamentary seats and Venizelos himself was not elected, in spite of his political and diplomatic successes.

The Greek royalists, with Constantine I back on the throne, decided to advance further into Anatolia, although they had promised during the election period to bring the soldiers back home. On the other hand, Allied financial support for the Greek forces was withdrawn, and strained relations developed with the departure of Venizelos to Paris. After a new offensive on March 23, 1921, and bloody fighting, especially in June and July, the Greeks captured Kutahya and Eski Shehir. Marching under a broiling sun through the Anatolian Desert they crossed the Sakarya River, some fifty miles from Ankara.

In the meantime, improvements in Turkey's diplomacy achieved striking successes. By October 1921, France and Italy had withdrawn from Anatolia, while the Soviet Union signed a treaty with the Turkish nationalists recognizing them and arranging the borders between Russia and Turkey.

As the Greek army advanced from Smyrna toward Ankara, Turkish resistance was organized, primarily by Yörük Ali Efe and the efficient leader Kemal Ataturk, who later became president of the republic.[7] Kemal was known as the hero of Gallipoli, where he was victorious against the invasion by the Allies in 1915 for which Winston Churchill, Britain's navy minister, was primarily responsible. The Turks did not react intensely against the loss of the external provinces, but the invasion of the homeland itself aroused fierce resentment, especially by the

Map 3.1
Proposed Partition of Turkey under the Treaty of Sèvres

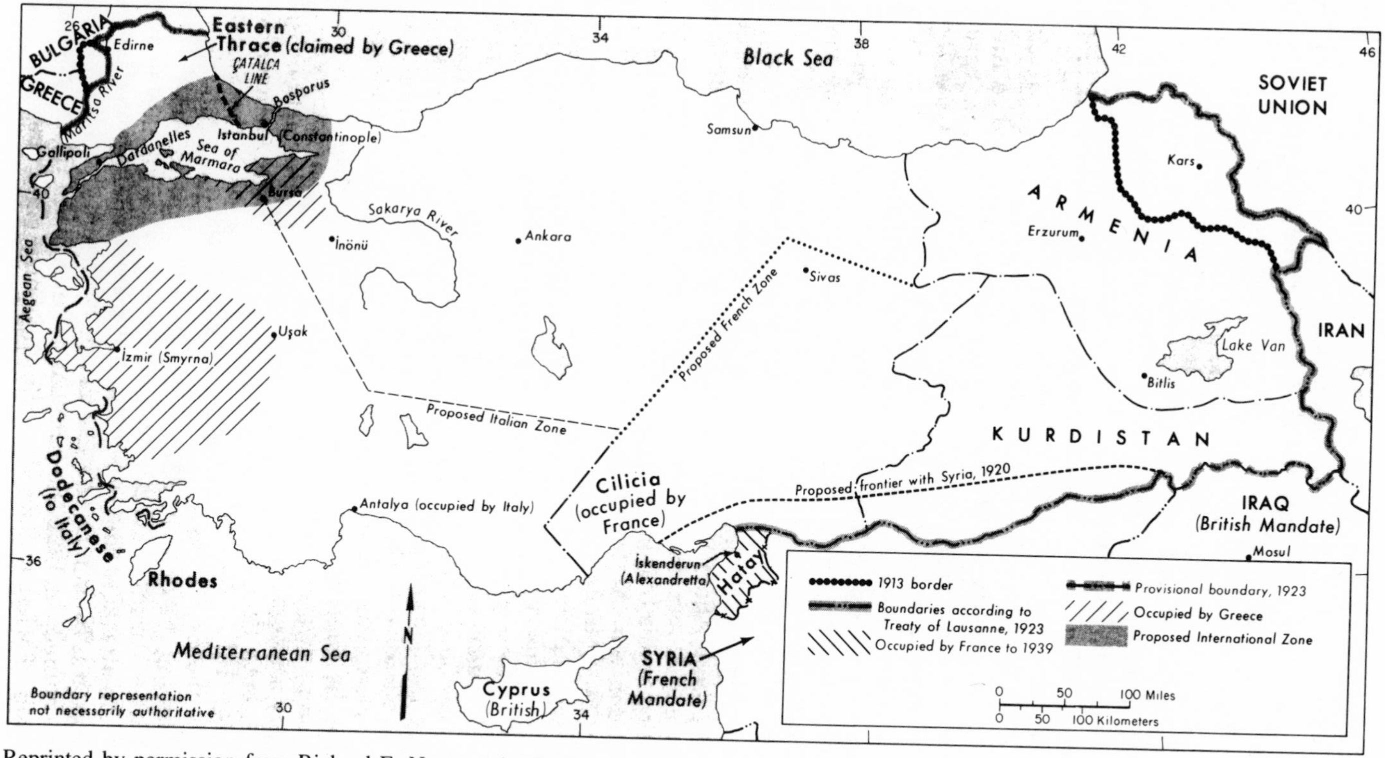

Reprinted by permission from Richard F. Nyrop, ed., *Turkey: A Country Study*, Third Edition, Washington, D.C.: The American University, 1980, p. 45.

nationalists under Kemal Ataturk, who rejected the Treaty of Sèvres outright. In the meantime, Kemal's forces were armed secretly by France and openly by Russia. Lenin supported the "liberation" Turkish forces against the "imperialistic" aims of the Greeks, who were supporting the expedition of the Allies against the Bolsheviks.

On August 26, 1922, the Greek army, with unreliable communications and limited supplies, under heavy artillery fire and a ferocious attack by the Turkish infantry, broke and fled in panic back to Ismir (Smyrna) with heavy losses. On September 9, the victorious Kemal came to Ismir hoping to stop the massacres and terror inflicted by the Turks on the Greek and Armenian populations. "For days the streets were hideous with murder and pillage,"[8] while half of the city was destroyed by fires whose marks are still visible today. A number of Allied vessels (U.S., British, French, and Italian) anchored off Smyrna refused to allow the terror-stricken people to embark for protection. The Turkish massacre and cruelty continued to the degree that George Horton, the American consul, stated that "a feeling of shame that I belong to the human race" prevailed. About 125,000 Greeks and Armenians were killed in Smyrna alone.

On October 11, 1922, an armistice was signed at Mudanya, which represented by Allied surrender to the demands of the nationalist Turks. A week later, Lloyd George, the British prime minister, who encouraged the Greek army and the palace to undertake the adventure in Asia Minor, handed in his resignation. On July 24, 1923, the Treaty of Lausanne was signed, under which Greece lost eastern Thrace and the Smyrna zone, while a compulsory exchange of some 400,000 Turkish nationals with 1,500,000 Greek nationals was stipulated.[9] About 500,000 Greeks were killed. This was the Greek tragedy of ten years of war and some 4 million refugees (from Russia, Asia Minor, and eastern Thrace). In spite of the severe economic and social suffering, the new blood and talent imported with the refugees contributed to the development of the country thereafter.

Reconciliation and Cooperation

To avoid dependence on great powers Venizelos strove to establish friendly relations with neighboring nations, such as Italy (September 28, 1928), Yugoslavia (March 17, 1929) and, particularly, Turkey. With Italy, all important differences were settled, except the status of the Dodecanese Islands. With Yugoslavia, more privileges were given in its use of the Salonika Free Zone. Full diplomatic relations were established with Bulgaria.

With concessions by both sides, Greece and Turkey achieved friendly relations and on June 10, 1929, an agreement was signed. Turkey agreed to accept the Greeks in Constantinople (Istanbul) as permanent residents and Greece paid 425,000 pounds for the property of the Turks who left Greece.

More important treaties were signed on October 30, 1930, when Venizelos went to Ankara, and in 1931, when Ismet Inonou, the Turkish foreign minister, went to Athens. In addition to the cordial relations established at that time, economic relations were improved and trade between the two countries increased. Moreover, a new spirit of friendship and cooperation was created when more agreements were enacted by all Balkan nations on commerce, transportation, tourism, and other services.

During the depression years (1929–1934) severe economic hardship came to both countries, especially to Greece, where gross trade declined 70.5 percent in value, with total imports at 587.28 million gold francs as against exports of only 279.87 million gold francs.[10] In spite of the economic hardship of that time, relations between Greece and Turkey improved greatly, not only on economic but on political matters as well.

THE ESTABLISHMENT OF MODERN TURKEY

During the Balkan wars and World War I, the Ottoman Empire slipped to its doom. The heterogeneous population that inhabited its farflung and unwieldy area, the differences between Muslims and Christians, and the economic, social, and military disturbances at home and pressures from abroad were among the main causes of decline.

The disintegration of the Ottoman Empire was associated with territorial claims and occupations by the victorious Allies. So, "the sick man of Europe," as Tsar Nicholas I of Russia described (1833) the Ottoman Empire, was dismembered, as Britain, France, and Italy took over Arab and other provinces.

Another element of crisis in the empire came from the Young Turks. After the suppression of their movement in 1876, they started an underground movement that flourished, especially in Salonika. Advocating racial and religious equality and the end of autocracy, the movement, represented by the Committee of Union and Progress, was supported by some young army officers, including Enver Bey and Mustafa Kemal. Although the Young Turks managed to introduce some reforms, especially in 1909 and 1910, they faced serious problems of inflexibility on the part of the Moslem judicial institutions that dominated the Ottoman society. Moreover, the formation of the Balkan League in 1912 by Greece, Serbia, and Bulgaria and their concerted attack on Turkey in the autumn of that year liberated almost all the European sections of the Ottoman Empire. On the other hand, the alliance of Russia with Britain, France, and Italy made some Young Turks favor alliance with Germany and war against the Allies, who wanted the partition of Turkey. Thereafter the Young Turks became, to a large extent, nationalistic and abandoned their movement for reforms for equality and progress. However, they were able to record some progress. With French advisers, they reformed the tax system toward eliminating the curse of the old regime of tax-farming, while with British supervisors they reformed the customs duties. In any case, their movement subsequently helped the westernization and modernization of Turkey.

After the Greco-Turkish war and the rise of Kemal Ataturk, the borders of today's Turkey were determined (Treaty of Lausanne, July 24, 1923) and economic reforms were introduced. Ataturk (meaning "father of Turkey") wanted the de-Islamization and westernization of Turkey. This transformation, although slow and painful, reached partial fulfillment, at least in economic development terms.

Among the major reforms introduced by Kemalist nationalists were: abolishment of the sultanate and caliphate, the fez was outlawed and the veiling of women discouraged, new civil penal and commercial codes based on European models and a new constitution were adopted, a new alphabet based on Latin was introduced, women could vote and hold office, and a state capitalist control of the public sector (*etatism*) was introduced with the new constitution.

The Young Turks, influenced by the Russian Revolution and the English Fabian ideas, were enthusiastic about state control over the economy of the Ataturk regime, according to which if the private sector did not perform well then the state would interfere and even take over productive operations. At that time and especially during the 1930s, protective tariffs were raised, transport rates were reduced, and lands for industrial sites were granted, particularly for sugar and textile factories.[11]

The five-year plan, which was announced by Ataturk in 1935, incorporated a number of reforms for the modernization and development of the Turkish economy. Investment in plant and equipment, not only by the private but also by the public sector, was emphasized. Public sector investment was to be financed through taxation. Direct taxes, which were about 30 percent of total taxes, included income taxes that were graduated from 15 to 45 percent. Indirect taxes, about 60 percent of total taxation, provided the largest part of government revenue.[12]

During the prewar and early post–World War II periods, the economy of Turkey was primarily based on agricultural production, mainly tobacco and grain. Mining, textiles, leather, and food processing were also important. After the economic reforms of Kemal Ataturk, protective tariffs were raised, domestic savings were encouraged, and highways, railroads, and other public works were built. Agricultural productivity and self-sufficiency were emphasized. Industrial progress was also pursued but less intensively. The government of Ismet Inonu (1938–1950) continued to emphasize the agricultural sector at the neglect of the industrial sector. During the years of "emergence" of the Turkish economy (1923–1950), the lack of entrepreneurship and the weakness of the private sector were largely responsible for the rapid growth of state economic enterprises (SEEs). However, the policy of self-sufficiency pursued by the Turkish policymakers during that period did not permit much trade expansion with neighboring Greece.

Gradually, and particularly in the 1930s, Germany penetrated and established a firm position in Turkey. The Germans trained the Turkish army, projected and assisted the construction of the Berlin-Baghdad Railway, and invested in a number of industries.[13] During World War II, the Turks managed to preserve neutrality and stay out of the ordeal and the destruction of war faced by other countries, particularly Greece.

Due primarily to World War II conditions, economic growth in the 1940s was impressive. High growth rates of the GNP (Gross National Product) continued in the 1950s as well, due mainly to an increase in the nonagricultural labor force rather than to productivity growth.

However, the gap in per capita income between the urban industrial workers and the rural workers was and still is large. Moreover, the opening of the economy to the West increased the propensity to import without a substantial increase in exports. Then the government's optimistic policies, projecting great leaps forward, proved largely ineffective because of the difficulties of changing a culturally and religiously conservative society in a short period. This is a familiar phenomenon in developing nations such as Turkey. There it could be observed as early as the intensive developmental efforts of Kemal Ataturk years ago.

The Armenian Tragedy

After the victory of Russia over the Turks in 1877–1878, the Treaty of Berlin was concluded in June 1878. It permitted Britain to take Cyprus and sanctioned the gradual replacement of Turkey in Europe by the Balkan states, while Armenia, Crete, and Macedonia were designated as objects of the Great Powers. The Turkish sultan Abdul Hamid II, ''The Great Assassin,'' who had been associated with the Bulgarian massacres of 1876, utilized religious passions for political ends and resorted to organized genocide of the Armenian Christians, extending not only to the mountains of Armenia bordering Russia, but also to the streets of Constantinople (1894–1896, 1909).

Article 61 of the Treaty of Berlin, designating Armenia as an area of concern for the Allies, served as a pretext for inflaming the Turks' hatred of the Christian element and became the cause of its ruin. This led to the formation and execution of a diabolical scheme of extermination of the Armenians in Istanbul and in Armenia proper by Turkish soldiers and wild Kurdish horsemen. Among other crimes, women were sold as slaves after being bestially violated. In the words of the historian Arnold Toynbee, ''The intermittent sufferings of the Armenian race have culminated in an organized, cold-blooded attempt on the part of the Turkish rulers to exterminate it once and for all by methods of inconceivable barbarism and wickedness.''[14]

A systematic slaughter of some 1.5 million Armenians, including women and children, took place on April 24, 1915, close to the Russian borders. Those who survived the massacre were ordered to make a long disastrous walk, ''a death march,'' toward the Syrian borders. Most of them perished from hunger, hardship, and torture or were hanged along the way, especially in the desert of Der-Es-Zor.

The premeditated, systematic annihilation of the Armenian people in 1915–1923 has been recognized. However, scholars trusted by the Turks, such as Ezel

Kural Shaw and Bernard Lewis, do not agree as to the number of people killed. While Armenians claim that as many as 2 million were massacred, writers sympathetic to the Turkish arguments base their calculations on the Ottoman census of 1914 and argue that the Armenian population was only 1.3 million. They contend that 400,000 Armenian people were actually transported in 1915–1916, some 700,000 fled to the Caucasus, western Europe, and the United States, and 100,000 remained in Turkey. Therefore, they estimate that about 300,000 were slaughtered.

Regardless of whether there were 300,000 or 2 million, or, more probably, 1.5 million people who perished, the truth is that these horrible atrocities by the Turks between 1915 and 1923 aimed at the extermination of the Armenians. In addition to the ones slaughtered in their homes, many died during their transfer or "death march." Clemenceau had to admit that "the history of mankind has never presented such an example of organized horror." Mothers saw their children die of starvation in their arms. A little girl told her mother that when she died she did not want to give her body to the others to eat because they did not give her meat from the others' bodies while she starved. This was an organized Hitler-like genocide of worldwide importance.[15]

In 1987, the European Assembly recognized the Armenian genocide in the sense of genocide defined by the General Assembly of the United Nations. However, it also recognized that the Turkey of today must not be held responsible for the tragedy of the Armenians belonging to the Ottoman Empire.

During the period of the Armenian genocide by the Turks, many Armenians fled to the Armenian Soviet Socialist Republic. There they erected a monument in memory of the massacre, which is still open to visitors and tourists. The author visited this monument during a research trip to eastern Europe. An eternal flame, under a high metallic arch, and a historical account of the Armenian ordeal in the background are the sad characteristics of this place.

Another ordeal of the Armenians occurred in Smyrna in 1922. When the Greek troops retreated from the disastrous expedition into Asia Minor, Smyrna was burned and pillaged, raped and wrecked by the Turks. "The Armenians, with nowhere to go, were slaughtered although they played no part in the Greek recklessness."[16] As Ernest Hemingway reported, the retreating Greeks, on the other hand, smashed the legs of their loyal mules so that they might never carry Turkish masters.

To avoid being caught and persecuted by a recalcitrant Turkey, the Armenian people, with one of the most ancient civilizations in the world, are still fleeing their homeland to other countries and scrambling for a safe position elsewhere. It is estimated that only about 60,000 Armenians remain in Turkey now, primarily in Istanbul, and about 6 million are spread all over the world, mainly in the Soviet Union and the United States. This is the tragedy of the Armenian people who continue to struggle for a sovereign homeland under difficult conditions.

United States congressional joint resolutions are presented from time to time to designate April 24 as a day of remembrance honoring Armenian victims of the genocidal massacre and dispersion in 1915. However, the American government discourages the approval of such a resolution on the ground that it would harm relations with Turkey, which is regarded as an important ally. To remember the ordeal of their ancestors, Armenians parade in New York on April 24 every year. As George Deukmejian, the governor of California, said, the idea is that mature societies admit their past mistakes to avoid repetitions similar to that of Hitler who decided he could get away with the extermination of the Jews because, as he put it, "Who still talks nowadays about the extermination of the Armenians?" (Or that of Cambodia in April 1975 and later, when about one-fourth of the people were destroyed.) In revenge, underground Armenian groups, such as the Justice Commandos Against Armenian Genocide and others, have resorted to bombing Turkish airline and tourist offices and assassinations of Turkish diplomats in different countries and cities, such as Paris, Lisbon, Geneva, Athens, and Los Angeles.[17]

The Kurdish Struggle for Independence

The Kurds, a fairly homogeneous Moslem tribal society of some 14 million people, are of Indo-European origin. They live in an area extending from western Iran (Kermansach) to northern Iraq and Syria but they are mostly located in the eastern provinces of Turkey, especially in the regions of Kars and Arntachan. Primarily, they belong to the Sunni branch of Islam, opposing the Shiite Moslems, sharing no common characteristics with the Turks, the Persians, or the Arabs. The region in which they live has been divided mainly among three countries (Turkey, Iran, and Iraq) and this makes it difficult for their union in one independent Kurdish nation. Moreover, each of these countries at times uses its Kurdish minority against the other neighboring countries for its own benefit, or makes alliances to coordinate policies toward annihilation of the autonomy-seeking Kurds.

These stubborn Kurdish people opposed the Seljuk Turks and later the Ottoman oppressors for a long time, but being under the antagonism of powerful Turkey and Persia, they could not achieve independence.[18] Kurdish nationalism expanded during the nineteenth and especially at the beginning of the twentieth century. The Treaty of Sèvres in 1920 gave to the victorious powers (mainly Britain, France, and Italy) the possibility to grant autonomy to the Kurds. However, with the Treaty of Lausanne in 1923, the Treaty of Sèvres was void and the Allies did not keep their promise. Since then, the Kurds have been continuing their struggle for independence.

After Turkey became a republic in 1924, the Kurds rose, from time to time, against Turkish oppression. Thus, in the uprising of 1924, some 15,200 Kurds were killed and 206 villages were destroyed. Also, similar revolts broke out in 1925 and 1930, as well as in 1937 and 1938. In the serious battle of Tunceli (Dersim) in 1938, the Kurds were defeated by the Turks. As a result, the Tunceli province was placed under martial law until 1946. The Soviet Union occupied northwestern Iran in 1945–1946 and allowed the creation of the state of Kurdistan (Mahaband). After the Soviets left, the Iranians reoccupied the new state and executed its president, Zaki Mohamant.

After World War II, the oppression of Kurds in Turkey began to relax in some ways, and some religious and nationalistic activities were tolerated. However, after May 27, 1960, the military dictatorship in Turkey again started prosecuting Kurdish separatists and sentenced some of them to death.[19]

Major Kurdish rebel attacks occurred mainly in Iraq after 1960. The Kurdish struggle for independence in Iraq forced the Baath party of Sadat Housein to recognize some form of autonomy and to include some of their leaders in the General Assembly. Also, limited but temporary autonomy was offered by Iran after the disturbances in March 1979, in which more than 100 people were killed.

Similar improvements in the status of the Kurds occurred in Turkey in the 1960s and the late 1970s, when liberalism was flourishing. The Kurds were attracted to liberal and leftist parties like the Turkish Workers party that was sympathetic to Kurdish aspirations. However, when the party was dissolved by the military regime in 1971, some Kurds began to form their own clandestine organizations. Others, like Serafettin Elci, joined the Republican People's party, a social democratic group. Elci served as minister of public works when this party was in power under Prime Minister Bulent Ecevit in 1978 and 1979 and supported the economic development of the backward eastern region where the Kurds lived.

After the armed forces came to power on September 12, 1980, the junta once again began to arrest and prosecute Kurdish nationalists, including Elci, who argued that the eastern region has been left to poverty and misery and that "it is natural that there should be reactions in an underdeveloped society that is oppressed."[20] Massive trials of Kurds have taken place since the military coup of 1980 for "illegal" activities inside Turkey and abroad (mainly in Sweden) aiming at introducing a language other than Turkish and "attempting to divide the Turkish nation into ethnic groups."[21]

At present, the largest Kurdish segment lives in Turkey, where unemployment is high and people feel neglected. The economic backwardness of the area and the Kurdish independence movement are responsible for disturbances and violence from time to time. Some 8 to 10 million Kurds are believed to live in Turkey. They are among the poorest people of the country. Diyarbakir, the capital of what Kurdish clandestine nationalists call Kurdistan, Van, and other cities around the river Tigris are known for poor housing, unpaved streets, and economic backwardness. Turkish security and armed forces are busy in their drive against Kurdish nationalist organizations, said to number about ten. A principal clandestine Kurdish organization is Apo, a name derived from that of its leader, Abdurrahman Ocal. These organizations that demand independence put slogans on walls and elsewhere in Turkish and Kurdish and call for "Freedom for Kurdistan." Frequently visitors can hear a student, a clerk, or a writer declare:

"I am Kurdish, not Turk." The separatists are centered mainly in high schools and universities.

However, there have been no serious revolutions since the insurrections in the 1920s and 1930s. It is estimated that about 80 people of Kurdish origin are sitting in the 635-number Turkish Parliament. Although Turkish authorities try to understate the Kurdish movement for self-determination and independence, the problem remains and at times becomes serious as disturbances and massive trials occur.

Kurdish separatist fighters have been conducting hit-and-run raids, especially in recent years. Sometimes, Kurds in Turkey receive help from Kurdish camps in Iraq. Under a 1984 agreement between Turkey and Iraq, Turkey is permitted to carry out operations against these camps on Iraq territory. Turkey has conducted a number of raids with aircraft and ground forces. However, Iran objects to such operations, saying they help Iraq. In May 1983, Turkish infantry crossed the Iraqi borders hunting and killing Kurdish separatists.[22] In August 1986, Turkish planes entered Iraq and bombarded Kurdish camps. In a similar air attack on March 4, 1987, it was estimated that 100 people were killed. Some 30 planes from the Batman and Diyarbakir airfields were used for raids against three locations in Iraq.[23] In the previous attack 242 partisans, fighting for self-determination, and 211 civilians were killed.

EFFECTS OF THE CONFLICTS OVER CYPRUS

The strategic position of Cyprus attracted the involvement of the Great Powers in its affairs for the promotion of their own interests. From ancient times through the Roman and Byzantine periods on to the Ottoman and British occupations, and primarily during its recent postliberation years, the island has had a turbulent history that perhaps no other region can match. It survived many invasions, occupations, and intrusions by a number of superpowers.

Greek warriors returning from the Trojan expedition with their fleet, in about 1200 B.C., were misdirected by strong winds and sailed to Cyprus. They were mainly Arcadians, under General Agapenor, and they settled in the area of Paphos where they built the sanctuary of Goddess Aphrodite.

In July 1570, Cyprus fell to the Ottomans, in spite of the heroic defense by a mixed force of Greeks and Italians under the command of Bradadin, an experienced Venetian general. With the Treaty of Berlin, concluded in June 1878, the island passed from Ottoman Turkish hands to Britain, which annexed it outright in 1914. At the end of World War II, the population of the island (600,000) was and still is approximately 80 percent Greek and 18 percent Turkish.

After World War II, the Cypriote Greek majority wanted an end to the British occupation and in the 1950s started guerrilla fighting for liberation. On August 29, 1955, the British, following their usual diplomatic practice of divide and rule, organized a conference in London, in which Turkey was invited to participate as a third member in the arrangements for Cyprus's independence. This three-member conference became and still is the source for serious conflicts between Greece and Turkey over Cyprus.

On September 6–7, 1955, some three to four days after a pro-Cyprus demonstration in London, new serious disturbances broke out in Istanbul, and to a lesser extent in Smyrna, because of bomb explosions in the house where Kemal Ataturk was born and in the Turkish consulate, both in Salonika. Although the damage was not severe, the media, especially newspapers in extra editions, and the Turkish foreign minister and other government officials exaggerated the events. Then a mob of youngsters demonstrated and proceeded to burn stores and houses owned by Greek people in Istanbul. The police and the responsible authorities of the Menderes government did not offer protection.[24] In Smyrna, though, violence was not as serious as in Istanbul and destruction was less severe. However, attacks in Smyrna against Greek officers, working in the NATO offices, and their wives had serious emotional effects in Greece. In Ankara, though, the chief of prefecture (nomarchis) offered enough protection and avoided serious disturbances.

As a result, a new wave of refugees left Istanbul for Greece to avoid atrocities. Of 80,000 Greeks living there, only a few thousand remained. The explanation of the Menderes government, which neglected to provide needed policy and army protection, was that the disturbances were instigated by "red agents."

In the late 1950s, Greece and Turkey tried to improve their political and economic relations through high-level political contacts. Constantine Caramanlis, prime minister of Greece, visited Ankara in 1959 and had friendly discussions with Menderes, the prime minister of Turkey, and other government officials. Celal Bayar, the president of Turkey, also visited Athens.

In 1960, Cyprus secured its independence from British control.[25] However, the issue of the Greek majority rule versus the Turkish minority rights remained after Cyprus became an independent republic. Internal stress and conflicts caused major crises in 1964 and 1967, during which Greece and Turkey verged on war. In 1964, United States president Lyndon Johnson warned against a Turkish intervention in Cyprus, threatening that the United States would not defend Turkey against a possible Soviet attack.

In 1964, a Turkish discriminatory decree (No. 6/3801/11.2.64) was imposed against Greek citizens that deprived them of their rights to carry out legal dealings with regard to the transfer of property. This measure is in contradiction to the association agreement between Turkey and the EEC, and Greece is using it to refuse entry of Turkey into the EEC.

In July 1974 the right-wing military junta in Athens, which governed Greece since 1967, conducted a coup against the government of Cyprus under Archbishop Makarios III.[26] Some 650 Greek army officers assigned to Cyprus's National Guard, according to the 1960 independence agreement guaranteed by Greece, Turkey, and Britain, were used to install Nicos Sampson as president, after overthrowing the legitimate president, Archbishop Makarios. They aimed mainly at enosis, union of Greece and Cyprus.

On July 20, some 6,000 Turkish troops, reinforced over the next few days by more than 25,000 additional troops with U.S. equipment, invaded and occupied some 40 percent of Cyprus, in spite of UN Secretary Council resolutions and objections of Britain, the United States, and the EEC. Some 200,000 Greek Cypriot refugees out of a total population of 600,000 fled to the south and about 10,000 Turkish Cypriot refugees were flown to northern Cyprus. At that time and later the Turks sent in settlers from Anatolia to colonize areas and properties that belonged to Greek Cypriots.

In protest over the continued occupation of Cyprus by Turkish forces, the United States Congress imposed an embargo on military assistance to Turkey. The embargo seemed not to have had much practical results and was lifted in 1978. In 1983, Decktash, the leader of the Turkish Cypriots, declared the creation of a separate Turkish Cypriot republic, which was not recognized by any nation but Turkey. After so many years and despite the repetitive resolutions of the United Nations for the withdrawal of the Turkish troops and settlement of the Cyprus conflict through negotiations between the Greek and the Turkish communities, the problem still remains unsolved and irritates the relations of Greece and Turkey, especially in the Aegean Sea.

Thus, Cyprus, Aphrodite's isle, which has always been a pawn of the Mediterranean chessboard, is still a source of contention between Greece and Turkey, as Turkish troops have occupied about 40 percent of the island since 1974.

NOTES

1. William McGrew, *Land and Revolution in Modern Greece, 1800–1881* (Kent, Ohio: Kent State University Press, 1985), chap. 10.

2. Leften Stavrianos, *The Balkan since 1453* (New York: Holt, Rinehart and Winston, 1958), 296–99.

3. For the dismal economic conditions and the efforts toward stabilization in 1943–1946, see Gail Makinen, "The Greek Hyperinflation and Stabilization at 1943–1946," *Journal of Economic History* 156, no. 3 (September 1986): 795–805.

4. Winston Churchill, *Memoirs of the Second World War* (Boston: Houghton Mifflin, 1959), 885–86. For the British influence on Greece and its replacement by Americans, see Heinz Richter, *British Intervention in Greece* (London: Merlin Press, 1986), 201–19.

5. Walter Lippmann in the *Herald Tribune*, April 1, 1947, reprinted in Stephen Rousseas, *The Death of a Democracy: Greece and the American Conscience* (New York: Grove Press, 1967), 84. More on American aid in Harry Psomiades, "The Economic and Social Transformation of Modern Greece," *Journal of International Affairs* 19 (1965): 194–205; and C. Munkman, *American Aid to Greece* (New York: Praeger, 1958), chap. 4.

6. Harry N. Howard, *The Partition of Turkey: A Diplomatic History, 1913–1923*

(New York: Howard Fertig, 1966), chap. 7. Also Lawrence Evans, *United States Policy and the Partition of Turkey, 1914–1924*. (Baltimore: Johns Hopkins University Press, 1965), chap. 10.

7. Geoffrey Lewis, *Modern Turkey* (New York: Praeger, 1974), 63–74.

8. Lewis, *Modern Turkey*, 84. Similar horrible events occurred in other cities as well. Thus, in Pergamus some 600 people were burned in a church by the Turkish army.

9. For firsthand information about the ordeal of the refugees, from Ernest Hemingway, see Charles Fenton, *The Apprenticeship of Ernest Hemingway* (New York: Farrar, Straus and Young, 1954), chap. 8; and Arnold Toynbee, *The Western Question in Greece and Turkey* (New York: H. Fertig, 1970), chap. 7.

10. Stavrianos, *The Balkans since 1453*, 666. For more details on Balkan cooperation, see Nicholas Gianaris, *The Economics of the Balkan Countries: Albania, Bulgaria, Greece, Romania, Turkey, Yugoslavia* (New York: Praeger, 1982), 48–52; Robert Kerner, *The Balkan Conferences and the Balkan Entente, 1930–1935* (Berkeley: University of California Press, 1963), chaps. 2–6; and Leften Stavrianos, *Balkan Federation* (Hamden, Conn.: Archon Books, 1964).

11. Stanford Shaw, *History of the Ottoman Empire and Modern Turkey* (London: Cambridge University Press, 1976–1977), chap. 6. For the argument that many of the Young Turks, including Djavid Bey and Mustafa Kemal (Ataturk), were hidden Jews, *doenmehs* (the renegades), see Joachim Prinz, *The Secret Jews* (New York: Random House, 1973), 118–22.

12. Philip Price, *A History of Turkey: From Empire to Republic* (London: Allen and Unwin, 1965), chap. 7.

13. Wayne Vucinich, *The Ottoman Empire: Its Record and Legacy* (New York: D. Van Nostrand, 1965), 178–79.

14. Vahan Kurkjian, *A History of Armenia* (New York: Armenian General Benevolent Union of America, 1964), 299. See also Gerard Chaliand, *The Armenians, From Genocide to Resistance*, trans. Tony Berrett (London: Zed Press, 1983); and Moses Khorenatsi, *History of the Armenians*, trans. R. Thomson (Cambridge: Harvard University Press, 1978).

15. Kevork Bardkjian, *Hitler and the Armenian Genocide* (Cambridge, Mass.: Zoryan Institute, 1985), chap. 4. Also, "The Sorrows of Armenia," *New York Times*, April 26, 1983, sec. A; Doris Cross, "The Unanswered Armenian Question," *New York Times*, March 26, 1980, sec. A.

16. Kurkjian, *A History of Armenia*, 302. See also International League for the Rights and Liberation of Peoples, *A Crime of Silence: The Armenian Genocide* (London: Zed Books, 1985), chaps. 1–3; and Frederic Raphael, "Where History's Sweep Conquers the Visitor," *New York Times*, January 18, 1987.

17. For more details, see "Inconvenience vs. Armenians," *New York Times*, May 4, 1985, editorial; "Turkish Envoy in Lisbon is Killed by Gunman," *New York Times*, June 8, 1985, sec. A; "Turks Assail Armenian Terrorists," *New York Times*, March 6, 1981, sec. A; and Marvine Howe, "Turks, Angry at 'Passivity,' Mourn Slain Diplomats," *New York Times*, March 13, 1981, sec. A.

18. Xenophon, in his *Anabasis*, mentioned that "the Greeks . . . had been seven days passing through the country of the Kurds, fighting all the time . . . " and that they suffered more than from the king of Persia. Edgar O'Ballance, *The Kurdish Revolt: 1961–1970* (Hamden, Conn.: Archon Books, 1973), 15.

19. Derk Kinnane, *The Kurds and Kurdistan* (London: Oxford University Press, 1964), chap. 4.

20. Marvine Howe, "Turks Imprison Former Minister Who Spoke up on Kurd's Behalf," *New York Times*, March 27, 1981; also, Fredirick Barth, *Principles of Social Organization in Southern Kurdistan* (Oslo: Universitets Ethnografiske Museum, 1953), chap. 1.

21. For example, on November 1980 some 200 Kurds were arrested and prosecuted by the Turkish military. Also, 2,331 Kurds were arrested and 447 were tried in April 1981, while 97 of them were punished by severe penalties or death; Marvine Howe, "Turkey Opens Campaign Against Kurdish Rebels," *New York Times*, April 1, 1981, sec. A.

22. "Turkish Troops Reported to Battle Iraqi Troops," *New York Times*, May 31, 1983, sec. A. Skirmishes near Diyarbakir, between Kurdish separatists and Turkish soldiers, are reported from time to time. At least 700 people, 200 security members, have been killed since mid–1984. Alan Cowell, "Turkey Admits Inroads by Kurdish Guerrillas," *New York Times*, October 22, 1987, sec. A.

23. "Turkey Says Its Planes Raided Kurdish Guerilla Bases in Iraq," *New York Times*, March 5, 1987, sec. A. For other raids, see also *Proini*, New York, March 5, 1987 and June 22, 1987; and "Spring in Turkey, and Kurds' Insurgency Revised," *New York Times*, May 17, 1987, sec. A.

24. Some 4,000 stores, 2,000 houses, and 29 Greek and some Armenian and Catholic churches, as well as a number of schools, were destroyed. Also, the funerals in Tsisli and Paloukli were profaned. More details in the reports of the British Counselor Michael Steward, Istanbul, September 22, 1955 in the Archives of Foreign Office. Also *ELEF-THEROTYPIA*, January 8–13, 1985.

25. For the independence agreement, signed in Zurich, and its aftermath, see Stanley Kyriakides, *Cyprus: Constitutionalism and Crisis in Government* (Philadelphia: University of Pennsylvania Press, 1968); and Lawrence Stern, *Wrong Horse* (New York: New York Times Publishing Co., 1980).

26. For the rule of the Greek junta and its effects on Cyprus, see Andreas G. Papandreou, *Democracy at Gunpoint: The Greek Front* (New York: Doubleday, 1970); and Chris Woodhouse, *Karamanlis: The Restorer of Greek Democracy* (Oxford: Clarendon Press, 1982), chaps. 8–9.

II

DOMESTIC ECONOMIC
PROBLEMS

The preceding chapters of Part I examined briefly the historical trends of Greece and Turkey. The following chapters of Part II deal with such domestic aspects as natural and human resources and their productivity, developmental problems of the agricultural, industrial, and service sectors, and fiscal and monetary policies for economic stability and growth, with emphasis on problems of taxation, inflation, and unemployment.

Greece channels large amounts of investment into the housing and services sectors at the neglect of the manufacturing sector; while Turkey, being a less developed country, is based heavily on the primary or agricultural sector, mainly to provide the basic necessities to its rapidly growing population. Because these two countries constitute the natural gateway of Europe and Asia, common investment ventures are needed to improve their transportation network.

The market economies of Greece and Turkey face serious problems of large deficits in the budgets of the central governments and the budgets of public or semi-public enterprises. Such deficits lead to inflation and/or domestic and external borrowing. To reduce budget deficits and inflation, austerity measures and other fiscal and monetary policies are used by both countries. Tax incentives, subsidies, and credit facilities are also provided to encourage productive investment and reduce unemployment especially in less-developed regions.

Modern technology of mass production and better investment opportunities require large markets and big enterprises, especially in industry. These factors point to the need for improvement in economic relations and even common policies, not only on transportation but also on tourism and trade between these neighboring nations.

4

Resources and Productivity

LAND AND NATURAL RESOURCES

Greece and Turkey are in the eastern Mediterranean Sea at the crossroads of Europe and the Middle East, separated by the Aegean Sea and the Evros River in Thrace. To the north, Greece borders on Bulgaria, Yugoslavia, and Albania. Turkey borders Bulgaria (in eastern Thrace), the Black Sea, and the Soviet Union. To the west, the Adriatic and Ionian seas separate Greece from Italy. To the east, Turkey borders Iran; to the northeast, the Soviet Union; and to the south, Iraq, Syria, and the eastern Mediterranean.

The major ports are Piraeus, Salonika, Patras, Kavala, and Herakleion in Greece, and Istanbul, Izmir, Trabzon, Samsun, and Iskenderun in Turkey. The principal rivers are the Evros River on the Greek-Turkish border; the Nestos, the Strimon, and the Axios in northern Greece; the Pineios and the Acheloos in central and in western Greece; and the Alpheios in the Peloponnesus. In Turkey, the main rivers are the Sakarya in the northwest; the Euphrates and the Tigris in the southeast; the Menderes (Hermes in ancient times), the Gediz, and the Dalaman in the west; the Goksu and the Ceyhan in the south; and the Great Zab, the Murat, and the Coruh in the east. A number of fertile valleys are located primarily along these rivers.

Mainland Greece is an integral part of Europe, composed of varying mountains, the largest of which is the Pindus range in the northern part of the country. It is mostly a rugged goat highland with no meadows, similar to Homer's description of the island of Ithaca. With about 2,800 islands in the Aegean and Ionian seas the total area is 132,000 square kilometers. The islands in the Aegean, with numerous gulfs and bays, may be the remaining high mountain peaks and plateaus of Plato's Atlantis, a lost continent sunk into the sea many centuries ago.

Turkey is part of the great Alpine-Himalayan mountain belt and one of the more active earthquake regions of the world, as is Greece. Thus, a violent earthquake in Erzincam on December 28, 1939 caused about 160,000 deaths.

A structurally complex terrain, Turkey gives the appearance of a plateau between two mountain ranges, the Pontic Mountains along the Black Sea and the Taurus Mountains bounding the Mediterranean Sea and the Arabian Platform and converging in the eastern part of the country. Most of Turkey's total area of 779,000 square kilometers is composed of high plains, with a median altitude of 1,128 meters. Large plains are located around Tuz Golu (Salt Lake). The highest mountain is Ararat (with a peak of 5,166 meters) along the borders with the Soviet Union and Iran, in Turkish Armenia.

The most important cultivated plains of the western part of the country are those of Antalya, Usnurm, Bursa, and Truva (Troy). The central plateau is, for the most part, bare and mountainous, used primarily for grazing. Wooded areas are mainly confined to the northeast and the northwest. Frequent dust storms with a yellow powder are blowing in the summers, and heavy and lasting snows fall in winters. The eastern region consists of wild or barren wasteland, while the climate is severe and rough, from the highlands in the north (called Turkey's Siberia) to the mountains of Kurdistan (land of the Kurds). However, there are some fertile basins, such as the Mus valley close to Lake Van. Extensive mountains of barren limestone are covered by bare rocks. There are also many low, tillable hills where running water is usually absent. Most of the soil is poor, and in many areas resources are meager.

Both countries are situated on the temperate zone, with the warm Mediterranean climate prevailing on the shores. High temperatures in the dry summers force people to take a siesta, stimulate tourism, and promote the production of olives, grapes, figs, peaches, and other fruits. There are thousands of miles of wildly beautiful and strategic coasts. The geographical position of these two countries, halfway between the tropics and the cold North, attracts northerners, who come to enjoy the warmth and natural beauty. Their location, which has been an important factor in both their past and their present, has often been called a curse by the inhabitants as it beckons invaders and superpowers and attracts large numbers of visitors who alter the cultural conditions of the area.

Both countries are rich in mineral resources, which have hardly been located, let alone exploited. Presently, mining contributes a small part (less than 5 percent) to the value of total production in Greece and Turkey. However, it is expected that the increase in world demand for metal and subsoil resources will eventually make this sector more valuable.

The main mineral products of Greece and Turkey are bauxite, lignite, nickel, iron, chromite, and copper. Greece is a leading country in the production of bauxite in western Europe, and Turkey leads in the production of chrome (table 4.1).

Known major minerals in Turkey include iron ore, copper, chrome ore, boron, lignite, coal, oil, asbestos, and manganese. Although mining contributes only a small percent to GNP, it provides the raw material for key manufacturing industries such as iron and steel, aluminum, cement, and electric power. Important mineral exports include copper, boron, and, primarily, chrome. Some 82 percent

Table 4.1
Mining and Quarrying Products (thousand metric tons)

	Greece		Turkey	
	1970	1984	1970	1984
Brown Coal, Lignite	8,081	21,667	3,992	8,200
Iron ore	380	572	1,663	2,207
Bauxite	2,283	2,435	52	296
Chromite ore	19	35	302	196
Copper	n.a.	n.a.	20	32
Lead ore and Zinc ore	10	21	5	13
Magnesite	755	1,598	300	499
Nickel ore (m.t.)	8,600	14,888	n.a.	n.a.
Silver (m.t.)	13	56	n.a.	n.a.
Zinc ore	9	23	24	32
Salt	113	191	648	1,089

Note: n.a. = not available
In a few cases earlier years' data were available.
Source: United Nations, *Statistical Yearbook,* various issues.

of U.S. imports of chromium come from Turkey, Yugoslavia, and South Africa. The public sector dominates about 80 percent of mining output. Etibank, Turkey's largest state enterprise, is the holding company for most of the government's mineral resources.

At present, there is no significant petroleum production in either country. On the Greek island of Thasos, near the port of Kavala, some 30,000 barrels of crude oil per day are produced. (A Canadian-U.S.-West German company exploits this oil field.) Oil production in Turkey declined from 3.6 million tons in 1969 to about 2.5 million tons presently. Production takes place in fields close to the borders of Iran, Iraq, and Syria. Shell Oil Company is the main producer, followed by the government-owned oil company and a few other private enterprises. Proven crude petroleum reserves are estimated at 20 metric tons for Greece and 57 metric tons in Turkey. The government oil company owns and operates the Turkish section of a pipeline from Iraq's Kirkuk fields to near Dortyol. Also, a pipeline of about 500 kilometers transfers oil from Batman to Dortyol, on the Mediterranean coast. To satisfy growing demand for energy, both countries expect to transfer gas from the Soviet Union through long pipelines under construction.

Neither country produces nuclear energy as yet, as neighboring Bulgaria and other European countries do. Consideration of the construction of nuclear energy projects has been discouraged after the accident at Chernobyl in the Soviet Union in April 1986.

Hydroelectric power provides about 10 to 15 percent of the total energy production for Greece and 40 percent for Turkey. Other forms of energy production with good potential in both countries are that of geothermal, solar, and wind energy. Already, a good number of buildings are using solar energy, especially in Greece to provide hot water. Also, wind energy is provided in a number of islands and coasts in the Aegean. Strong winds come from the Dardanelles (Hellespont) straits near Troy, as Homer pointed out centuries ago. However, energy production is not sufficient to cover the rapidly growing demand generated by the combination of industrialization and urbanization, particularly in Turkey, where perhaps more than half of the rural villages lack electricity.

Energy consumption increased dramatically in the postwar years in both countries, particularly in Greece. From 460 kilograms of coal equivalent in 1960, it increased to around 2,200 kilograms per capita at present for Greece, while for Turkey it increased from 245 to around 900 kilograms of coal equivalent over the same period.[1] Energy imports were 54 percent of revenues from merchandise exports for Greece and 53 percent for Turkey in 1984. That is, more than half of the revenue from commodity exports is used to pay energy imports.

HUMAN RESOURCES

The population of Greece is about 10 million, compared to 8 million in 1950 and 7 million in 1937; that of Turkey is about 54 million, compared to 21 million in 1950 and 17 million in 1937.[2] The rate of growth of population is relatively low for Greece (1.0 percent per year) but very high for Turkey (2.2 percent per year). It was estimated by the World Bank that by the year 2000 the population of Greece would be 11 million, while that of Turkey would be 65 million. Life expectancy at birth is 75 years for Greece and 64 for Turkey.

Small Slav minorities exist near the northern borders and Moslems on the eastern borders of Greece. In Turkey, a large Kurdish minority (more than 10 million of the population) exists in the eastern borders.[3] There are also Zazas (150,000 in 1965), distant relatives of the Kurdish population, Armenians (62,000, mainly in Istanbul and Kastamonu), Greeks (50,000 primarily in Istanbul and Izmir), Lazes (26,000), Serbo-Croats (18,000), and Jews (mainly descendants of refugees expelled from Spain in 1492). Small minorities of Vlachs (dispersed descendants of the ancient Thracians) and Gypsies are scattered in Greece and Turkey. Most of the people in Greece belong to the Greek Orthodox Church. According to the census of 1965, there were 31 million Muslims in Turkey, 207,000 Christians (74,000 Orthodox), and 38,000 Jews (a decline from 77,000 in 1945, due to emigration to Israel). The head of the Orthodox Church is the ecumenical patriarch of Constantinople (Istanbul); other religious leaders are the Gregorian (Armenian) patriarch and the chief rabbi, also in Istanbul. For the first time since 1589 Dimitrios I, the patriarch of the world's 150 million Eastern Orthodox Christians, visited the daughter churches of Russia and other east European nations.[4]

The rapid growth of the Moslem population presents problems not only for Turkey but for other countries, such as Bulgaria, with its large Moslem minorities, as well as Germany and other European countries with sizeable numbers of Turkish immigrants. There are complaints by Turkey that Bulgaria is engaged in an assimilation campaign forcing changes of Moslem names, demolishing mosques, and forbidding the Turkish language. However, there are similar complaints from Cyprus that Turkish troops, which occupy almost 40 percent of the island, are forcing out Greek Cypriot refugees and are repopulating the area with Turks transferred from eastern Turkey and from Bulgaria. The Bulgarian argument is that there is no Turkish minority but only a group of Bulgarians forcibly "Islamized" under Ottoman rule who want to restore their ancient Bulgarian names.[5]

Turkey, a Moslem country, has low percentages of women participating in the labor force. This is particularly so in industry, where the active female population is only 5 percent, compared with 20 to 30 percent in Greece and the other Balkan countries. Historically, the inferior status of women in Turkey is due mainly to traditional conditions and religious beliefs.[6] Although polygamy was abolished by the reforms of Ataturk, the economic and social role of women is still limited. However, training and utilization of more female labor for the improvement of home and child services, family planning, sanitary conditions, and family budgeting can increase production without intensifying the problem of unemployment.

Greece is in a better position on matters of health and education. The ratio of population to physicians is 390 to one for Greece and as high as 1,500 to one for Turkey. Daily calorie supply per capita is 3,600 for Greece and 3,100 for Turkey. The number of people enrolled in secondary education, of the age group 12 to 18, is 82 percent for Greece and 38 percent for Turkey. The number of people who are enrolled in higher education, of the age group 20 to 24, is 17 percent for Greece and only 7 percent for Turkey.

The percentage of urban population, in cities over 500,000 persons, is 70 percent for Greece (compared to 51 percent in 1960) and close to 50 percent for Turkey (compared to 32 percent in 1960). On the other hand, the percentage of the active population, between the ages of 15 and 64, is 64 percent for Greece and 58 percent for Turkey. In Greece, the labor force in agriculture is 29 percent, in industry 28 percent, and in services 43 percent, while in Turkey the figures are 58 percent, 17 percent, and 25 percent, respectively.

Unfavorable socioeconomic conditions in Greece and Turkey pushed the population out of poor regions into the cities and abroad. The transfer of capital and labor from rural regions to industrial centers is the result of domination relationships between the core regions and the periphery.

Modern Turkey is a rapidly urbanizing country. Its urban population increased from 19 percent in 1950 to 47 percent in 1980, an increase of 16 million people. The regions of Marmara and southern and western Turkey absorb the largest part of migrant workers. The main provinces exporting labor, which benefit from investment priorities, include Rize, Erzincan, Trabzon, Gumushane, Cankiri, Kastamonu, Bilecik, and Tekirdaz. The main receiving provinces include Ankara, Istanbul, Izmir, Hatay, Adana, Zonguldak, and Samsun.[7]

Large proportions of migrants in the cities work in small trade and other shops, mainly as self-employed persons. Such small shopkeepers enjoy some degree of monopoly because of location, and they contribute to inflation by raising prices arbitrarily to make profits.

Long-run development leads to the agglomeration of cities, as more people tend to move into urban centers in order to enjoy higher income, the "bright lights," and other amenities of cities that act as magnets for peasants from the countryside. Such urban "demand pull" and "supply push" trends create problems of housing, pollution, sewage, unemployment, and crime for overcrowded urban centers. However, the fact that people continue to flow into the cities means that there are more advantages for them in the cities than in the villages. As a result, urbanization continues, mainly in Turkey, where urban population is close to 50 percent.

Greece and Turkey are among the countries that lose large numbers of professionals and scientists, primarily to the United States, Canada, France, and West Germany. This is so because political affiliations and nepotism, rather than merit and achievement, prevail in these two "brain-losing" countries. On the other hand, "brain-gaining" countries offer favorable economic and research conditions and an assuring appreciation for the work of scientists. To reverse the trend of "brain drain" and to encourage repatriation of scientists, educational reforms have been introduced but with limited results.

According to UNESCO (United Nations Educational, Scientific, and Cultural Organization) statistics, there were 31,509 Greek students abroad in 1981 and 14,606 from Turkey, as well as 10,127 from Cyprus. The United States, France, and Britain were the main recipient countries. There were 311,880 foreign students in the United States, 114,121 in France, and 56,000 in Britain in 1981.

Extensive emigration, especially to West Germany in the 1960s and the 1970s, reduced unemployment in both countries.[8] Such emigration mitigated the problem of surplus labor and disrupted what John Kenneth Galbraith calls the "poverty equilibrium" in the poor sectors of the economy. The governments of Greece and Turkey provide a number of incentives to facilitate repatriation of immigrant workers. They include subsidies, tax reductions, and other benefits to attract know-how and investment by the people working abroad.

ECONOMIC GROWTH

Economic growth, that is, increase in production, can be achieved through increments in the factors of production, technological advancement, net gains from foreign trade, and structural transformation from a predominantly subsistent agriculture to a more productive industrial economy. However, such a transformation has not materialized to a satisfactory degree and a large proportion of labor is engaged in agriculture, where low income prevails, especially in Turkey. From the point of view of economic development, Greece can be classified as being at a stage of intermediate development, while Turkey can be considered as struggling to move toward the self-sustained stage of growth.[9]

During the postwar years, both countries achieved high rates of economic growth, ranking among the top 5 percent of high-growth nations in the world. In the 1980s, though, there was a slowdown of real growth, mainly because of the relatively low level of investment in plant and equipment and the international recessionary trends. The availability of a large supply of labor, part of which was transferred from the rural to the industrial and services sectors, seems to be the major factor for the high rates of growth in postwar Greece and Turkey. Moreover, emigration of underemployed workers to West Germany, especially in the 1960s and 1970s, helped to increase labor productivity and growth in these two countries. Overinvestment in housing, on the other hand, helped preserve high rates of growth in the Greek economy during the postwar years, but it has used up excessive resources with simultaneous shortages in urban infrastructure and industrial development. Recent declines in construction, however, led to the downturn of economic growth, while the neglected industrial sector started to affect the overall growth performance.

The annual growth of GDP (Gross Domestic Product) in Greece and Turkey in the 1960s and 1970s was 5 to 6 percent on the average, but in 1980–1985 it dropped to 4.8 percent in Turkey and less than 1 percent in Greece (table 4.2). The largest decline occurred in the manufacturing and services sectors. More or less, a similar behavior in postwar growth rates can be observed in the European Economic Community. For both countries, average gross investment as a ratio to GDP was about 20 percent annually and the incremental capital-output ratio (ICOR) was 3.3 for Greece and 4.0 for Turkey in 1960–1985.[10] Manufacturing and services generally had low ICORs and housing had high ICORs. Per capita GDP in U.S. dollars in 1985 was $3,294 for Greece and $1,157 for Turkey, compared with $7,593 for the EEC.

The overall or national ICORs, that is, gross investment over GDP changes, were higher in Turkey than in Greece during the last two decades. This means that less capital per unit of output was used in Greece than in Turkey. This in turn does not mean that capital is more productive in Greece than in Turkey, because other factors, mainly labor, must be considered along with the ICOR. In order to determine in which country or sector the productivity of capital, or the rate of return on capital, is higher, the relative share of capital should also be calculated. For example, if the relative share of capital to production (ΔR) were 30 percent and the ICOR 3.3, then the rate of return on capital (r) would be 9.1 percent, or $r = \Delta R/ICOR = 0.30/3.3 = 0.091$. If in Turkey $\Delta R = 0.40$ and ICOR $= 4$, then $r = 0.10$, and so on for the particular sectors of the economy.[11]

Table 4.2

Economic Growth and Investment (constant prices)

	Greece			Turkey		
	1960–70	1970–80	1980–85	1960–70	1970–80	1980–85
Average annual Growth of GDP (%)	6.9	4.9	0.8	6.0	5.9	4.8
Agriculture	3.5	1.7	0.2	2.5	3.4	3.3
Industry	9.4	5.3	-0.8	9.6	6.6	4.2
Manufacturing	10.2	6.4	-0.9	10.9	6.1	4.0
Services	7.1	5.7	2.1	6.9	6.8	4.3
Investment (GFCF) as percentage of GDP	21.3	19.0	19.8	18.3	22.4	18.9
National ICORs (GFCF/ΔGDP)	3.4	5.2	1.3	3.4	4.5	4.0
Agriculture	1.9	4.1	0.5	3.5	3.2	3.7
Manufacturing	2.0	3.0	1.1	2.1	2.9	3.2
Housing	14.9	14.8	7.0	14.6	11.5	22.8
Services	1.9	3.1	0.4	2.1	1.9	1.0

Note: The closest year's data available were used.
Source: World Bank, *World Development Report,* various issues; OECD, *National Accounts,*
various issues, and *Economic Surveys: Greece,* various issues.

If we multiply the relatively constant ICOR slope by the GDP for a year, we can estimate the capital stock of the countries considered. For Greece it was $110.2 billion (33.4 × 3.3) and for Turkey $198.4 billion (49.6 × 4.0) in 1984, at current prices (table 4.3). If we divide the capital stock by the labor force, we find that the capital/labor ratio (capital per worker) was $29,200 ($110.2 billion/3.5 million) for Greece and $13,800 ($198.4 billion/14.4 million) for Turkey. The average productivity of labor (GDP/labor) was $9,500 for Greece and only $3,300 for Turkey, that is, the average Greek worker is producing about three times as much as the Turkish worker.

For the ten EEC members, total output was $2,916 billion in 1984 and the capital stock $28,464 billion ($2,916 × 9.76). The estimated capital/labor ratio was $268,000 ($28,464/106) and the average productivity of labor $27,500 ($2,916/106), that is, about three times that of Greece and nine times that of Turkey. This is due primarily to larger capital accumulation and the higher skills and know-how in the advanced western European countries.

New ideas, new technology, and big money are needed to stir the lethargic industrial investment conditions in these two countries. Probably a consortium

Table 4.3
Output, Capital Stock, Labor Force, Capital/Labor Ratio, and Productivity of Labor in Greece, Turkey, and the EEC, 1984 (U.S. dollars, constant 1980 prices)

	Greece	Turkey	EEC
Output (GDP in billion dollars)	33.4	49.6	2,916.4
Estimated Capital Stock (billion dollars)	110.2	198.4	28,464.0
Labor Force (millions)	3.5	14.9	106.1
Estimated Capital/Labor Ratio (thousand dollars)	31.5	13.3	268.3
Productivity of Labor (GDP/Laborers in thousand dollars)	9.5	3.3	27.5

Note: For EEC, the ten member nations of 1984; for ICOR, average of 1960–1984, constant 1980 prices; for labor force, total civilian employment.

Source: Calculations were based on OECD, *Economic Surveys: Greece, Economic Surveys: Turkey,* and *National Accounts,* various issues.

of industrialists and entrepreneurs or a special "Industrial Fund" may be needed to amass large amounts of money for investment in competitive industries for tools, machinery, and other manufacturing products. Public monopolistic and inefficient enterprises as well as controls on prices, interest rates, and wages (determined by governmental interventions) act as drawbacks to private investment, which accounts for about 70 percent of the total investment in manufacturing in both Greece and Turkey. It should be noted here that the incremental capital output ratio in manufacturing is comparatively low (around 2) and, *ceteris paribus*, small amounts of investment can be used for large amounts of output.

Investment preference should be given to industries that use domestic resources and produce products satisfying primarily domestic demand. As such are mining industries (iron, aluminum, cement, marble, etc.) and firms producing metals and similar products with many forward and backward linkages, which can substitute imports and increase exports. Large firms with vertical concentration could apply modern mass-production technology and use cheaper labor, so that they could be able to compete with similar big firms.

Investment in real terms increased in Greece at an average annual rate of 9.3 percent in the 1960s and 2.8 percent in the 1970s. But in the 1980s, investment rates became negative. A major reason for the decline in the investment rate in recent years is the announcement that there would be a policy of "socialization" of industries and the introduction of supervising councils by the government, first in enterprises and then in a sectoral level. These types of "public" councils created an unfavorable climate for investment. Such experiments, although largely abandoned, created uncertainty and fear on the part of investors. Also, wage and price controls and other anti-innovative and bureaucratic measures led to investment pessimism.

Problematic Enterprises and Efficiency

To improve investment and production conditions in public enterprises, the Law 1365/1983 provided for a system of "socialization," requiring that labor representatives together with representatives of the Chamber of Commerce, the Association of Greek Industries, and local authorities participate in management. However, the consequent decrees resulted in such socialization taking a "decorative" form in practice. It turned nationalized firms into a worse nationalized form of management. Six out of nine members of the Management Council are government appointees and three are representatives of the employees of the enterprise in which they work. Automatically, decisions are made according to the desires of the government and the party in power, which appoints the large majority of the board of directors.

On the other hand, the Advisory Assembly, consisting of nine government representatives, nine representatives from the employees, and nine representatives from other social groups (Association of Greek Industries and Chambers of Commerce or Exports) but none from consumers, has no power and is largely a public relations body, which assembles every three months.

It may be proper to try the system of self-management for a few public enterprises, such as the Aluminum of Greece, LARKO, Olympic Airlines, Public Power Corporation, Organization of Telecommunications of Greece, and Organization of Railways of Greece. However, the board of directors should be chosen entirely from the people working in each enterprise, while the employee-owners should bear risks and accept reduction in wages and benefits in cases where their enterprises have losses. Also, privatization, through selling stocks to the public, a form of Schumpeterian people's capitalism, may make these enterprises more efficient.[12]

Some 43 problematic enterprises in Greece, including Pyrkal, Aget, Piraiki-Patraiki, the Skalistiri group, and Athinaiki Hartopiia, are under the supervision of the Organization for the Rehabilitation of Enterprises (OAE) (Law 1386/1983). Presently, many problematic firms are under reorganization and could possibly be transferred or sold back to private investors. This is so, mainly because the government poured money from its budget into the rescue of these problematic enterprises without results—a process that resembles the Pythos (sieve) of Danaides in ancient mythology, that is, the curse of the daughters of Danaus to pour water forever into a vessel full of holes.

Around 20 of these inefficient firms are in the process of being sold to the private sector by auction, 17 would be sold to private and foreign investors, including the old stockholders, and the above 5 to 6 big firms would be transferred to individuals if they would not become efficient and profitable. The same fate is expected for other problematic firms outside the OAE, such as the Tsimenta Halkidos Corporation and other weak firms. In addition to Greek investors, interest to buy such enterprises was expressed by other Europeans and mainly by Americans through the City Bank, the First Boston Bank, and General Electric.

The Turkish government also enacted (in 1986) a comprehensive law to privatize some 40 state-owned companies, commonly known as State Economic Enterprises (SEEs). These companies or organizations account for about 40 percent of Turkey's industrial production and 60 percent of fixed investment. Among them are Arcelik, which makes household appliances; Eregli steel plant; Tofas, the car-making subsidiary of Fiat; Celebi, a chartering subsidiary of the national Turkish Airlines; Usas, which provides airport ground services; Turban, a chain of tourist hotels; and five plants belonging to Citosan, the state cement corporation. Several of these big concerns are trading on the embryonic Istanbul Stock Exchange, which is expected to receive a big boost as a result of privatization.

Because of the overstaffing and their obsolete management techniques, these inefficient enterprises are a burden on the treasury, and the government wants to reduce the heavy subsidies and eliminate bureaucratic etatism, through privatization. In many cases, the personnel employed in such enterprises are offered shares on favorable terms.[13]

URBANIZATION AND DECENTRALIZATION

In Turkey, and more so in Greece, government policies, directly or indirectly, encouraged the movement of labor and other resources to urban centers during the postwar years through credit, infrastructural and educational facilities, and other public services. The long neglect of the countryside led to dualistic rigidities and distortion in the allocation of resources. As a result, the gap between the advanced and the subsistence regions became larger, and rural areas remained backward compared to industrial centers. Regional development policy may be considered responsible for the maldistribution of income and wealth in both countries. It would seem that the gap in per capita income among regions widened during the postwar period.[14] Despite favorable policy pronouncements, there was poor performance in the less-developed regions of these countries in both industrial and overall growth. The lack of proper regional planning and the conscious or unconscious political emphasis on urban centralism may be responsible for such a widening regional gap.

To eliminate interregional differences, the governments of both countries provide investment incentives such as tax concessions, generous depreciation allowances, and even labor subsidies. Such a policy can be used as a development model, a paradigm, for other countries as well. Investment incentives may also be provided by local authorities to private enterprises. They may include capital grants, community development projects, and possibly subsidies for development in disparate regions.

On the other hand, foreign investment, along with domestic investment, has been concentrated in limited areas, such as Athens-Piraeus and Salonika in Greece and Istanbul, Ankara, and Iskenderun in Turkey, introducing advanced technology and large-scale industries. These developmental trends created, in many cases, economic enclaves that proved to be detrimental to regional industrialization.

Turkey presents a wide range of regions, with a relatively advanced west, an intermediate center, and a very poor eastern region. Greece also has a variety of regions that belong to different stages of development. Epirus, central Peloponnesus, and nonirrigated islands are classic examples of less-developed regions.

To reduce inequalities, Greece provides generous rewards to employment-creating investment in backward areas (Law 1262/1982). The whole country is divided into four regional categories: developed (A), intermediate (B), backward (C), and frontier (D) regions. Depending on the classification, the incentives provided vary from region to region. Thus investors may receive grants of from 20 to 50 percent of their investment, plus interest subsidies of from 30 to 50 percent on the money they may borrow (up to 30 percent of total investment). The investor then can invest in poor regions (C) using only 25 percent of his or her own capital. Regions characterized as the poorest (C category) include parts of northwestern Greece (Epirus), the central Peloponnesus (Arcadia, the Kalavrytan province of Achaia), parts of Crete, and similar mountainous and deprived areas on the mainland and the islands. Moreover, from 20 to 30 percent of ploughback (undistributed) profits may be exempted from taxation as long as they remain with the enterprises for reinvestment in these poor areas. Generous depreciation allowances, 25 to 150 percent higher than the normal depreciation rates, and subsidies for professional training are also provided.

Shore land is a unique and valuable resource for domestic and foreign investment for both nations because of its esthetic and recreational importance. To preserve its beauty and accessibility, measures with noneconomic objectives may be needed. Large parts of the shore land are separated by sea from the great majority of the people. Accessibility by automobile or by regular boat service is limited by barren rocks and cliffs, which give much of the picturesque shore land a wild and craggy beauty. Furthermore, acquisitions of shore lands by domestic and foreign speculators tend to monopolize the most desirable areas. Foreigners tend to buy valuable shore lands from the poor peasants and erect barriers, excluding other people from the beaches and often tending to treat the landless peasants as servants. In addition, there are comments that this type of "invasion," particularly in Greece by EEC investors, leads to a demeaning shock, cultural demoralization, and abuse of the legendary hospitality of the locals.

From a regional point of view, west Turkey and northern and central Greece (in which Attica is included) are the most prosperous regions, with substantial industry and a thriving agriculture. In Greece, Thessaly, Macedonia, the coastal Peloponnesus, Thrace, and, to some extent, Crete produce substantial amounts of agricultural products, mainly wheat, grapes, olives, cotton, and tobacco. Epirus, many Aegean and Ionian islands, and the western, central, and eastern Peloponnesus (with the exception of the plains of Corinth and Argos) are poor in both industrial and agricultural production.

At present the concentration in the Greater Athens area is very striking, and herculean efforts are needed to alleviate the serious illness created by such unhealthy urbanization. About half of Greece's national employment is concentrated in the area of Athens. The dominance of Athens is obvious also in resource-oriented industries such as food, tobacco, textiles, leather and its products, chemicals, rubber, wood and cork, paper and its products, and basic metals. Only in small-scale handicraft employment, mainly in footwear, textiles, and woodworking, is Athens' role smaller compared to other areas, particularly Macedonia.

Turkey also provides generous incentives for domestic and foreign investment, especially in less-developed areas. Such incentives include capital grants of up to 20 percent of the total investment cost, allocation of government land for private investments, credit facilities, and exemption of taxes, duties, and other fees.

In spite of the decentralization benefits offered, people continue to move from the countryside into the urban centers, mainly Istanbul, Izmir, Samsun, and Iskenderun. Istanbul in particular has become a mammoth city in recent years. From 1 million inhabitants a few decades ago, it has over 6.5 million today. Such a population explosion has brought urban blight to the city and the nearby shores of the Golden Horn (the waterway that runs from the Bosporus to the heart of the city). The waterside areas crumbled, lined with slum houses, decrepit workshops, and primitive factories. In many cases, they function as dumps for industrial waste and sewage.

The famous trade center and capital of great empires, founded in the seventh century B.C. by Ionians giving it the name "Byzantium" (from the architect Byzas of Megara), the city of Emperor Constantine, Constantinople, now Istanbul, faces problems of decay. Population presure leads to overnight erections of shanty dwellings on the city outskirts, while the nearby green countryside is paved over with concrete. Currently, though, local authorities spend millions of dollars (more than $13 million in 1987 alone) to improve the area and decentralize the city.

One of the main reasons for concentration in urban centers is the convenience of these places for raw material imports. Other reasons involve the existence of high power capacity, which is needed for modern factories, and, for skilled workers, the significantly higher wages in these areas compared to other cities and regions. This is so because previous capital investment was largely concentrated in these urban centers. However, the cost of living, especially that of housing, is higher in the large cities than in the other provinces. This, together with the recent problems of pollution and congestion, may lead to a gradual decentralization from the cities back to the countryside.

NOTES

1. United Nations, *Statistical Yearbook*, various issues; and Richard Nyrop, ed., *Turkey: A Country Study* (Washington, D.C.: American University, Foreign Area Studies, 1980), chap. 14.

2. There are about 0.8 million Greeks and 1.5 million Turks in West Germany. Also, there are about 0.5 million Greeks in Australia, a larger number in Canada, and 2.5 to 3 million in the United States. For the background and policies on Greek and Turkish emigration, see Ronald Krane, *International Labor Migration in Europe* (New York: Praeger, 1979), chaps. 13 and 14.

3. George Harris. *Turkey: Coping with Crisis* (Boulder, Colo.: Westview Press, 1985), 16.

4. Geoffrey Lewis, *Modern Turkey* (New York: Praeger, 1974), 212–13. Also, "Mission to Moscow," *Time*, September 14, 1987, 66.

5. Henry Kamm, "Bulgarian-Turkish Tensions on Minority Rise," *New York Times*, October 4, 1987.

6. Such beliefs prevail primarily among the Moslem population. For example, in southern Sudan, "a reasonably sound wife costs about 40 head of cattle, with perhaps a few goats and chickens thrown in." John Goddard, "Kayaks down the Nile," *National Geographic Magazine* 107, no. 5 (May 1955): 173. In Constantinople a seventeenth-century sultan (Ibrahim the Mad) ordered his 1,001 concubines trussed and tossed into the Bosporus, and then filled the Great Harem of Topkapi with new ones. *Time*, September 13, 1971, 39.

7. OECD, *Economic Surveys: Turkey*, various issues. Marmara and Central Anatolia are the main regions of Turkish migrants abroad. See Rusel Keles, "The Effects of External Migration or Regional Development in Turkey," in Ray Hudson and Jim Lewis, eds., *Uneven Development in Southern Turkey* (New York: Methuen, 1985), 54–75.

8. The pressure of unemployment and emigration will probably be reduced when the two nations reach stationary population. According to the estimates of the World Bank, for Turkey this will be in 2075 with 100 million people, while for Greece this will be in 2065 with 11 million people. To reduce unemployment, Greece and more so Turkey continued to export labor. Nicholas Gianaris, *Greece and Yugoslavia: An Economic Comparison* (New York: Praeger, 1984), 113; and Suzanne Paine, *Exporting Workers: The Turkish Case* (London: Cambridge University Press, 1974), chap. 3.

9. W. W. Rostow thinks that, for Turkey, the takeoff started after 1933, when import substitution in light industry began. See his *The World Economy: History and Prospects* (Austin: University of Texas Press, 1978), chap. 39.

10. Using a simplified version of the Harrod-Domar model, without gestation lag, we

can calculate the rate of investment required to achieve a certain rate of economic growth as follows:

$$g = \frac{j}{v} - \pi$$

That is, $j/5 - 1\% = 4\%$, and $j = 5\,(4+1) = 25\%$, where g is the per capita growth of income or output, j is investment as percentage of income, v is the ICOR, and π is the rate of population growth. Nicholas Gianaris, "The Instability of the Incremental Capital-Output Ratio," *Socio-Economic Planning Sciences* 3, (August 1969): 119–25.

11. Nicholas Gianaris, "International Differences in Capital-Output Ratios," *American Economic Review* 60 (June 1970): 465–77; and Maria Negreponti-Delivani, *Analysis tis Ellinikis Oikonomias* (Athens: Papazisis, 1981), 39.

12. For a further review, see Nicholas V. Gianaris, *The Economics of the Balkan Countries: Albania, Bulgaria, Greece, Romania, Turkey, Yugoslavia* (New York: Praeger, 1982), 58–78; and T. Kostopoulos, *Beyond Capitalism: Toward a Nomocratic Society* (New York: Praeger, 1986), chap. 6.

13. Kenneth Mackenzie and Orkun Akpinar, "Turkey's Privatization Program Picks up Steam," *Wall Street Journal*, May 26, 1987.

14. Problems of income distribution in the valuable articles in Aydin Ulusan, *Political Economy of Income Distribution in Turkey* (New York: Holmes and Meiers, 1980); and Nicholas Gianaris, *The Province of Kalavryta: A Historical and Socioeconomic Review* (New York: National Herald, 1983), 75–97. For the change in *etatism* and the abandoning of the policy of supporting inefficient state economic enterprises (SEEs), see George Kopits, "Turkey's Adjustment Experience, 1980–85," *Finance and Development* 24, no. 3 (September 1987): 8–11.

5

Sectoral Resource Allocation

STRUCTURE OF PRODUCTION

In Turkey, and more so in Greece, there has been an unbalanced sectoral growth policy during the postwar years. Turkey, following the example of other developing economies, tried to develop the industrial sector, while Greece, consciously or unconsciously, stressed the services sector at the expense of others, primarily the manufacturing and agricultural sectors. The share of industrial production to total GDP is close to 35 percent for Turkey and 30 percent for Greece, compared with 21 percent and 26 percent, respectively, in 1960. The share of services to GDP currently is around 47 percent for Turkey and 53 percent for Greece, compared with 38 percent for Turkey and 51 percent for Greece in 1960. On the other hand, the share of agricultural production (including cattle raising and fishing) to total GDP is around 18 percent now for both countries, compared to 41 percent for Turkey and 23 percent for Greece in 1960.

The relative decline of agriculture and the growth of industry and services is a universal economic trend, and it would be difficult for these two countries to avoid such a developmental process. However, Turkey followed the usual historical trend of advancement from agriculture to industry to services, while the economy of Greece moved, to a large extent, from agriculture directly to services, neglecting industrialization. Greek policymakers, realizing that the open economy of Greece cannot catch up with the other industrial countries, started recently to emphasize technological development, primarily in microelectronics, bioengineering, alternative energy sources, and other scientific and high-technology areas.

Policymakers in both countries, particularly in Greece, have not done enough to discourage movement of human resources and capital from the countryside to urban centers. Moreover, foreign investments have concentrated in a few areas that have public utilities and market facilities. As a result of such sectoral and regional concentration, the gap between the advanced (industrial) and the subsistence (agricultural) sectors has been widening. The "backwash effects" from the poor to the rich regions have been more powerful than the "spread effects" from the advanced to the backward sectors. As a result, income disparities persist and urbanization continues.

It seems that both countries need an unbalanced growth policy in favor of decentralization to correct previous unwise policies that led to unhealthy urbanization. They would be ill advised to pursue a strategy of balanced growth, that is, a program of simultaneous investment in mutually supporting industries throughout the whole economy. Although such a policy has the advantage of making sectors and industries each other's customers, progress at snail's pace by a deliberate unbalancing of the economy would induce decision making and action through tensions and incentives for entrepreneurs at the local and national levels.

Initiation of development through a chain of unbalanced growth sequences with emphasis on those sectors and industries that present maximum backward and forward linkages would, most probably, result in high and sustainable rates of growth.[1] For Greece and Turkey, manufacturing industries processing agricultural and mining products, with backward and forward linkages, seem to present good opportunities for investment and potentially high rates of productivity. What is needed mostly is transfer of technology close to the raw materials, investment financing, and improvements in the transportation and distribution networks.

Development financing is one of the weakest links in economic policy. Policymakers in Greece and Turkey form development plans and, using explicitly or implicitly a version of the Harrod-Domar model with constant capital output ratios, project investment requirements to achieve certain rates of economic growth. The next serious question is how to finance the required investment. Are domestic savings and foreign sources sufficient to finance projected investment?

The financing of gross capital formation in Greece and Turkey comes primarily from savings (about 2/3 of the total) and consumption of fixed capital or depreciation (about 1/4). Higher depreciation rates can be observed in more industrialized countries, such as Britain, France, West Germany, Italy, and the United States (where they vary from 50 to 60 percent of total saving), primarily because of higher capital accumulation. Total saving, as a percent of GDP, is 11 percent for both countries. About 70 percent comes from households, 10 percent from general government, and around 10 percent from corporate and quasicorporate enterprises. In developed countries, however, corporate saving is higher. For the United States and Britain, for example, it is about 30 percent, and for West Germany 20 percent. The savings-to-income ratio in Greece and Turkey is declining through time, mainly because of a growing marginal propensity to consume, due primarily to the phenomenon of the demonstration effect.

AGRICULTURE

From ancient times, land cultivation and cattle raising were the main occupations of the people in the area. During the Roman, Venetian, and Byzantine periods, the feudalistic system of Western Europe prevailed in large parts of the two countries. Large segments of land were owned by the land barons, the nobles, and the Church.

During the Ottoman occupation of Greece, land was divided into large and small regions governed by pashas and *sadjakbegs*. Smaller regions were governed by other Turkish chief (*voivodas*) and local *kodjabashes*. The followers and collaborators of the Ottomans were rewarded with gifts of land after each military victory. The best land and even whole villages (*chifliks*) belonged to the Turkish local rulers (*beys*). Heavy taxes on produce were levied every year, in addition to the taxes imposed on the Christian *rayahs* as a punishment for not converting to Islam (*haratsi*). Under such conditions, many people gave their property to monasteries, which were exempt from property confiscations, and the previous owners cultivated the land on behalf of the Church. Large and rich farms and properties were accumulated by the monasteries, most of which were distributed back to the tillers after the liberation of Greece from the Turks.

In the postliberation years, agricultural reforms were initiated in the Balkans, including Greece. Large estates or litifundia, particularly in fertile plains, which were unfairly acquired or inherited during Turkish domination, were distributed to the previously exploited peasant masses. Moreover, the gradual influence of Western capitalism and the trend toward a market agricultural economy increased the dependency of the farmers on middlemen and loan sharks, as well as on exports to European markets. Exports of mainly tobacco, fruits, and other agricultural products to Germany were intensified before World War II. However, the distribution of land through inheritance and dowry led to its subdivision into small strips (stamps) scattered in different places.

As mentioned previously, huge estates remained with the Greek Orthodox Church after the Turks were defeated during the War of Independence and afterwards. In April 1987, the Greek government passed a law to take over these estates and transfer them mainly to agricultural cooperatives. This property of some 70 monasteries is composed of around 370,000 acres of forest and agricultural land, as well as hotels, marble quarries, and office blocks, at an estimated worth of about $1 billion. Greece's most famed monastery, Mount Athos near Salonika, is exempted. However, church officials object to this action and threatened to abandon independence established in 1850 and to return to control by Constantinople (Istanbul), under the ecumenical patriarch, who is the spiritual leader of all Eastern Orthodox churches. They object especially to the establishment of the new lay-dominated administrative committees that would control the Church's economic affairs.[2]

Agriculture has long been the primary economic activity throughout Turkey. It employs more than half of the labor force of the country. However, per capita production of food declines in absolute terms, primarily because of rapid population growth. The largest part of the interior and the west is wheatland, while the east is mostly grassland for livestock raising. Fruits, cotton, and tobacco are the major crops of the western and the Mediterranean regions of the country, and hazelnuts, tobacco, and products of mixed farming prevail in the north.

Expansion of wheat cultivation, at the expense of meadows and grasslands, resulted in destruction of tree cover, loss of topsoil, and low productivity. Due to the Islamic inheritance, land is fragmented into small scattered farms, as it is in Greece. As a consequence, mass-production technology is difficult to apply. Over two-thirds of the farms in Turkey consist of five hectares or less, while less than 5 percent are more than twenty hectares. As a result, leasing, share-cropping, and joint ownership of parcels of land are common.[3] However, in southeast Anatolia feudal-like landlords and many landless families prevail, although Kemal Ataturk stressed the need for upper and lower limits of ownership. Land reforms after the 1920s and especially in 1973 have not changed conditions much.

New decentralization measures, taken recently in Greece and to a lesser extent in Turkey, encourage voluntary collectivization and the establishment of agro-industrial cooperatives in the countryside, with the aim of organizing the un-protected farmers. These measures, though, have had limited success.

Both Greece and Turkey have good subsoil but, mostly, poor soil resources. Many mountains are covered with bare rocks. About a third of the land is covered by forest, and the large numbers of low hills are without natural irrigation. The warm, mostly dry climate promotes the production of olives, vegetables, grapes, and other fruits, especially in Greece and western Turkey. The temperate climate of the region and the extensive beautiful coasts attract tourists and investors.

Greece produces the largest amount of tomatoes in western Europe (about 2.3 million tons) next to Italy (9.6 million tons), while Spain produces 2.1 million tons and France 880,000 tons. There is strong competition from Italy and Spain not only in tomatoes but in peaches, grapes, watermelons, peppers, and cucumbers. For lemons and oranges, Greece has a good market in the eastern European countries, which absorb about 90 percent of total exports, compared to only about 3 percent by the EEC. The main importers of Greek lemons are the Soviet Union (40 percent), Poland (22 percent), Czechoslovakia (11 percent), Yugoslavia (10 percent), and Romania (7 percent). For Greek oranges, the main importers are Romania (30 percent), the Soviet Union (23 percent), Poland (14 percent), Czechoslovakia (10 percent), Yugoslavia (7 percent), and East Germany (7 percent). The major crops of Turkey are wheat, barley, cotton, sugar, beets, hazelnuts, and tobacco.

In Greece, the most important agricultural area in the production of wheat (about half of total production), cotton, tobacco, peaches, apples, and other fruits is Macedonia. Thessaly is next in the production of grain, cotton, and tree crops. Thrace produces wheat and tobacco, and Sterea Hellas, Peloponnesus, and Crete are the major regional producers of olives, grapes, and oranges. Epirus and most of the poor islands produce little aside from oranges and other fruits. In the mountainous areas of Greece and Turkey agricultural and pastoral activities are dominant. However, low land productivity forced many inhabitants to leave these regions in search of a better livelihood.[4] Livestock products contribute about one-third of the gross value of agricultural output in Turkey and less than that in Greece.

The cooperative movement in both nations intends to provide the small farmers with marketing facilities for selling their products and buying the needed tools and materials. The governments of both countries usually purchase large amounts of wheat and other products, and the agricultural banks and the cooperatives are responsible for collection and warehousing. Also, sizeable agricultural subsidies are provided to the Greek farmers by the EEC every year.

Cooperatives deal with such products as olives and olive oil, dairy products, wine, tomatoes, and fruits. However, when private merchants offer more cash down payment, they can break the cooperatives. The prevailing disorganized marketing for many agricultural products creates a parasitic class of a multitude of local dealers and wholesalers, which raises distribution costs and inhibits effective marketing.

As mentioned previously, in both countries, where private ownership prevails, there is extensive subdivision of land into small lots (stamps) scattered in different places. In such a division of land into small parcels, mainly because of inheritance and dowry, it is difficult to use tractors and other machines of mass production that increase land and labor productivity. However, production incentives on such privately owned lots are high, particularly for crops such as vegetables and fruits that require labor-intensive methods of cultivation and harvesting.

Some farmers realized that ownership of small, widely scattered lots is not conducive to high productivity and voluntarily agreed to exchange them and/or to form cooperatives for more efficient use. In Greece, where there are limited large grass pastures, goats prevail, while in Turkey more sheep and cows are raised. Hot, dry weather conditions in southern Greece and western and southern Turkey promote the production of olives, figs, raisins, tobacco, cotton, and similar products; while production of corn, wheat, potatoes, and oats prevails in the north. Turkey is ranked fourth in Europe, excluding the Soviet Union, in forests. To increase the efficiency of the agricultural sector and to stimulate food production, investment in rural sectors was encouraged and incentives to the farmers were provided in both countries. However, the size of land holdings may not be sufficient for the use of modern technology.

Greece has far less sheep and cattle but more pigs than Turkey. In Greece milk is produced by cows, sheep, and goats in almost equal amounts, while in Turkey more milk is produced by sheep. During the last two decades, the number of cattle and sheep remained constant or declined slightly while that of pigs increased in Greece. The number of horses, asses, and mules declined dramatically in both countries.

Greece produces primarily barley, rice, tobacco, and cotton; Turkey produces mainly wheat, corn, potatoes, wool, and forest products. Turkey has more threshers and tractors than Greece (table 5.1).

Greece is known for production of *ouzo* and Turkey for a similar product

Table 5.1

Selected Agricultural Products (thousand metric tons) and Livestock (thousand head)

	Greece			Turkey		
	1970	1980	1984	1970	1980	1984
Cattle	997	950	800	13,235	16,607	17,200
Sheep	7,680	8,000	8,500	36,351	46,026	48,707
Pigs	383	1,020	1,324	18	13	11
Horses	255	120	100	1,110	807	703
Asses	376	253	230	1,938	1,331	1,208
Milk	1,358	1,700	1,716	4,293	5,472	5,805
Wool	8	10	11	47	61	61
Tractors (thous. units)	62	140	165	105	435	512
Threshers (thous. units)	4	6	7	9	14	14
Barley	737	929	896	3,250	5,300	6,500
Cereals	3,377	5,334	5,651	18,031	24,414	26,338
Maize (corn)	511	1,279	1,992	1,040	1,240	1,500
Cotton	111	116	150	400	500	586
Eggs (hen, thous. m.t.)	96	119	126	96	207	252
Oats	107	83	72	415	355	316
Potatoes	756	1,084	980	1,915	3,000	3,200
Rice	79	80	91	13,270	234	280
Tobacco	95	117	137	150	234	210
Nitrogenous fertilizers	201	333	418	243	807	891
Wheat	1,931	2,970	2,646	10,081	16,554	17,235
Potash	17	44	48	11	29	25
Forestry (roundwood) (mill. cubic meters)	3	3	3	34	23	19
Fish	98	104	100	184	427	567

Note: In some cases earlier years' data were available.

Source: United Nations, *Statistical Yearbook*, various issues.

known as *raki*, which are distilled from the juice of grapes and are flavored with anise seed. Sultans have always been famous grapes and are used mainly for wine making, notably in the Corinth and Attica regions of Greece and the Marmara and Izmir plains of Turkey.

Turkey, along with other Middle Eastern countries, is known for the production of opium, especially morphine and heroin. According to the U.S. Bureau of Narcotics, Turkey is producing about 200 tons of opium per year, compared with 150 tons in Iran, 200 tons in Pakistan, and 100 to 150 tons in Afghanistan. The price per kilogram of morphine in Turkey is about $3,500 to $5,000 and that of heroin $8,000 to $15,000 (with purity of 60 to 90 percent). In its efforts to curb production and distribution of narcotics, the United States agreed in the early 1970s to pay compensation to Turkish farmers to stop producing opium. However, the Turks maintained that the amount to be paid would cover only one-twelfth of the loss to the country, estimated at about $300 million per year (including processing and transportation of the crop, mainly to Europe). It was estimated that the loss to the producers of Afyonkarahisar alone was close to $7 million per year.[5]

INDUSTRY

During the last century, the European powers of that time, primarily Britain, France, and Germany, moved with industrial capital into Greece and Turkey to exploit new resources and markets. Private or government loans and investments were used to finance mainly the construction of highways, railways, and other infrastructural projects. One of these projects was the railroad connecting Belgrade with Salonika and Constantinople, which was constructed at the beginning of this century and runs through Turkey to Baghdad. The governments of Greece and Turkey increased taxes and tried to stimulate exports to finance industrial investment, but the flooding of their markets with western products prevented rapid industrialization. Moreover, high tariffs on agricultural machinery and other industrial products created a few monopolies or oligopolies and aggravated the plight of the peasants, who had to pay high prices for such products.

High unemployment in the cities and surplus rural labor led to extensive emigration of Greek peasants, primarily to the United States, during the interwar years. However, investment in such cottage industries as flour milling, tanning, pottery, textiles, the processing of olives and other agricultural, dairy, and mineral products provided employment for some workers. Many seafaring Greeks, on the other hand, were employed in vessels and steamships built mainly by wealthy emigres. The Turks, though, did not have the same opportunities for emigration and remained mostly in the rural sector.

After World War II, Greece and Turkey were left with very limited, if any, industrial capacity. From then on, both countries paid limited attention to industrialization while short-run services and residential construction in large cities were emphasized. Lack of confidence and economic and political instability were responsible for the extensive channeling of savings into housing and services. In addition, commercial banks lent their support to a few monopolistic or oligopolistic firms that were concentrated in large cities. Because of the heavy air pollution in the industrial cities, corrective measures have been taken to reverse this trend of industrial concentration. As a result of the increase in petroleum and raw material prices in the 1970s, both countries experienced a slowdown in their industrial growth in recent years. Table 5.2 shows the main manufacturing products of Greece and Turkey.

At present, per capita annually, Turkey produces about 13 kilos of meat, mainly pork and veal, and Greece produces 36 kilos; the annual per capita production of cheese is around 20 kilos in Greece and 3 kilos in Turkey. In comparison with Greece, Turkey produces about twice the amount of tobacco, about three times the amount of sugar, and about twice the amount of cotton

Table 5.2
Manufacturing Products (thousand metric tons)

	Greece			Turkey		
	1970	1980	1984	1970	1980	1984
Meat	233	381	357	537	518	624
Butter	6	6	6	113	116	135
Cheese	142	189	199	94	126	135
Wheat flour	526	1,016	927	1,855	1,437	1,582
Sugar	188	198	326	643	1,140	1,654
Wine (thous. hecto-liters)	4,532	5,224	5,400	440	390	370
Beer (thous. hecto-liters)	777	2,560	2,850	480	2,533	3,226
Tobacco products (millions cigarettes)	17,029	25,017	26,207	37,253	51,977	61,500
Cotton yarn	42	135	137	178	420	232
Wool yarn (pure)	11	14	11	30	4	5
Sawn wood (thous. cubic meters)	272	380	390	2,471	4,650	4,117
Tires (thousands)	n.a.	n.a.	n.a.	1,139	2,929	3,777
Ethylene	13	14	14	43	42	56
Phosphate fertilizers	104	170	194	61	564	621
Cement	4,848	12,340	14,196	6,373	14,802	13,595
Crude steel	435	1,067	755	1,312	1,700	2,479
Aluminum	91	184	158	18	34	30
Lead	15	21	4	3	3	4

Note: n.a. = Not available

In some cases earlier years' data than 1984 were available.

Source: United Nations, *Statistical Yearbook*, various issues.

yarn. Energy production, in coal equivalent, is about 8.6 million tons in Greece and 17.6 million tons in Turkey, annually.

Both nations offer investment incentives for industrial development and economic decentralization. Generous grants, sizeable loans with interest subsidization, tax exemptions, high depreciation allowances, and other benefits are granted for such investments by individual companies, cooperatives, and foreigners. Grants up to 50 percent of the cost of investment and other similar benefits are given, depending on the backwardness of the area and the industrial sectors in which companies and individuals invest. With such investment, private firms and agro-industrial cooperatives are encouraged to integrate their operations vertically and horizontally from basic production to manufacturing and advanced distribution in such products as cereals, dairy products, fruits, cotton, olive oil, and other products, providing processing, storage, and marketing facilities. However, in practice they have not been very successful so far.

In Turkey, but primarily in Greece, industry has been concentrated in a few, mostly urban, areas. Emphasis on manufacturing in the countryside requires the improvement in infrastructural facilities in the form of better transportation, communications, and technical training.[6] The establishment of small or middle-size factories in the countryside, producing flour, textiles, shoes, and pottery, and processing olives, grapes, and similar products, would provide the market for each other's products in rural regions and reduce migration to urban centers or abroad. Moreover, the development of industries related to cattle raising and dairy products, fisheries, and minerals would create additional demand and provide additional income which would have a multiple economic effect in these regions. Yet, feasibility studies on production possibilities and effective marketing of the related commodities produced will be necessary before each investment venture is undertaken. Through trial-and-error experience, entrepreneurs could proceed to establish, first, labor-intensive and, later, capital-intensive projects. Such industries are needed not only to absorb disguised unemployment but also to provide vocational and on-the-job training.

About half of the 40 largest industrial firms in Greece and a smaller number in Turkey are foreign owned. Many of the remaining firms are largely subsidized. It seems though that the policies of supporting industries through subsidization proved to be a failure. Such policies appeared to shield the inefficiency of such firms that are moving toward bankruptcy or takeover by other firms or the government and/or by their employees and workers.

About half of Greece's population (4.1 million) live in the Athens-Piraeus area and their suburbs. Also, a large part of industry is located there. Such a concentration of industry in the area and the urban explosion over the last three decades have made Athens the city most affected by pollution in western Europe, followed by Nice and Milan. Thus a brown cloud of pollutants, called *nefos*, hovers over Athens for much of the summer. This cloud is a photochemical smoke, composed of nitrogen oxide, hydrocarbons, and peroxylacetyl nitrate, and sometimes is formed as low as 30 yards from the ground. *Mutatis mutandis*, this same holds true for Istanbul as well. New decentralization measures and other urban disamenities are expected to drive people and industries back to the countryside where investment benefits and fresh air prevail.

In both nations, many enterprises, which are family-owned oligopolies, enjoyed protection in the past and to some extent now, especially in Turkey. Such "sleeping" enterprises might have neglected innovative activities and have enjoyed high rates of profit under the umbrella of protection. Under growing competitive conditions, though, they have to introduce more efficient methods of production in order to survive.

Most Greek and Turkish enterprises are small and middle-size firms, employing ten persons or fewer and are primarily in the food, canning, shoes, ceramic, and cosmetics industries. They depend primarily on overworked family members and hesitate to group themselves into large economic units that would be able to implement modern technology and methods of mass production and achieve economies of scale. To overcome this hesitation and to encourage the establishment of modern production units with high efficiency, investment and tax incentives are provided by the governments of both nations.

TOURISM AND OTHER SERVICES

Tourism and the services sector in general are of vital importance for both countries, especially for Greece. The old and new discoveries of archaeological collections at Athens (Acropolis), Crete (Cnossus), Mycenae, Pilos, Tiryns, Macedonia (Vergina), and in other places of Greece, related to classical and Hellenistic periods, as well as Byzantine art objects, attract waves of tourists throughout the year who wish to satisfy their curiosity about and expand their knowledge of ancient history. On the seashores of mainland Greece and the Ionian and Aegean islands tourists can dawdle over ancient sites and wine-dark water.

Natural beauties and the dry climate of Greece and Turkey continue to attract large numbers of foreign tourists. The picturesque beaches and the rich history, as well as the innumerable archaeological monuments primarily in Greece, make the area one of the most popular destinations for international tourists. With the Olympic Games in 1996 expected to be held in Greece, in commemoration of the centenary of the first such games of modern times (1896) held in Athens, tourism would be enhanced. Moreover, if the Olympic Games were held at their birthplace (Olympia) in the Peloponnesus (where they started in the seventh century B.C.) on a permanent basis, as is contemplated, the Greek economy and tourism in particular would be greatly improved.

On the beaches of western Anatolia, tourists can enjoy the sunshine and pleasant weather and visit neighboring places of historical importance. Cities such as Istanbul (Constantinople), with the largest population in Turkey; Izmir (Smyrna), the third largest city in Turkey; Bergama (Pergamus), with its famous library of some 200,000 volumes in its Hellenistic heyday; Ephesus, one of the

Seven Wonders of the World with the ancient temple of Artemis, which the author searched recently; and Bordum (Halicarnassus) are some of the attractive places with ancient monuments and historical importance. Other touristic areas of archaeological importance include Aphrodisias, with the famous Odeon Temple; Sardis, the capital of ancient Lydia where the first coins were struck; and Troy, the famous site of the conflict between Myceneans and Trojans provoked by the abduction of the legendary, beautiful Helen of Sparta in the thirteenth century B.C.

Istanbul, though, like Athens, faces problems of car congestion and pollution. In the 1950s, the population of the city was less than a million. Now it is between six and seven million. Within the city there are some 600,000 cars and trucks, and hundreds more are added every day, far more than the strained highways can take. Serious traffic jams can be observed daily on the Galata Bridge over the Golden Horn. On the streets, a visitor may buy silk rugs or a vendor's cooked mussels and sliced lemon, or even the dance of a Gypsy's trained bear. There are not many riding on camels anymore, and not many people wear fezzes. Commerce, which was practiced mainly by Greek, Armenian, and Jewish minorities previously, is not very efficient. Efforts are made by the municipality to decentralize and Europeanize the city, which has a rapidly growing population. Also, thousands of Iranian fugitives from the Islamic revolution enter the city every month.

A well-known monument in Istanbul (Constantinople) of historical, religious, and touristic importance is Hagia Sophia, which means "Divine Wisdom" in Greek. The cathedral, which the Byzantine emperor Constantine consecrated as the basilica in 325 A.D., burned down twice. The present building was constructed by Emperor Justinian between 532 and 537. Sultan Mohammed II transformed the church into a mosque on May 29, 1453 when he conquered Constantinople. However, the secular revolution of Kemal Ataturk, which started in the 1920s, restored Hagia Sophia to its historical importance as part of universal culture. In 1980, Prime Minister Suleyman Demirel's government set aside part of Hagia Sophia, known as the Imperial Gallery, as an Islamic sanctuary. This move brought criticism from Ataturk's disciples, who saw and still see it as a dangerous concession to the fundamentalists and a step in the Islamic revival.

Increasing numbers of tourists are also visiting the attractive Mediterranean coasts in southwestern Asia Minor and the ancient sites nearby. The region that Homer, Herodotus, and Alexander the Great knew as Lycia holds a prominent place. At the port of Patara, which St. Paul left on his way to Rome, an amphitheater overlooks a valley and the silted-over harbor of the old city. Excavation by French archaeologists in the 1960s in the valley of the river Xanthos uncovered Byzantine and Roman constructions and other ancient monuments. The beautiful sarcophagus in the city of Xanthos, dating from the fourth century B.C., was shipped to London in 1842. The British Museum has sent back a plaster replica of the marble that once surrounded the Monument of the Harpies, rising above the amphitheater, and the so-called Lion Pillar.

Table 5.3
Tourist Arrivals by Country of Origin, 1983 (in thousands)

Origin	Greece	Turkey
Britain	889.0	84.4
Germany, W.	728.5	174.9
U.S.A.	406.9	188.9
Italy	327.6	57.6
France	299.5	88.2
Austria	195.4	73.8
Sweden	189.9	14.0
Switzerland	173.8	35.5
Yugoslavia	55.4	60.3
Turkey	43.4	-
Greece	-	138.7
Total	4,778.5	1,625.1

Source: United Nations, *Statistical Yearbook,* 1985, Table 12.

Although annual revenue from tourism in Turkey increased substantially, from about $200 to $400 million during the last ten years, the number of tourists has remained about the same (around 1.2 million).[7] This may be due to a pervasive notion among Moslems that tourism is immoral. Prevailing dictatorial conditions and the issue of human rights, as well as the belligerent position of Turkey against Cyprus and the Aegean Sea, may also be considered responsible for such an unfavorable climate for tourism in the area despite the attractive locations and the expensive advertisement by the Turkish government.

The annual number of tourists in Greece increased from 2 million in 1974 to 4 million in 1979. More than 7 million tourists visit Greece per year at present. As a consequence, revenue from tourism increased substantially, accounting for more than one billion dollars per year. At present, the largest number of tourists in Greece and, more or less, in Turkey come from the large EEC countries, the United States, Austria, and Sweden. Periodic devaluations of the drachma and the lira aim to attract tourism, in addition to the beneficial effects on the balance of trade through cheaper exports and more expensive imports. Large numbers of Yugoslav tourists come to Greece and Turkey, but a limited number of Turks visit Greece every year (table 5.3).

Large numbers of Greeks traveled to Italy (437,000), Britain (85,000), and Germany (77,000) in 1983, while many Turks traveled to Bulgaria (2.7 million), Iraq (365,000), Italy (224,000), Yugoslavia (118,000), Syria (92,000), Germany (62,000), and other EEC countries, during the same year.

There are about 1.5 million Turks and 800,000 Greeks who are immigrant workers in West Germany. These workers send part of their earnings back home to their relatives or for investment in manufacturing, housing, trade, and other ventures. Total immigrant remittances amounted to $900 million for Greece in 1984, compared to $1.1 billion in 1981 and $700 million in 1973. In Turkey, they were $1.7 billion in 1985, compared to $2.1 billion in 1982.[8] Such remittances are used to pay part of the sizeable trade deficit, while emigration helps reduce unemployment in Greece and, primarily, in Turkey.

It is estimated that, by the year 2025, up to 50 million Muslims, primarily Turks, will have arrived and settled in Europe. The birth rate per year in Turkey is more than double that of Greece and even higher than that of the four large EEC nations (with a total population of 230 million). With a slackening of the rules of admission of Turkish workers to the Community, a great multiplication of the present number of Turkish immigrants is expected to take place. While remittances to Turkey would greatly increase, a significant change in the demographic composition of western Europe may occur.

The importance of the service sector is expected to increase with the gradual transformation of the economies of Greece and Turkey from agriculture to industry and to services and their stronger relations with the EEC countries. The long-run developmental process, which has been followed by the developed countries as well, suggests that higher priority should be given to the sector of services because industrialization would be difficult due to EEC competition. Although productivity measurement is difficult in services, improvements in the methods of the computation of output per unit of time, via computers and other techniques, may give better comparative results regarding sectoral and subsectoral efficiencies.

Similar to what other EEC countries have done in upgrading educational services and technological resources and stemming the drain of talent, Greece and Turkey established cabinet departments or other services, with high expectations for transferring and introducing new technology.

In addition to the development of alternate energy sources, such as solar, wind, and geothermal energy, where these countries have a comparative advantage, information technology, earthquake engineering, biotechnology, and self-fertilizing plants can be used for the advancement of the pharmaceutical, agricultural, and services sectors of Greece and Turkey.

The use of computers in such services as communications, transportation, office work, banking, and other professions would help to increase the productivity of the service and other sectors. Furthermore, the rapid spread of supermarkets and self-service stores, which can be observed in both countries, is expected to increase output per unit of time and make this sector more productive.

Improvement in the efficiency of the service sector is expected to be achieved through the use of telecommunications, passenger cars, and a wider spread of mass media via television, radio, and printed material. Greece has about 1 passenger car per 10 persons and around 35 telephones per 100 inhabitants. Turkey has about 1 car per 50 persons and 7 telephones per 100 persons. There are also about 350 radios and 175 television receivers per 1,000 persons in Greece and 120 radios and 120 television receivers per 1,000 in Turkey. Annual fairs, such as that in Salonika, film festivals, athletic meetings (at times with other Balkan groups, known as Balkaniads), and theatrical and other joint performers help to improve the economic and cultural relations between the two nations.

TRANSPORTATION

Although both countries enjoy natural endowments of excellent ports, the railway system of Greece and Turkey is old and inadequate, partly because of the rough terrain and partly because of neglect due mainly to the rapid development of automobile, sea, and air transportation. Much of the rail equipment is obsolete and the cost of operation is high. The main line runs from central Europe to Yugoslavia and it continues south down the Vardar (Axios) valley of Salonika and through Thessaly to Athens. This line and most of the other rail lines in the two countries have standard track gauges. However, there exist a number of narrow-gauge lines in Greece such as that of Volos-Kalabaka and those in Peloponnesus.

European, primarily German, companies had been mainly responsible for the construction of the Berlin-to-Baghdad railroad and a few other links into Turkey (based on the ninety-nine year concession of 1902), mostly to facilitate exports of mining and other agricultural products. The first State Economic Enterprise (SEE) was the state railroad company that extended the lines to Ankara and other areas of the country, so that the railroad system accounted for about three-fourths of surface freight traffic. The lines of Istanbul-Ankara-Erzurum, Izmir-Adana-Dortyol, and north-south between Samsun and Iskenderun are the main traffic corridors. There were about 8,000 kilometers of track carrying some 14 million tons of freight (60 percent of which was minerals and ores) in 1976. However, in the postwar years the road system has been rapidly developed so that the length of surface roads increased from 24,000 kilometers in 1950 to more than 50,000 kilometers at present.[9]

Trucking from Europe to the Mideast, via Greece and Turkey, has become a profitable operation in recent years. More than 180,000 tons of cargo, worth around $300 million, cross Bosporus Bridge every month. Turkey charges $800 for each loaded truck. In spite of the frustrations of delays, especially at border points, and the hazardous conditions of mountain roads, truckers continue to travel, making more than $1,200 per trip.

The use of automobiles brought many changes in Greece and Turkey during the interwar years and afterward. It stimulated road building, it provided transport for agricultural products, and it accelerated the relocation of urban population in the industrial centers. As mentioned previously, Greece has 1 passenger car per 10 persons and Turkey has 1 car per 50 persons. Although considerable efforts have been made to improve the road systems in both countries, many roads are in bad condition. Besides the national roads, running primarily through central Europe and Yugoslavia down to Salonika, Athens, and Patras in Greece, and from Salonika to Istanbul to Ankara and the Turkish interior, many regional and local roads have been developed. However, in the effort to link even small villages with national or central roads, particularly in the mountainous parts of both countries, many of these roads were badly constructed and, consequently, are underutilized.

Both countries have extensive shores, and sea transportation is vital, as are port services. However, despite the natural endowment of excellent harbors in both countries, some ports often become the bottlenecks or the white elephants of economic development. Since demand for port services is quite inelastic, it is expected that ports can generate revenue for further expansion.

It would seem that higher prices are supposed to be charged in times of traffic congestion and lower prices in times of port underutilization. Although there are economies of scale, particularly in large ports such as those of Piraeus, Salonika, Patras, and Kavala in Greece, and Istanbul, Izmir, Trabzon, and Mersin in Turkey, it is difficult to measure them in order to optimize port operations. Appropriate price distinctions between port congestion and port underutilization would improve allocative efficiency and allow many ports to replace public subsidies with port-generated revenue. Otherwise, vessel owners using the port facilities would surely apply their own congestion charges to cargo and shipping rates.

At the same time, some degree of competition among ports might exist. Different port managers in the same country or in other neighboring countries might try to draw some more traffic to generate more revenue. Development policies on port facilities should be coordinated with similar policies on inland transportation so that the uninterrupted flow of passengers and commodities may be secured. This is particularly so for Greece and Turkey, who together constitute a natural gateway for central Europe to the countries of the Middle East.

In addition to the main ports of Piraeus and Salonika, with heavy traffic, other Greek ports are being developed. They include Kavala, Corfu, Preveza, Patras, Herakleion, Rhodos, and primarily Volos. In the port of Volos alone more than 5,000 vehicles and 6 million tons of cargo, primarily from the EEC countries, are loaded every year for the Middle Eastern countries, while the ferries from Volos to Tarsus and Latakia, Syria, handle about 2,700 trailer trucks per month. Also, heavy traffic can be observed in a number of Turkish ports, especially those of Istanbul and Izmir. Other important ports that need further development include Trabzon, Samsun, and Zonguldak in the Black Sea, and Antalya, Mersin, and Iskenderun in the south.[10] The main oil terminals handling domestic and Iraqi crude are near the port of Iskenderun.

To improve transportation between the EEC and the Middle Eastern countries, Greece and Italy agreed to collaborate on the construction of a 22-mile road linking the Greek ports of Igoumenitsa in the west and Volos in the east and to modernize these two ports. The EEC will finance 80 percent of the work. Turkey should be interested in the development of such transportation lines that could facilitate its trade with the EEC. Eleusina, one of the important ports of Greater Athens (less than ten miles to the west of the city), is used primarily for tankers, while the ports of Patras, Corfu, Rhodos, and Herakleion are largely used for passenger shipping. Because of the long coastlines in both Greece and Turkey and the large number of inhabited islands in Greece, coastal shipping continues to be an important means of transporting passengers and goods internally.

Shipping, however, because of its international nature, is very sensitive to economic slowdowns and worldwide recessions. Thus, during periods of slump (such as that of the early 1980s) the shipping industry is caught in a severe squeeze as too many ships chase too few customers. Under such conditions many tankers, bulk cargo vessels, and container ships, which belong mostly to small independent shipowners, are laid up in berths, primarily in Eleusina and Piraeus in Greece, or in scrapyards for dismantling. As a result, freight rates drop and the value of ships declines, while loans using ships as collateral are rolled back or go unpaid.

NOTES

1. Nicholas V. Gianaris, *Economic Development: Thought and Problems* (West Hanover, Mass.: Christopher Publishing House, 1978), 84–110.

2. Alan Cowell, "Greek Bill Would Tax Church Land," *New York Times*, March 15, 1987.

3. Joe Pierce, *Life in a Turkish Village* (New York: Holt, Rinehart and Winston, 1964), chaps. 5–7; and Paul Magnarella, *Tradition and Change in a Turkish Town* (New York: John Wiley and Sons, 1974).

4. Anne Krueger, *Turkey* (New York: National Bureau of Economic Research, 1974), chap. 4; Ron Ayres and T. Thomson, *Turkey: A New Era* (London: Euromoney Publications, 1984), chap. 9. See also related articles of Marios Nikolinakos and Helmuth Toepfer in *Uneven Development in Southern Europe*, ed. Ray Hudson and Jim Lewis (London: Methuen, 1985).

5. Bernard Weinraub, "In Reagan's Drug War, Congress Has the Big Guns," *New York Times*, March 15, 1987, p. E5; and Lewis Geoffrey, *Modern Turkey* (New York: Praeger, 1974), 217–18, from *Milliyet*, December 1, 1972.

6. For industrial investment in Greece 1961–1980, see A. F. Freris, *The Greek Economy in the Twentieth Century* (New York: St. Martin's, 1986), 166–74. For Turkey's industrial development, see Bertil Walstedt, *State Manufacturing Enterprise in a Mixed Economy: The Turkish Case* (Baltimore: Johns Hopkins University Press, for the World

Bank, 1980), chap. 4; Max Thornberg, Graham Spry, and George Soule, *Turkey, An Economic Appraisal* (New York: Twentieth Century Fund, 1949), chap. 5; and Walter Weiker, *The Modernization of Turkey* (New York: Holmes and Meier, 1980).

7. There are more bedrooms on the island of Rhodes alone than in the whole of Turkey. Ron Ayres and T. Thomson, *Turkey: A New Era*, 74. For growing tourism in Lycia, see Tom Wicker, "Travels in the Ages," *New York Times*, October 1, 1987.

8. OECD, *Economic Surveys: Greece* (Paris: January 1986), 41; and OECD, *Economic Surveys 1985/1986: Turkey* (Paris: September 1986), 21.

9. Richard Nyrop, ed., *Turkey: A Country Study* (Washington, D.C.: American Univerity, Foreign Area Studies, 1980), 176–78.

10. Nicholas V. Gianaris, *The Economies of the Balkan Countries: Albania, Bulgaria, Greece, Romania, Turkey, Yugoslavia* (New York: Praeger, 1982), 121–22. More on Greek shipping in Heraklis Haralampidis, *Naftilia kai Oikonomiki Anaptyxi* (Shipping and Economic Development), (Athens: Center for Economic Research and Planning, 1986); Wray Candilis, *The Economy of Greece, 1944–66* (New York: Praeger, 1968), chap. 5; and Nikos Vernadakis, *Econometric Models for the Developing Economies: A Case Study of Greece* (New York: Praeger, 1978), 35–37.

6

Fiscal Policy

IMPORTANCE OF PUBLIC FINANCE

With a growing public sector in Greece and Turkey, the subject of public finance for both countries acquires great importance not only on matters of financing government expenditures but also on matters of countercyclical policy. Since these two countries are currently facing relatively high rates of inflation and high unemployment rates, policymakers have a rough time implementing public policies to solve this economic dilemma. Although it is difficult to curb inflation and increase employment with fiscal measures alone, government policies on taxes and expenditures, nevertheless, play a vital role in these matters.

Governmental policies on expenditures and taxation are of great importance in determining income and wealth distribution, investment allocation, and growth performance. Recent policies, emphasizing reduction in inflation and an increase in factor productivity, have generated more attention regarding the use of public finances for achieving these goals. Such policies aim at stimulating saving and investment even at a sacrifice of vital social programs.

On the other hand, the growing proportion of older people in the population presents new problems of financing social security and transfer payments in both Greece and Turkey, regardless of their economic philosophies. Furthermore, both economies have moved gradually toward large public sectors, while serious efforts toward decentralization have been made mostly as a result of bureaucratic inefficiencies. These elements indicate that there is a notable drift toward structural similarities in the fiscal systems of the two countries.

It seems that structural changes and reforms are needed in the public sector to raise more revenue through higher productivity. This is particularly so for Greece and Turkey with an overburdened bureaucracy and a complicated public sector. Recent inflationary pressures have led to significant distortions in the fiscal systems of many economies, including those of Greece and Turkey. As a result, the public sector absorbs large amounts of national income mainly in the form of taxes and heavy borrowing, despite criticisms of misallocations and low performance by this sector. For that reason arguments for public spending reduction, tax indexing, and decontrolling the economy are growing. There is a well-accepted principle that "if you tax something, you get less of it. If you subsidize something, you get more of it."

With higher levels of development and higher per capita income, it is to be expected that direct taxes or taxes on personal income and profits will acquire more importance than indirect taxes, that is, taxes on goods and services. Indeed a more open policy toward domestic and foreign trade, higher urbanization and monetization of the economies of Greece and Turkey, and the relative growth of salaried workers will create a favorable climate for structural changes in taxation toward larger direct taxes.

The transfer of resources from the agricultural to the more money-using industrial and service sectors, which can be observed in these two countries, is also favorable toward an increase in revenue from direct taxes. The same thing can be said for government policies toward more employment and a more equitable income distribution. Such policies increase public sector spending and expand the tax base. Increases in nominal income because of inflation and increases in real income because of productivity growth offer fertile ground for further expansion in direct taxes and public expenditures.

A serious problem in public policy is how to finance government services in such a way that additional expenditures (marginal costs) for each public purpose will equal additional or marginal benefits. If there is a deficiency in the quantity and quality of government services and public administration, this will have an adverse effect on the private sector and the economy as a whole.

Out of the three main alternative means of financing public expenditures, that is, taxation, issuance of government securities, and creation of money, it would seem that the first alternative is the most anti-inflationary for the Greek and Turkish economies. Money creation, on the other hand, is clearly inflationary when it exceeds the real rate of economic growth, given that income velocity of money is currently constant or growing in both nations. The issuance of government bonds is not widespread in these economies, as is the practice of borrowing from the banks.

The occasional and temporary nature of governmental economic policies during the postwar years created a serious structural problem in the economies of Greece and Turkey. Such policies, affected by the sociopolitical instability of these countries, led to a large tertiary sector at the expense of neglecting the secondary sector, especially in Greece, and to some extent the primary sector as well. As a result, a large class of middlemen and self-employed persons in services was created with income almost double that of salaried persons and farmers. These high incomes result primarily from high profits realized by oligopolistic or local monopolistic distributors and traders, who, in turn, spend the bulk of their earnings in unproductive, quick-profit ventures, such as speculation on urban lots or apartments and imported luxury goods. These high profits are also used to increase the demand mainly for consumer goods, pulling prices up without offering much to improve productivity and employment.

Public policies in Greece and Turkey seem to focus too much attention on consumption and not enough on investment to increase productive capacity. To induce the private sector to consume less and save more, fiscal reforms, a decrease of regulations, and the introduction of policies intended to increase investment are needed to spur production incentives and expand supply. In that way, spending for investment would replace spending for consumption. To reverse the slump in savings that starves investment and feeds consumption, stimulation of long-term investment incentives for individuals and enterprises is required in these market economies.

Emphasizing reduction of overspending, through reforms, would not be an economic panacea, but it might be expected that it would help stimulate investment, revive productivity, combat inflation, and encourage exports. It would, most probably, have an anti-inflation and anti-recession function, helping to solve the dilemma of simultaneous inflation and unemployment that plagues Turkey and Greece. Also, faster depreciation (higher deductions from taxable income for the cost of a productive asset) and low capital-gains taxes create an incentive to invest in more efficient equipment, which leads to higher enterprise productivity, more jobs, and less inflation. Such fiscal devices allow old enterprises to renew aging facilities and young enterprises to satisfy their appetites for modern capital equipment.

GOVERNMENT EXPENDITURES

Greece and Turkey face serious fiscal problems regarding the formulation and balancing of government budgets. At times, lack of fiscal discipline and socioeconomic instability make things worse. In recent years, fiscal deficits do not contribute much to investment. Politicians find it more acceptable to reduce investment and future growth than to cut subsidies and wages of the civil servants and face social unrest. As a result, real capital formation is reduced in Turkey and more so in Greece.

Fiscal operations in general, and government spending in particular, weigh heavily in the aggregate demand and the economic performance of these nations, depending on political and territorial disturbances. Defense expenditures are relatively large in both countries. Technological changes in weaponry, rapidity of obsolescence, and the nature of the equipment-intensive military establishment increase government outlays and impose a heavy burden on the budgets. In addition, subsidies allocated to a number of economic sectors and production units are responsible for large portions of government spending.

Another cause of rising budget expenditures is the increasing cost for public services due to inflation, which runs at high rates, particularly in Turkey. Moreover, population mobility and its concentration in urban centers augment the need for public services and municipal facilities. The ever-increasing use of cars, buses, and planes for transportation as well as the need for more electric power and other public utilities necessitate growing public investment because the private sector is either unable or hesitant to undertake and implement long-term capital investment.

The growing role of transfers and the problem of adjusting income distribution among different groups of population, mainly among different regions, are additional causes of governmental intervention and an increase in budget expenditures. Such expenditures, together with welfare payments, which aim at reducing large income inequalities, are growing rapidly, especially in Greece. Moreover, improvements in medical services and technology move the population bulge farther up the age scale and intensify the fiscal problem of social security payments.

The economic role of government, which expanded during the recent decades while pursuing social objectives, is under intense criticism. Mandated spending programs, such as interest payments, unemployment benefits, and other welfare costs, are difficult to control by government because, whether explicitly or implicitly, they are indexed and increase with rising prices. Such spending based on indexed entitlements, which are considered in economic theory as automatic stabilizers, may, on many occasions, stimulate inflation. From that point of view, it becomes difficult for the governments of Greece and Turkey to exercise fiscal discipline, reduce budget deficits, and implement anti-inflationary policies.

Increases in wages and salaries of civil servants, which absorb sizeable amounts of government expenditures, are largely indexed and follow, more or less, the rates of inflation through mainly discretionary decisions made by the responsible ministries or other public authorities. Also, social security payments are indirectly indexed to the cost of living. In the rural areas of Greece and more so of Turkey, the social security programs provide limited payments and are largely based on conventional obligations of relatives to look after the aged and the infirm, although such programs have been satisfactory for urban centers.

A more difficult problem in these quarreling nations arises in defense spending. Many defense items, such as planes, tanks, guns, and the like, are purchased abroad. As long as the prices of such items keep going up, larger amounts of government expenditures are required for their purchase. The domestic economy, then, is drained of valuable financial resources while inflationary pressures persist.

In addition to its social function, the public sector in these countries plays an important role in the performance of the overall economy. As a matter of practice, the public and private sectors are largely complementary and interdependent. Through the creation of an environment conducive to private investment, and through the establishment of needed infrastructure, as well as provision for regulation or the absence of it, the public sector can have a decisive impact on the private sector and the economic development of the countries involved.

In Greece and Turkey, as in many other market or planned economies, the public sector provides a wide range of economic and social services in such areas as education and vocational training, provisions of electricity and water, transportation, communications, infrastructural investment, and a host of other activities that affect production, distribution, and growth. Although there is no way to escape the interaction between the public and private sectors, it is difficult to determine what policies or what blends should be adopted by each country. For the public sector to be more of a benefit than a burden in the economy, good public management, sound industrial and agricultural policies, and an effective fiscal system are all important.

Although there are signs in these economies that indicate public spending is approaching its economic and political limits, the public sector continues to expand rapidly, particularly in Greece. The governments of these countries recognize that they cannot have economic growth without incentives to invest, which can be achieved by shifting resources from the governmental consumption sector back to the investment sector. That is why government consumption spending, which rose rapidly during the postwar years, started tapering off in Turkey and, as expected, in Greece, not so much because of the disorganized popular resistance but because the governments of these countries began taking the lead themselves. However, this task is difficult, especially for Greece, because of the reaction of many vested interests that have already been created in the past and the disturbances expected in the future.

However, in these nations, where people still tend to look to government to solve their problems, public spending is expected to be high. As mentioned previously, such spending takes place mainly in the form of subsidies in the areas of health, social security, education, transportation, housing, and agriculture, as well as in defense expenditures. The gradual reduction in income inequalities necessitates additional spending by the respective governments, primarily in the form of consumption or subsidizing the transfer of wealth from one group to another.

Such spending has the advantage of improving income distribution, but often reduces incentives to work and slows down economic growth. Thus, while public spending for social insurance against illness or unemployment may raise the level of social welfare, it may, at the same time, exaggerate budget deficits and drain investment funds. Also, government spending in advanced education may prove to be socially counterproductive as long as it is used for training young people in honorific professions for which there is no demand and no satisfying jobs available. This is another serious fiscal problem in both Greece and Turkey.

In the middle or less developed countries, such as Greece and Turkey, public sector capital formation seems to be vital for development because the private sector is hesitant to undertake tangible investment, especially in the long run. Thus, in some cases, the public sector invests in big projects for purposes of reducing unemployment and stimulating development. Nevertheless, nondevelopment spending, as a proportion of total public share, continues to be high. As a result, self-reliant and government-promoted industrialization becomes weak and in many instances the state accumulation policy proves to be less effective than planned.

As is the case with many developing countries, the share of the state and local governments in the total public spending is relatively low and is expected to gradually increase more than that of the central government. Central influence on local government expenditures started diminishing and policy recommendations for reintegrating public expenditure control and planning become more and more ineffective.

GROWTH OF BUDGETARY SPENDING

Regarding government expenditures, it would be proper to distinguish between operating or current budgets and capital budgets. Other countries, notably Sweden, and U.S. state and local governments, as well as private enterprises, are making such distinctions. Capital expenditures are investments that would pay off in the future. Only depreciation, that is, wearing-out capital, should be included in current expenses. Therefore, government investments in roads and bridges, health, education, and the like should be considered as capital expenditures. As such, they would benefit present and future generations through positive returns and social externalities. From that point of view, budget deficits would be reduced substantially if government capital expenditures are excluded from current budgets. Likewise, the government debt would be reduced if capital assets created by budget expenditures are excluded.

For long-run financial stability and growth in the economies of Greece and Turkey a balanced current (ordinary) budget, in which the investment budget is not included, should be the main objective of fiscal policy. Moreover, infrastructural changes and new investment opportunities, financed through budgetary expenditures or current account surpluses, would stimulate development without disturbing monetary stability in the long run.

In addition to central and local governments, the public sector includes also the public enterprises in both nations and the revolving funds in Turkey. The consolidated budget of the central Turkish government includes, in addition to taxes and expenditures of the public sector, some sixteen annexed budgets of special agencies, such as state irrigation and hydroelectric dams administrations, highway administration, state monopolies, imports, forests, and six universities and academies.[1] The ministries and the public agencies submit their requests for funds to the ministry of finance, for the next fiscal year, beginning January 1 in Greece and March 1 in Turkey.

After the approval by the parliament in Greece and the senate and the national assembly in Turkey, the budget bill is completed and the ministry of finance is responsible for its implementation. The budgets of both nations include current expenditures for consumer goods and services, investment spending, and transfers. For long-term projections of public sector revenue and expenditures, five-year development plans are formulated. Annual modifications of the plans are common, while supplementary funds are usually appropriated throughout the year.

Both nations follow, more or less, the Keynesian prescription for deficit spending, as do many other market economies. Such deficit spending can be financed by selling bonds or other government securities to the public. In this case, competition between the government and the private sector for scarce economic resources is intensified.

Some major questions to be asked in connection with the trend of growing public expenditures and their deficit financing are (1) Is the relative expansion of the public sector producing adverse macroeconomic effects by crowding out private investment or is it only a question of private consumption being replaced by government consumption? (2) Is this expansion the result of a growing demand for government services on the part of the taxpayers and, therefore, are they willing to bear the burden of additional taxation in case borrowing is undesirable? (3) Are high government expenditures and budget deficits the result of high military spending due to mistrust and conflict between these two nations over Cyprus?

The financing of public sector investment, to supplement private investment, calls for a curb on public consumption. Excessive current public expenditures and the resulting budgetary deficits, so familiar in Greece and Turkey, upset monetary and current account equilibria. To have equilibrium of supply and demand and to ensure that more savings are allocated to productive investment, reductions in consumption spending by the public sector, accompanied by fiscal incentives to the private sector, are needed. Such fiscal incentives may include reduction in income tax rates, investment credits, and tax levying on nonproductive property and luxuries consumption.

Relationship of Government Expenditures to GDP

Government consumption expenditures, as percentages of gross domestic product (GDP), were higher and growing in Greece but declining in Turkey in recent years (tables 6.1 and 6.2). In the EEC member countries, as a group, such government expenditures were growing from 14 percent of the GDP in 1960 to close to 20 percent presently, almost the same as those in the United States. The dramatic increase of general government expenditures in Greece in recent years was due primarily to the distributional policies and the social philosophy pursued by the government, especially in 1981–1985. Large amounts of money were spent for increases in the salaries of the employees of the public sector and for pensions, which led to budgetary deficits and kept inflation at high levels. Also, high government expenditures were needed to implement decentralization programs and to rescue inefficient public and private enterprises.

The decline in the proportions of government expenditures in Turkey in recent years was due primarily to the austerity measures introduced after 1980 and the privatization of a number of inefficient government enterprises, the deficits of

Table 6.1
Government Consumption Expenditures as a Percentage of GDP (current prices and exchange rates)

Country	1960	1970	1980	1985
Greece	11.7	12.7	16.4	20.0
Turkey	10.6	13.1	12.6	8.5
EEC	14.1	15.2	18.6	18.5

Source: OECD, *National Accounts,* various issues; and IMF, *International Financial Statistics,* various issues.

Table 6.2
Elasticities of Government Consumption Expenditures, with Respect to National Income (national currencies, current prices)

Country	1950–60	1960–70	1970–80	1980–85
Greece	1.01	1.13	1.38	1.46
Turkey	0.92	1.27	0.96	0.63
EEC	1.02	1.22	1.33	1.09

Source: OECD, *National Accounts,* various issues; and IMF, *International Financial Statistics,* various issues.

which were covered by the governmental budgets. However, Turkey continues to spend large amounts of money on defense, as Greece also does, and on subsidization of products produced mainly by foreign investment.

Some 3 percent of revenue from direct taxes and portions of the revenue from lotteries and casinos are used by the newly created Turkish Administration of National Defense.[2] It is worth mentioning that the Turkish government signed contracts to buy 160 F–16 planes from General Dynamics, costing about $40 million each, as did Greece for 60 F–16 planes.

The elasticities of government consumption related to national income are positive and growing for Greece during the postwar years and for the EEC in 1950–1980. The average elasticity for Greece was 1.01 in the 1950s, 1.13 in the 1960s, 1.38 in the 1970s, and 1.46 in the 1980s. For Turkey, it was 0.92 in the 1950s, 1.27 in the 1960s, 0.96 in the 1970s and 0.63 in the 1980s. For the EEC, it changed from 1.02 in the 1950s to 1.33 in the 1970s and declined to 1.09 in the 1980s. This means that, in the 1950s, government spending for consumption increased almost equiproportionally with the increase in income in Greece, Turkey, and the EEC. However, it increased proportionally more for all countries considered in the 1960s and even more for Greece and the EEC in the 1970s. In the 1980s, it increased for Greece and declined for the EEC and Turkey. Therefore, public expenditures increased more than the total economy for Greece, during the three postwar decades, but they leveled off or declined, in recent years, for the EEC and Turkey.

TAX REVENUE

General government revenue over national income (average taxes) increased in Greece from 20 percent in the 1950s to 26 percent in the 1960s, 30 percent in the 1970s, and 35 percent in the 1980s. In the case of Turkey, general government revenue changed from 23 percent of national income in the 1960s to 26 percent in the 1970s and thereafter.[3]

A similar pattern of changes can be observed in marginal taxes during the postwar years. Such positive marginal tax rates indicate that the tax structures in both countries have built-in flexibility; that is, independent of any relative decision, taxes change automatically with changes in national income.

The percentage increase in tax revenue over the percentage increase in national income (income elasticity of taxation) was positive and higher than 1 for Greece (1.35) during the last three decades, while for Turkey it was positive and higher than 1 in the last two decades (1.30). These results indicate that taxes increased proportionally more than national income during the postwar years in both Greece and Turkey.

Such growing proportions of taxation, which were needed to finance ever-increasing public expenditures, support the Wagner hypothesis, which postulates that the share or the ratio of public spending or taxes to national product increases with the growth of per capita income.[4]

Tax revenue comes primarily from indirect taxes and direct taxes. Indirect taxes (mainly turnover taxes, stamp duties, and tariffs) are transaction-based taxes levied on national product, while direct taxes are person-based levies on national income. Indirect taxes are usually shifted forward and push prices up, especially in Greece and Turkey; direct taxes, that is, personal income, payroll, property, and corporate income taxes, tend to press prices downward and en-courage leisure.

The structure of the Greek tax system has not changed much during the postwar years. Direct taxes are a small proportion of total taxes. They absorb only 6 percent of GDP compared to 16 percent absorbed by indirect taxes. In Turkey, direct taxes absorb about 5 to 7 percent of national income compared to about 10 percent absorbed by indirect taxes.

For Greece, the portion of national income absorbed by central government taxes increased during the postwar years, from 13 percent in 1960 to 17 percent in 1970, 19 percent in 1980, and 23 percent in 1985.[5] Similar increases can be seen in direct taxes. The ratio of direct to indirect taxes increased from 22 percent in 1960 to 24 percent in 1970, 31 percent in 1980, and 40 percent in 1985. However, compared to that of other developed countries, this ratio remains very low.

For Turkey, central government tax revenue, as percentage of national income, changed from 16 percent in 1962 to 22 percent in 1970, 23 percent in 1980, and 19 percent in 1985. Moreover, direct taxes as a proportion of the total budget revenue increased from 30 percent in 1962 to 35 percent in 1970 to about 45 percent thereafter, while indirect taxes remained around 55 percent. As a result, the ratios of direct to indirect taxes increased from 57 percent to 81 percent.

In both countries, local government receipts, mainly those of municipalities and communities, are relatively small. For Greece, they account for only about 14 percent of the total (general government) taxes, compared to more than 60 percent of those of central government. In Turkey, such local government receipts account for only 5 to 12 percent of the total (general government) taxes, compared with about 80 percent of those of central government.

For both nations, state and local receipts declined continuously during the postwar years, as did state and local expenditures, until the very recent past. This means that, from the point of view of public finance, Greece and Turkey had a centralized system during the postwar years that continued to become even more centralized from year to year. Such a high degree of centralization in the public sector may be responsible for the high degree of bureaucracy that prevailed in these countries.

In contrast, state and local receipts in most developed countries absorb high proportions of general government revenues. For example, they absorb around 15 percent of total taxes in Italy, 29 percent in Great Britain, 34 percent in West Germany, 43 percent in the United States, 47 percent in Australia, 48 percent in Japan, and as much as 64 percent in Canada.

Another form of taxation to be considered by Greece and Turkey is the land tax, which may be a good source of revenue for municipalities and communities. Such a tax has the advantage of eliminating the holding of idle land for social prestige or speculation, while providing, at the same time, a degree of financial independence for local authorities. Moreover, it increases the incentives to transfer ownership of land from those who left the rural sector to the remaining farmers. It exercises pressure to broaden cultivation and stimulates agricultural production. The land tax then may help reduce the denudation of the countryside of its labor and other valuable resources. Therefore, a land tax, which may be progressive, can raise substantial amounts of revenue with low tax rates. This is so because it has a large base and there is not much evasion since land cannot be easily concealed and may be used as a security for tax payment. Particularly in Greece and Turkey, a land tax in the countryside may prove to be beneficial not only for purposes of revenue collection but, more importantly, to force the reconstitution of small pieces of land, scattered about in different places, into larger and more efficient farms.

Land taxes, which were used mainly before World War II for revenue, lost importance to other forms of taxation. These taxes, which were levied in cash or in kind, were based either on land valuations or on annual yields. Taxes based on the capital value of land stimulate higher production, through technical innovations and intensive cultivation, because additional production is free of taxes. From that point of view, some kind of low land taxes may be considered proper for Turkey and particularly for Greece to force sales of small lots by migrants to the remaining peasants who till them.

There are no capital-gains taxes and limited property taxes in Greece and Turkey. Urban property transactions are subject only to transfer tax applicable to all or most real estate transactions. It seems that profits coming from unearned increments in the value of shore land constitute a rational and equitable basis for taxation. Taxation on capital gains from urban and shore land sales would revoke what may be considered a subsidy for speculation by the present tax policy. On the other hand, transfer taxes in rural, denuded, backward areas should be reduced so that land transactions and investment can be encouraged and decentralization can be improved.

From April 1986, higher tax exemptions were introduced for property transactions in Greece. Thus, for married couples buying their first house or apartment the tax-exempt amount was raised from 2,400,000 to 3,000,000 drachmas, plus 800,000 drachmas for each of the first three children and 1,500,000 drachmas for each additional child. For single adults, these amounts are 2,000,000 drachmas for the first house or apartment and 700,000 drachmas for the first lot. Moreover, the tax-exempt value for buying agricultural and cattle-raising areas was raised from 100,000 to 125,000 drachmas per acre.

Because taxation on capital or wealth in both countries is limited or nonexistent, a tax on income from capital can be avoided by keeping capital stock idle. But this practice reduces the use of available resources and retards growth. In the case of keeping liquid capital stock, an inflationary money creation is similar to a tax.

Other forms of taxation include expenditure taxes (on personal income less savings) and betting or game taxes (lotteries, horse racing, cards), which are used by both countries.

Tax Evasion

Serious problems of tax evasion appear in both countries. To eliminate or reduce tax evasion and loopholes, both governments try from time to time to introduce vigorous tax laws. But measures such as the requirement that the origin of income be reported when property is bought or an investment is made proved only marginally effective. Instead, such measures discouraged investment and encouraged outflow of capital abroad. In a way, the cure turned out to be more harmful than the disease itself.

Tax evasion in Greece and Turkey seems to be rampant, probably the highest in Europe. Payoffs by tax evaders are common. Go-betweens collect payoffs from both the individual tax evaders and the officials in the ministry who usually agree to settle for a fraction of the tax assessed. Similar payoffs take place in other ministries for other activities, primarily for import licensing. This is part of the system of *rousfeti* or patronage that has plagued Greece and Turkey for many years. Businessmen get bank loans, parents obtain jobs for their children, and civil servants get their promotions and privileges through patronage, with little regard to merit or performance.

Sometimes, measures allowing the government to arrest tax evaders may be considered counterproductive, because the cost of arresting people and putting them in jail may exceed the amount of additional revenue to be collected. Probably, lower tax rates, fewer exemptions and loopholes, and a broader tax base would reduce tax evasion and bring in more tax revenue.

Harmonization of the tax systems of Greece and Turkey with those of the EEC would most probably lead to a change in the tax structure of these countries toward higher proportions of direct taxes (including social security contributions), relative to total tax revenue and would reduce tax evasion. However, social and political factors, in addition to pressures from groups of taxpayers that are powerful in Greece and Turkey, may delay such structural changes in the foreseeable future and tax evasion may continue.[6]

In the economies of Greece and Turkey, with growing service sectors, there are increasing opportunities to deal in cash to escape taxation. The internationalization of financial services also provides additional escape routes. Thus, the "underground economy" is enlarged at the expense of the "above-ground" income reported. In addition to the unreported income from illegal gambling, drug dealing, burglaries, and other criminal activities, much income is collected "off the books" primarily by business and professions ranging from the practice of medicine and law to driving taxis, renting rooms, and a host of other activities. It is estimated that up to 50 percent of the disposable income escapes taxation in these two countries, compared to about 15 to 20 percent in the United States. Such underground dealing is forcing savings into cash or non-earning assets that cost tax evaders money.

To make the tax system more equitable and to reduce tax evasion, the Greek government introduced an estimated minimum of income needed for basic living conditions for professionals such as doctors, lawyers, and other people offering services. However, care should be taken to avoid overtaxing professionals who receive a salary, upon which they pay taxes, and earn more income from additional services they offer. Thus, a doctor serving in a small town who receives a taxable salary from the Institute of Social Insurance (IKA) should not also be subjected to the above estimated minimum income regulation. This would be in accordance with the needed decentralization policy pursued by the government.

DIRECT TAXES

Direct (income) taxes, the main source of government revenue, were also used in ancient times. Classical Athens (Solon's Laws) and Rome relied on income taxes, progressive in character, as did medieval Europe. However, the rise of industry and the expansion of domestic and primarily foreign trade in Greece and Turkey, as in other developing nations, led to the extensive use of indirect taxes. The increasingly pecuniary nature of economic life, though, and the quest for an improvement in income distribution call for a shift to direct taxation in the form of income and/or property taxes.

Direct taxes of the central government, which normally reside at their original impact point and are not shifted forward or backward by the bearer of the burden, account for close to one-third of total tax revenue in Greece and more in Turkey. They increased from 17 percent of total tax revenue of the central government of Greece in 1960 to 28 percent in 1984. For Turkey, they increased from 30 percent to about 45 percent, respectively. Greece and Turkey seem to follow trends of growing direct taxes, similar to those prevailing in the EEC and other developed market economies.

Highly progressive taxes have detrimental effects on investment and production incentives. They can lead to lower tax revenue because of the resulting disincentives for work and the expected lower levels of investment and production (supply-side arguments). Raising taxes by increasing tax rates beyond a certain point may decrease total revenue by reducing the tax base. This is analogous to the raising of prices by monopolists in order to increase profits, which may lead to a decrease in total profits because of a proportionally larger decrease in demand. Greece, Turkey, and other countries such as the United States, West Germany, and Britain are in the process of reviewing or implementing measures to reduce high tax rates and encourage investment in productive enterprises. However, tax incentives to producers for investment stimulation and industrial growth should not be used to shore up obsolescence and perpetuate inefficiency.

In Greece, different tax rates prevail for different classes, such as merchants, self-employed persons, clerks, and pensioners. Merchants pay the highest tax rates, followed by professionals and clerks. With a recent law, 1364/1982, Greece introduced a property tax similar to that of France. Thus for owners of real estate property worth between 25 and 35 million drachmas the tax is 0.5 percent. For every additional 10 million drachmas property value, the tax rate increases progressively by 0.5 percent, but to no more than 2 percent. If the person's spouse also has property, the above tax rates (from 0.5 to 2 percent) start on property worth more than 35 million drachmas (or more than $250,000). Such property taxes, with even higher rates than the ones mentioned above, seem to be needed by the government, not only for revenue but also for decentralizing urban centers, particularly Athens.

Corporations and companies (joint stock companies, limited liability companies, and proprietorships) in Greece are liable to pay income or profit taxes (Laws 3325/1955 and 3843/1958). Taxable corporate income is determined after dividends and fees of the executives are subtracted. The latter are subject to personal income taxes and are withheld and paid by the corporations. Ploughback or undistributed profits are subject to corporate income taxes. Dividends from stocks already listed on the Stock Exchange of Athens are subject to a tax rate of 38 percent if the stocks are personal and 41 percent if they are nonpersonal. If the stocks have not been listed on the stock exchange the rates are 43 percent and 47 percent, respectively. However, an amount of 25,000 drachmas per stockholder is deducted from the dividends of the same company and 100,000 drachmas per stockholder from all dividends from different companies.

Profits of enterprises are subject to taxes after the cost of operation, donations (to public, educational, religious, and athletic institutions), and depreciation are subtracted. Rates of depreciation vary from 4 to 15 percent for machinery, 8 percent for factory structures, warehouses, and hotels, 5 percent for other buildings, 20 percent for office furniture, 30 percent for hotel furniture, and 100 percent for tools and repair of instruments in operation (Decree 88/1973).

Domestic and foreign corporations pay 40 percent taxes on taxable income. However, for industrial and mining corporations whose stocks are listed on the Stock Exchange of Athens the tax rate is 35 percent. Moreover, there is a contribution to the Organization of Agricultural Insurance for the pensions of farmers, which, added to the tax rates above, raises them to 43.30 percent and 38.24 percent, respectively. To avoid double taxation, taxes paid on income earned in a foreign country and taxable in Greece are deducted from the taxes due.

Rent is subject to taxation. Net income from rent is gross income minus mortgage interest and a certain amount deducted for depreciation, insurance, other taxes, and repairs. In Greece, the deduction for depreciation is lower on rents from stores, offices, and warehouses, as well as on rents from open lots. On the gross income from rents (whether actual or imputed) of buildings in the Athens metropolitan area and Salonika a 3 percent special duty is imposed for waterworks.

Export incentives are provided through deductions from taxable income varying from 3 percent for industrial enterprises to 2 percent for agricultural enterprises and 1 percent for other exporting companies. Such deductions are under the pressure of elimination from the EEC.

Income from interest is not taxed in Greece and is taxed to a limited extent in Turkey. However, in the EEC countries such income is subject to taxes of about 35 percent. The same is true for other market economies, such as the United States, where income from interest is added and taxed together with other incomes, as is income from dividends. It would seem that, after certain exemptions, taxes on interest would encourage purchasing of more stocks and bonds and would increase direct investment.

Income Taxes

Both Turkey and Greece have a progressive income tax system. With inflation, when money incomes rise at the same rate as prices, real income remains the same. However, under progressive taxation, after tax, real incomes decline because tax rates increase as nominal or money incomes rise. Thus people find themselves sliding up the rate brackets and paying higher taxes although their real incomes remain constant or may even decline. The same thing can be said for nominal gains resulting from increases in the prices of assets because of inflation. From that point of view, the inflationary setting of the Greek and Turkish economies has had a major impact on income taxes. Both countries have implemented or considered measures of indexation to mitigate the taxpayers' real burden.

Changes in direct taxes are affected by changes in nominal incomes, which, in turn, are affected by inflation. As income increases, direct taxes are expected to increase even more, as long as progressive tax systems prevail. This is true for Greece and Turkey, where the elasticities of direct taxes with respect to national income are higher than one.

Personal income taxes can be levied on the total income from all sources (unitary system) or independently on each source of income (secular system). The last system, which prevails in Greece and Turkey, provides for different tax rates for wages and salaries, for professional income, property income, and profits from different sources.

Income taxes, which include taxes on personal income and taxes on profits, are about 5 to 6 percent of GDP for Greece, compared to 10 to 12 percent for Turkey and 13 to 14 percent for the EEC, the United States, and Japan. In Greece and Turkey, such taxes on income and profits, as percentages of GDP, were about half before 1970. For the EEC, they were about one-third less up to 1970, while for the United States they were about the same. It is expected that Greece and Turkey will increase income tax revenues, as a proportion of GDP, until they reach the revenue levels of the EEC and then level them off, as happened with the EEC and the United States. This seems to be the trend for nations with low and middle developed levels, that is, to follow the path of the more developed nations.

As percentages of total taxation, taxes on income and profits are 16 to 18 percent for Greece, 45 to 50 percent for Turkey, about 35 percent for the EEC, and 45 percent for the United States and Japan. Before 1970, these taxes were somewhat less in all the above countries except for the United States, where they were about the same or a little higher. These figures indicate that Greece is expected to gradually raise the income taxes, as proportions of GDP and total taxation, to the EEC levels. However, Turkey is expected to keep the same proportions of taxes on income and profits, which are close to those of the EEC, and to increase other indirect taxes, so that the proportions of income and profit taxes to total taxation will be reduced to the levels of the developed nations, notably those of the EEC.

In Greece and Turkey, the progressive tax rates reach high levels that are, more or less, comparable to those of the four large EEC countries. But the tax revenue collected is relatively small because of the limited tax base and the widespread tax evasion. Lower tax rates and a simpler tax system may bring about larger amounts of income tax revenue. From that point of view, it seems that as the tax burden rises, the morale for tax payment declines.

Personal income taxes, as proportions of GDP, are very low for Greece, compared to those of the EEC, but for Turkey they are close to those of the EEC. They are around 4 percent of the GDP for Greece, 8 percent for Turkey, and 12 percent for the EEC and the United States. Some twenty years ago, they were about half of what they are today for Greece and Turkey and about two-thirds of the current percentage for the EEC. As proportions of total taxation, though, taxes on personal income are about 14 percent for Greece, 28 percent for the EEC, 38 percent for the United States, and as high as 45 percent for Turkey.[7]

Among the EEC countries, Denmark (24) had the highest personal income taxes, as percentages of GDP, followed by Belgium (16), Britain, West Germany, Ireland, Italy, Luxembourg, and the Netherlands (10 to 12), while France, Greece, Spain, and Portugal had the lowest (4 to 6) percentages. More or less, the same ranking prevails for the taxes on personal income as percentages of total taxation.

The lowest personal income taxes, as percentages of GDP and total taxation, in Greece are due primarily to the limited tax base and not to the tax rates. The progressive tax rates in Greece vary from 12 percent for the first 200,000 drachmas taxable income to 49 percent (down from 63 percent) above 1,000,000 drachmas taxable income since 1987. The first 400,000 drachmas are not taxable. Thus, total personal income of 1,000,000 drachmas would pay 156,000 drachmas total taxes.

To increase tax revenue, without increasing tax rates, and to reduce the bracket creep, Turkey introduced tax changes, especially since 1984. In addition to the value added tax (VAT) of 10 percent (introduced on January 1, 1985), penalty rates for late payment were increased.

In 1986, personal income tax rates and brackets were again adjusted for fiscal drag in Turkey. The first income bracket was enlarged to TL (Turkish liras) 3 million, from TL 1 million, and the bottom rate was set at 25 percent, instead of the previous 30 percent. The highest tax rate was reduced from 60 to 50 percent and now starts at TL 48 million, instead of TL 25 million prevailing previously. However, corporation tax rates have been raised from 40 to 46 percent. At the same time, a system of advance payment of corporation taxes and income taxes for large-income earners was introduced.

Because the legal minimum wages and other fixed incomes had not been adjusted fully to inflation in Turkey, tax rebates on consumer expenditures were raised. Central authorities have shifted more responsibilities for expenditures to special funds, financed primarily by specific levies and receipts. Such receipts come mainly from sales of revenue-sharing certificates not shown in the public budget. More responsibilities were also shifted to local administrations, which benefit from a greater share in taxes collected.

Corporate income taxes are around 1 percent of GDP for Greece, 2 percent for Turkey, close to 3 percent for the EEC, and 2 to 3 percent for the United States. Among the four large EEC nations, Britain has the largest proportion (around 4 percent) of GDP absorbed by corporate income taxes, followed by Italy (3.8 percent), France (2 percent), and Germany (2 percent). As percentages of total taxation, such taxes were 3 to 4 percent for Greece, 10 to 12 percent for Turkey, and 7 percent for the EEC (11 percent for Britain, 9 percent for Italy, 5 percent for France, and 3 to 4 percent for Germany). In Turkey and Greece the corporation tax rate reaches 46 percent.

Social security contributions for Greece are about 12 percent of GDP as they are in the EEC. However, for Turkey, they are only about 1 percent of GDP. As percentages of total taxation, social security contributions are 35 percent for Greece, 29 percent for the EEC and the United States, and as low as 5 percent for Turkey. The low level of industrialization and the small percentage of the labor force in the nonagricultural sectors of the economy are primarily responsible for such small percentages of social security contributions in Turkey.

High income taxes destroy personal incentives to work, reduce productivity, and may have regressive effects. Although tax revenues in Greece and Turkey are not as high as in Western developed countries, further reductions in tax rates to stimulate production in these countries may pay for themselves by creating a surge in investment and new work effort, thereby increasing tax revenue and reducing budgetary deficits. Therefore, tax increases may be directed to the portion of income that is actually spent. Thus, a cut in personal income tax and/ or a reduction in social security payroll tax may be matched with a sale or value added tax, which discourages consumption and encourages savings and investment, especially in Greece and Turkey, where the propensity to consume seems to be high.

In Greece and Turkey, with progressive taxation, additional tax revenues are provided by inflation. This takes place through increases in income and spending, pari passu with inflation, and the automatic increases in rates under the progressive tax system. These additional revenues finance additional government expenditures that stimulate inflation (as long as they are not directed toward productive investment), and the public sector keeps on expanding. For the government, then, inflation seems to be a wonderful tax. This is a practicable way of transferring command over resources from consumers to the public sector, particularly in countries like Turkey, where the fiscal system is relatively inefficient and the number of taxpayers is not large.

INDIRECT TAXES

The largest part of government revenue in Greece and Turkey comes from indirect taxes. They account for about 70 percent of the central government revenue in Greece and 55 percent in Turkey. Indirect or in rem taxes include mainly turnover or sales taxes, excises, stamp duties, tariffs, and value added

Figure 6.1
Indirect Taxes as Percentage of National Income: Greece, Turkey, and the EEC,
1958–1985

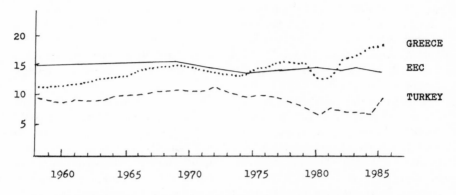

Source: OECD, *National Accounts,* various issues; and United Nations, *Yearbook of National*
            Accounts Statistics, various issues.

taxes. They are levied independently of the owner's ability to pay and are likely to be shiftable forward to consumers.

As percentages of national income, indirect taxes in Greece are not much different from those of the EEC and are higher than those of Turkey. They are mostly declining and around 8 percent of national income for Turkey and gradually increasing to about 19 percent for Greece. For the EEC they are constant and about 15 percent of national income (fig. 6.1). Although recent reforms tend to reduce the fiscal role of indirect taxes in favor of direct taxes, they still constitute a substantial portion of the budget revenue. This is because collection of indirect taxes is easier and manipulation by lower units is more difficult than in the collection of direct taxes. Further tax reforms, with a global and particularly EEC view, are needed to effect productivity, new technology, and competitiveness.[8] An adjustment of the indirect taxes should encourage capital formation and exports and discourage wasteful consumption.

Stamp duties (about 28 percent of total indirect taxes) were the largest portion of indirect taxes in Greece up to 1987, followed by turnover taxes (20 percent), petroleum products taxes (14 percent), tobacco taxes (9 percent), taxes on transport (6 percent), and taxes on real estate transfer (4 percent). Stamp duties were levied at 2.4 percent on invoices and 1.3 percent in other cases. Turnover taxes on domestic or imported manufactured goods were levied at 8 percent or less. Import ad valorem duties, primarily on luxuries, varied from 10 to 50 percent. Those indirect taxes or portions of them have been replaced by the value added tax in Greece introduced in 1987. There are no general sales taxes in Greece and Turkey such as one may find in many other countries, especially the developed ones. However, there are high turnover or value added taxes, tariffs,

Table 6.3
Elasticities of Indirect Taxes with Respect to Private Consumption (PRC),
Imports (IMP), and Gross Domestic Product (GDP) (current prices)

	PRC	IMP	GDP
Greece			
1950–60	1.44	1.56	1.35
1960–70	1.74	1.22	1.41
1970–80	1.10	0.74	1.41
1980–85	1.40	1.17	1.41
Turkey			
1950–60	0.85	1.31	0.85
1960–70	0.90	0.90	0.90
1970–80	1.04	0.58	1.05
1980–85	1.04	0.62	1.03

Source: OECD, *National Accounts;* and United Nations, *Yearbook of National Accounts,* both
various issues.

and other forms of indirect taxes that can be considered expenditure or consumption taxes.

Indirect taxes, as percentages of total taxes, are higher in Greece and Turkey
than in the EEC. From that point of view, an increase in direct taxes in Turkey
and more so in Greece, as well as structural changes in both direct and indirect
taxes, are expected to occur in the near future. One can expect that the same
situation will be encountered with other EEC members, notably Spain and Portugal. As mentioned earlier, a major tax reform introduced recently in Greece
and Turkey is the value added tax, in place of turnover and other complicated
indirect taxes.

High tariffs on imported goods, especially in Turkey, make their prices higher
compared with other countries. Elimination or reduction of such tariffs and excise
taxes, according to the directives of the EEC, would exert pressure on domestic
industries producing the same goods or close substitutes.[9] However, such a
competitive process would reduce inefficiency, despite the expected detrimental
effects on employment conditions.

As Table 6.3 shows, the elasticities of indirect taxes, with respect to private
consumption (PRC) and gross domestic product (GDP), were mostly higher than
one in both Greece and Turkey for all three decades considered. However, the

elasticities of indirect taxes with respect to imports (IMP) were less than one (except for 1950–60) and declining for Turkey and more than one for Greece (except for 1970–80). In the 1980s, the percentage changes in indirect taxes were higher than those in private consumption, imports, and GDP for Greece.[10] For Turkey, such changes in indirect taxes were almost equiproportional to changes in private consumption and GDP and declining with respect to imports, especially in the 1980s. Probably, after the recent introduction of VAT, indirect taxes will increase and these elasticities will be higher.

The Value Added Tax (VAT)

The value added tax is an expenditure tax collected upon the value of additional production. It discourages consumption spending in favor of savings and investments, which, in turn, are associated with high rates of economic growth. The use of VAT in both countries, and particularly in Greece, would gradually simplify the tax system, decrease tax evasion, and stimulate productivity. The VAT, as an indirect proportional tax on the value of all goods and services included in a firm's invoices reduced by the amount of previous VAT liability, is less painful and more easily collectible with low administrative costs.[11] Unlike turnover taxes, it discourages vertical concentration of enterprises, encourages competition, and assists policymakers in adjusting demand to the conditions of supply.

It is suggested that in countries such as Greece and Turkey with high rates of income taxes it would be proper to shift some burden away from taxes on income and profits toward a value added tax. Nevertheless, in order to soften the impact of the VAT on low-income people, a system of gradually decreasing income tax credits can be introduced that would make this tax progressive and fair.[12]

The membership of Greece and the eventual accession of Turkey to the EEC will mean a further decline in indirect taxes collected from imports, but the VAT is expected to increase tax revenue and help make up for the reduction of tariffs. But as long as the elasticities of total government expenditures in relation to GDP keep on growing, as they did during the postwar years, other forms of taxation, mainly income taxes, will also be used to reduce budget deficits.

The VAT can be defined as a tax upon the difference between the total value of output minus the value of purchased material inputs and is collectible at each stage of production. It taxes all factors of production, including labor, and encourages the transfer of capital from declining industries to the successful sectors and enterprises. Moreover, without distorting the efficient allocation of resources, it helps policymakers determine whether demand for consumer goods is growing in an inflationary way. However, additional value added taxes themselves would, more likely, be passed on to consumers through rising prices. From that point of view, exceptions may be needed in food and housing in order to soften the impact of VAT on poor families.

To spur production incentives and expand supply, there is a need in both countries for a reduction in regulations, the introduction of tax reforms, and the implementation of policies intended to reduce consumption and stimulate investment. With the enactment of such policies, total demand would not be diminished but the mix would be changed toward a greater replacement of consumption by investment. By taxing wasteful spending and even replacing personal income taxes with sales or VAT taxes, saving and investment would be encouraged and work incentives toward higher producivity would be stimulated. The VAT may also help reduce bureaucracy by simplifying the tax system. Although it may increase tax revenues, to the extent that it does not replace turnover and other taxes, it will, in the long run, replace many other tax regulations that are so complicated and confusing in Greece and Turkey. With the tax system being adjusted to EEC standards, taxes upon imports and domestic commodities will become the same. Moreover, vertical monopolization, which was encouraged by the previous turnover taxes, and the movement of capital and companies into countries with low taxes will be avoided with the VAT.

A modification and simplification of the tax system would also help small and medium-sized enterprises, since the disadvantages of the present turnover taxes, which favor vertical integration, would be eliminated. Instead, the way would be clearer for them to adjust their size in such a way that they can enjoy the best results from economies of scale and improved productivity. At the same time, their independence would be preserved. As a result, small, nonvertically concentrated enterprises, which are in the majority in Greece and Turkey, would find themselves in a relatively more favorable competitive position. They are the ones upon which the great pressure of EEC competition will fall and they need all the support they can get.

From the point of view of tax revenue, it would seem difficult for those two countries to replace completely the turnover and other indirect taxes with a VAT. As mentioned earlier, the VAT is collected at each stage of production and distribution, and is more successful in countries having a high level of industrialization with many intermediate stages of production. In Greece and Turkey, however, the proportion of industrial production to total production is relatively low and the in-between manufacturing stages are limited. For example, these nations would collect taxes at the first stage of metal production needed for cars or aluminum products, electrical equipment, and the like, but all the other stages up to the final product would take place in other countries that manufacture these products. Therefore, Greece and Turkey would not benefit much from tax revenues from the VAT levied at each intermediate stage. Moreover, they cannot collect tariffs on imports from the EEC, which account for about half of their total imports. Only at the final stage of sales, whether it be at the wholesaler or retailer level, would a VAT be collected. Although parts or the total amount of revenues from tariffs are or may be substituted by the VAT or other forms of taxes, there are or may be limitations to this type of tax substitution or "circumvention" of EEC regulations.

France or other industrial nations, for example, can afford to have low direct (personal income) taxes because of large revenue from indirect (VAT) taxes, but Greece and Turkey, with a large tertiary or services sector and limited tax-levying stages of manufacturing, may not be able to collect the needed revenue from the VAT. Under such conditions, they would be forced to increase income taxes or decrease public expenditures, both of which would be painful. A more desirable and efficient way out of this dilemma seems to lie with the rapid industrialization of these countries, with the main emphasis on import substitution and/or export promotion.

In Greece, the value added tax, which has been introduced since January 1, 1987, exempts from taxation exports and capital goods, so that investment and domestic production can be stimulated. Moreover, market monopolization is discouraged in favor of competition, while tax evasion is reduced. Most of the products and services are liable to pay a VAT at a rate of 16 percent, while other basic goods are to pay a VAT of 6 percent. For luxurious goods there are higher rates (33 percent), but food products are exempted. The sixth directive of the EEC provides that enterprises with sales of less than 10,000 European Currency Units (ECUs) are not liable to pay VAT. However, there are special treatments for special small enterprises, such as those with sales of less than 6 million drachmas and those involved in agriculture, travel, tobacco, and petroleum products.

The VAT is neutral, while the other taxes that have been replaced were favoring imports. Some turnover taxes, stamp duties, and other indirect taxes, though, have not been replaced by the VAT in Greece and Turkey and are expected to be abolished gradually in the coming years. On the other hand, intensive training and surveillance are required for the taxpayers to be familiar with the new taxes and their responsibilities.

In Turkey, the Value Added Tax (VAT) Law was published in November 1984, and, from January 1, 1985, a 10 percent VAT was levied on industrial, commercial, and agricultural goods and services, on professional activities, and on imports. A supplemental VAT was imposed on tobacco and tobacco products, and on alcoholic and nonalcoholic drinks. The VAT replaced production taxes and taxes on sales, sugar, transportation, advertising, and postal services. It was fixed at 6 percent for basic foodstuffs, effective from April 1, 1985, but later it was reduced to 3 percent and it became effeective in July 1985, while its collection was arranged to be made monthly instead of quarterly.

Corporation income taxes (46 percent) in Turkey are to be estimated and paid in advance, the amount being equal to 50 percent of monthly VAT liabilities. Simplified procedures for estimating tax liabilities were introduced during a transitional period for small businesses, farmers, and the self-employed. From that point of view, Turkey moved early to adjust its tax system to that of the EEC, while Greece was late in introducing the VAT, despite the pressures and the obligations from the EEC agreement for its implementation in 1984.

NOTES

1. Organization for Economic Cooperation and Development (OECD), *Economic Surveys 1985/1986: Turkey* (Paris: September, 1986), 26; and Richard F. Nyrop, ed., *Turkey: A Country Study* (Washington, D.C.: American University, Foreign Area Studies, 1980), 137–39.

2. Defense spending is about 15 percent of total central government expenditure for both countries. World Bank, *World Development Report, 1986* (New York: Oxford University Press, 1986), 222–23.

3. OECD, *Economic Surveys: Turkey*; and OECD, *National Accounts;* various issues. In developed countries, total tax revenue varies from 30 percent of national income for Japan and the United States, to 45 percent of GDP for the EEC, and 60 percent of National Material Product (NMP) for the Soviet Union.

4. For similar conclusions regarding other countries, see Richard Musgrave and Peggy Musgrave, *Public Finance in Theory and Practice,* 3d ed. (New York: McGraw-Hill, 1980), 322–33.

5. Some form of differential land tax is favored by Alan Prest, *The Taxation of Urban Land* (Manchester, England: Manchester University Press, 1981).

6. For comments on tax harmonization and problems of substitution, see the valuable articles in Carl Shoup, ed., *Fiscal Harmonization in Common Markets* (New York: Columbia University Press, 1967); also Nicholas Gianaris, "Fiscal Policy: Greece and the EEC," *Spoudai* 15 (January-March 1980): 1–11.

7. OECD, *Revenue Statistics of the OECD Member Countries* (Paris), various issues.

8. Nicholas Gianaris, "Indirect Taxes: A Comparative Study of Greece and the EEC," *European Economic Review* 15 (1981): 111–170. For tax reform arguments see Alan Prest, "The Structure and Reforms of Direct Taxation," *Economic Journal,* 89, (June 1979): 243–60; also, G. Gilbert and M. Mouillart, "E Dynamiki Ton Forologikon Domon Stis Hores tou OOSA" (The Dynamics of the Tax Structure in the Countries of the OECD), *Oikonomia kai Koinonia* (April 1981): 83–93.

9. For customs duties in different categories of imported goods in Greece, see Greek Government, *Statistiki Epetiris Dimosion Oikonomikon* (Statistical Yearbook of Public Finance), various issues.

10. The regression coefficient of indirect taxes on private consumption for Greece (0.22) was almost the same as that of the EEC for the period of 1960–1984 as was the coefficient of indirect txes on inflation (0.15). However, the regression of indirect taxes on imports gave a smaller coefficient for the EEC (0.45) than that of Greece (0.57). The difference may be justified because of the higher tariffs in Greece than in the EEC.

11. In accordance with the articles 99 and 100 of the Rome Agreement, establishing the EEC in 1957, and Greece's accession agreement of 1980, Greece introduced the VAT in 1987. Turkey introduced the VAT in 1985.

12. For the renewed widespread interest in consumption taxes, see articles in Joseph Pechman, ed., *What Should Be Taxed: Income or Expenditure?* (Washington, D.C.: Brookings Institution, 1980); also, David G. Davies, *United States Taxes and Tax Policy* (Cambridge, Mass.: Cambridge University Press, 1986), chap. 4.

7

Monetary Policy and Inflation

CHANGES IN MONEY SUPPLY

In both Greece and Turkey, there is a significant increase in money supply, which is related to the growing public sector and rising prices. When the velocity of money (the ratio of CDP over money supply) remains relatively constant or grows, the increase in money supply over and above the real economic growth leads to an increase in prices. In some cases, though, the increase in money supply is so dramatic that it not only overcomes a possible declining velocity and the growth in real production but it also generates a significant rate of inflation.

An important reason for increasing the money supply is to finance budgetary deficits. When tax revenues are not sufficient to cover governmental expenditures, the governments of these countries frequently create money, mostly to purchase goods and services, to pay their employees and to pay off previous debts.

Fiscal needs, therefore, affect monetary policies and force both governments to cover budget deficits by printing new money, regardless of the prevailing economic and market conditions. In Greece and to a lesser extent in Turkey, politicians tend to press for the creation of money to finance local projects, particularly when election time approaches. However, extra money creation, which leads to a limited positive inflation rate, may be fiscally desirable to discourage hoarding and to encourage productive investment.

By exercising monetary monopoly and printing additional money, the governments of these two nations can obtain real revenue. Depending on the transactions demand for money, individuals will give up real goods and services to obtain additional money in order to facilitate transactions, even if the price level is somewhat higher than previously. Moreover, by paying off previous debts with monetary units that have somewhat less value per unit than before, these governments gain real revenues, as they do through progressive taxation.

Given that government domestic borrowing from the general public is not extensively used in both countries, an increase in money supply is the main source of financing public sector deficits. As a result, money supply for Greece increased from 54 billion Greek drachmas (GDs) in 1970 to 309 billion in 1980 and 744 billion in 1985 (more than double in five years). For Turkey, money supply increased from 36 billion Turkish liras (TLs) in 1970 to 720 billion in 1980 and 3,256 billion TLs in 1985, that is about five times as much in five years.[1] Annual inflation remains around 15 to 20 percent for Greece, while ranging from 30 to 50 percent for Turkey.

Figures 7.1 and 7.2 show money supply and velocity of money for Greece and Turkey, respectively. Since income velocity of money remains constant, at around 5 for Greece, increases in money supply are primarily responsible for inflation. For Turkey, however, both money supply and velocity of money increased dramatically, especially after 1978, and raised inflation to high rates (fig. 7.2).

There seems to be a close relationship between the increase in budget deficits, the change in money supply, and the rate of inflation. In other words, the governments of Greece and Turkey print additional drachmas and liras to finance rising public sector deficits and this leads to an increase in inflation. Therefore, public sector deficits, including those of public enterprises, should be considered responsible for inflation.

Recent economic policies in Turkey by Prime Minister Turgut Ozal (Ozal-nomics), which resembled Reaganomics, were enacted to encourage private initiative and an open free market. Import and export rules were liberalized and the lira was floated.[2] In addition to austerity measures introduced, some 300 state-owned monopolies inherited from the Ottomans were and still are gradually being sold to the private sector; price controls on food and other items were lifted and a 10 percent value added tax was imposed. These supply-side policies and especially the elimination of price controls led to high inflation and an increase in government spending. Taxes were cut and the government had to borrow by issuing bonds with interest rates of 49 percent or higher. The buying power of the average worker fell, unemployment rose to 20 percent, and the rich got richer while the poor got poorer.[3]

Turkey and Greece try to mitigate inflation by stabilizing demand, mainly through moderation in the growth of the public sector. In addition, other measures, such as restrictive credit ceilings and income guidelines, are used for that purpose. However, the relatively weak outlook for external trade, cost pressures, and inflationary expectations present problems for anti-inflationary and economic growth policies in these countries.

In both countries, financial markets are imperfect and transmission of savings to productive investment is largely ineffective. Such market deficiencies and the endemic political and financial instability undermine the confidence of savers and investors and lead many households to save and invest in unproductive assets. From that point of view, the importance of the public sector in mobilizing saving and channeling it into productive investment is obvious. By providing

Figure 7.1
Money Supply (*M*) and Velocity of Money (*V* = GDP/*M*) for Greece (in billions of drachmas)

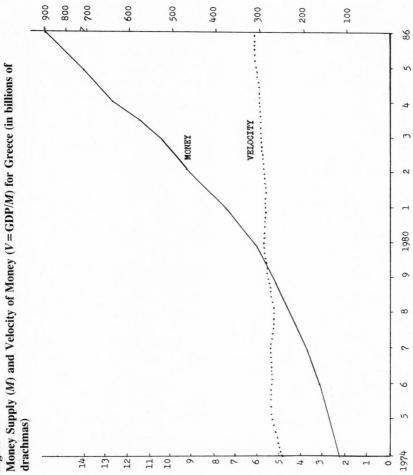

Source: Bank of Greece; and IMF, *International Financial Statistics*, various issues.

Figure 7.2
Money Supply (*M*) and Velocity of Money (*V* = GDP/*M*) for Turkey (in billions of liras)

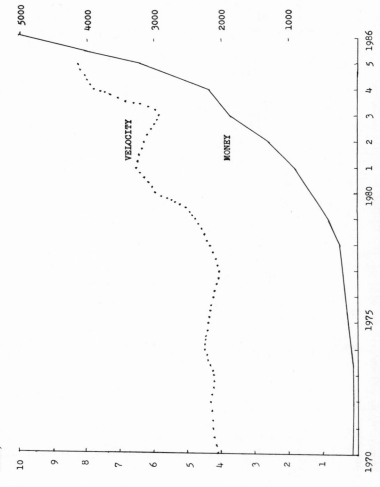

Source: IMF, *International Financial Statistics*, various issues.

saving incentives, such as tax exemption on income from interest, credit against taxes as a proportion of investment, and generous depreciation allowances, governmental policies can be instrumental in mobilizing saving and allocating funds to productive sectors and regions.

However, in their efforts to overcome inflexibilities in the financial markets, the Greek and the Turkish governments may use discretionary policies that may lead to inefficient resource allocation. Such policies may include intervention of the public sector in the financial markets as a borrower or lender and the establishment of unusually low interest rates in a monopolistic fashion.[4] In these cases, government interventions may impose market imperfections and distort efficient resource allocation. Individuals and corporations will rather try to borrow money with low interest rates than use their savings. On the other hand, if the central banks or the governments of these countries bail out troubled commercial banks or other enterprises, it could cause a new surge of inflation.

Restructuring the banking system to encourage competition and to determine exchange rates objectively should be the monetary policy of both nations. However, more centralization and government controls to serve the party or the individuals in power are used instead of liberalizing the banking system. Thus, as a result of a major restructuring of the Turkish industrial banks, Andalou, a state-owned bank, is expected to buy three other banks, including Etibank, Sumerbank, and Denizcilik Bankasi. These three banks specialize in mining, textiles, and shipping, respectively. About half of the new capital needed by this larger banking institution is expected to be raised on the Istanbul Stock Exchange.

The main commercial banks of Greece, the National Bank of Greece, the Commercial Bank of Greece, and the Ioniki Bank, were nationalized in the 1970s. However, under the control of the government, they extended loans to a number of inefficient "problematic" firms, mainly due to political pressures. Now they face problems of defaults of some of their client enterprises with heavy debts. Ioniki itself is in trouble because its manager was involved in scandals, giving large gifts to his favorite soccer team and being biased to the party in power.

For more investment in productive businesses, favorable loan terms and a tax structure favoring small firms and those that create new employment should be considered by the monetary or fiscal authorities of Greece and Turkey. Perhaps the widespread practice of borrowing funds from the private sector, by investment banks or other public enterprises in these countries, should continue for investment in long-term infrastructural projects where private firms are hesitant to invest. If borrowing, though, takes place to finance consumption, then the government competes with productive enterprises for a finite supply of lendable money, and the rate of investment will decrease.

Negative Interest Rates

In Greece and Turkey, the widespread practice of keeping interest rates artificially low in order to stimulate investment in particular sectors tends to dis-

Table 7.1
Inflation, Nominal Interest Rates, and Real Interest Rates in Greece

Year	Inflation	Deposit Interest Rates Nominal	Real
1975	13.4	9.6	-3.8
1976	13.3	8.9	-4.4
1977	12.1	8.5	-3.6
1978	12.6	10.0	-2.6
1979	19.0	11.9	-7.1
1980	24.9	14.5	-10.4
1981	24.5	14.5	-10.0
1982	21.0	14.5	-6.5
1983	20.2	14.5	-5.7
1984	18.4	15.4	-3.0
1985	19.3	15.5	-3.8

Note: For inflation, consumer price index, and nominal interest rates, the widely known postal savings interest rates were used.

Source: IMF, *International Financial Statistics* (IFS), various issues.

courage the mobilization of saving and to encourage the inefficient use of resources. Moreover, this practice of capital subsidization is associated with greater centralization in decision making concerning the rationing of capital. However, a well-conceived, albeit limited, structure of government regulations on credit markets may be required to discourage the development of monopolistic practices that may be utilized by major banks with strong ties to industries. This has been a familiar phenomenon in Greece and Turkey in which central banks and monetary policies are under the direct control of the government and the political party in power.

The central banks can steer GNP by raising or lowering interest rates. Real rates—nominal rates minus inflation rates—have been negative in Greece and positive in Turkey in recent years (tables 7.1 and 7.2). Their turnabout requires an increase in nominal interest rates in Greece, as happened in Turkey, or, better, a decrease in the rates of inflation, which necessitates a reduction in spending and investment. This, in turn, is expected to lead to a severe recession and high

Table 7.2
Inflation, Nominal Interest Rates, and Real Interest Rates in Turkey

Years	Inflation	Interest Rates Nominal	Interest Rates Real
1975	19.2	9.0	-10.2
1976	17.3	9.0	- 8.3
1977	27.1	9.0	-18.1
1978	45.4	10.0	-35.4
1979	58.7	7.3	-51.4
1980	110.2	10.0	-100.2
1981	36.6	28.5	- 8.1
1982	30.8	45.0	14.2
1983	32.9	45.3	12.4
1984	48.4	51.4	3.0
1985	45.0	53.0	8.0

Note: For inflation, consumer price index, nominal interest rates, and discount rates (end of period).
Source: IMF, *International Financial Statistics* (IFS), various issues.

unemployment for some time. From that point of view, a gradual reduction in inflation and an orderly adjustment of the nominal interest rates would be less painful in stabilizing the economy first and achieving higher economic growth with less unemployment and higher real income later.

FINANCING BUDGET DEFICITS

Greece and Turkey face major budgetary deficits that are the main sources of inflation, monetary instability, and foreign trade deficits. For Greece, central government deficits increased from 1.7 billion Greek drachmas (GDs) in 1960 to 5.2 billion in 1970, 53.4 billion in 1980, and as high as 506.6 billion GDs in 1985. As percentages of GNP, they increased from 1.6 percent in 1960 to

1.7 percent in 1970, 3 percent in 1980, and 11.3 percent in 1985. For Turkey, central government deficits increased from 3.6 billion Turkish liras (TLs) in 1970 to 160.8 billion in 1980 and 2,049.7 billion TLs in 1985. As percentages of GNP, they increased from 2.4 percent in 1970 to 3.6 percent in 1980 and 7.4 percent in 1985.[5]

Deficit financing through borrowing may lead to inflation because it absorbs primarily private saving, which is used mainly for government consumption. This is the way for government to shove other borrowers aside in order to finance the deficit. Inflation, in turn, poisons entrepreneurial initiatives and directs investment to short-term speculative ventures or to real estate business, which is usual in Greece and Turkey.

A good part of inflation may be due to monetizing central government deficits, which has become a familiar practice in both nations. Increases in money supply and the rates of inflation were greater in Turkey compared to those of Greece, particularly in recent years. Therefore, it is expected that inflation will be a more significant variable in economic policy for Turkey than for Greece.

To finance the huge public sector deficits, Greece and Turkey are using all three sources available, that is inflation, domestic borrowing, and foreign borrowing. The use of the first two sources of financing concerns these countries and their citizens and as such it is an internal problem.[6] The use of foreign borrowing, though, presents serious problems, because it leads these countries to a continuous economic hemorrhage and possibly to bankruptcy and dependence on foreign banks.

Although the rate of economic growth was high during the postwar years, in the 1980s it was low, mainly because of low rates of investment. Budgetary deficits absorbed large amounts of available saving, crowding out private investment and bidding interest rates to high levels. Moreover, substantial amounts of investment were channeled into housing and not much to industrial development and new technology, which are associated with high rates of long-term economic growth. In addition to housing investment, mainly in the large cities, emphasis was placed on small-scale trading and not much on industrialization for higher growth.

There were serious efforts in both nations for a better distribution of income and decentralization, mainly through public expenditures. However, without simultaneous increases in productivity, nominal wage raises were absorbed by an equal or higher increase in prices. Real income, therefore, remained the same, or rather declined in recent years, due to high rates of inflation.

The large deficits of the central government and the public enterprises create pressures for higher inflation and huge domestic and foreign debts. Public sector deficits and domestic debts can be covered by issuing new money. In this case and when the increase in money supply is larger than the increase in real economic growth, the difference would lead to higher prices or inflation. This is so because in Greece and Turkey the income velocity of money is constant or growing. The increase in money supply, therefore, is inflationary, as more monetary units are chasing the same products.

And all these problems because of the enormous spending by the public sector for nonproductive expenses, to finance, for example, festivities, to pay for expensive traveling of public officials, to employ extra and unnecessary personnel at home and abroad, to buy military hardware, to provide free education and health services, and to create new expensive government services that are expected to cost more than the benefits that are offered.

This is a policy of short-run enjoyments but long-run pains for these economies. Responsible public officials give the impression that the public purse belongs to them and that they have the right to spend for their political advantages, regardless of the resulting inflation and the responsibilities of present and future generations to pay the large debts created. From that point of view, some restrictions on public sector expenditures and debts should be imposed in both countries by a higher than simple parliamentary majority or a constitutional amendment.

When the government borrows money from its own banks and from individuals to finance its deficits, the annual interest and the amortization paid to the domestic debt-holders is money that remains within the country. If borrowing takes place through individuals or the general public, the government absorbs purchasing power from them, that is money which could be used for consumption or investment. If borrowing is made through the banks, which is a usual way of public sector financing in both countries, the governments take away primarily saving deposits of the people. This is an easy way of borrowing by the public sector of Greece and Turkey because all the major banks belong to or are under the control of the government.

To a large extent, borrowing from the banks accommodates public sector financing of deficits but absorbs funds that would be used primarily for capital investment. In addition to crowding out private investment, it drives up interest rates and increases the cost of new plants and equipment. From that point of view, productive enterprises and innovative entrepreneurs are deprived of one of the main sources of capital financing. Given that governmental deficit spending is largely channeled into consumption, it is no wonder productive investment is low and will continue to be low. Moreover, because the financial market in general and the bond market in particular are limited, investment financing becomes more difficult and more problematic for Greece and Turkey.

Budget Financing through Internal Debt

Internal or domestic borrowing takes place customarily through sales of government securities to individuals or the general public. However, in Greece and Turkey the governments borrow money mainly from the central banks and the commercial banks, which belong, directly or indirectly, to the government. Therefore, the government does not compete in the open market to acquire funds to finance its deficits, as is the case with the United States, for example. Instead, it "orders" its banks to extend loans to itself and the public sector in general. This policy brings about the misallocation of capital and deprives the economy of productive private investment.

Budget deficits, which are financed through domestic borrowing, increase the internal debt of the government and its interest payment. However, for every borrower there is a lender; for every debtor, a creditor. In government borrowing, the individuals and the institutions are the creditors. The government becomes poorer for owing more, but the lenders, the public, become richer for owning more. In addition to capital claims against the government, they receive annual interest as well. As people feel richer, they are inclined to spend more, thereby stimulating the economy. If there is unemployment, new jobs are created. If the economy is at the proverbial full employment, more spending leads to demand-pull inflation.

From time to time, the Greek and the Turkish governments issue bonds that are sold to individuals and institutions. Thus, the floating of a domestic bond loan in Greece for 30 billion drachmas (about $215 million) in November 1986 is a proper policy, as long as it is to finance investment. The loan was linked to the value of the European Currency Unit (ECU) and was similar to those made in Italy and elsewhere. The bonds carry a tax-free interest rate of 8 percent, fixed throughout their three-year duration.

Borrowing by the Greek government from the domestic banks was about $12 billion or 1,753 billion drachmas in 1985 (some 788 billion from the Bank of Greece and the rest, 1,013 billion, from the commercial banks), compared to 418 billion drachmas in 1980 and 35 billion drachmas in 1970. The Turkish government borrowing from domestic banks was $12 billion or 5,355 billion liras in 1984 (4,441 billion from the central bank and 914 billion from deposit money banks). Also, claims of these banks on government enterprises amounted to $480 million or 215 billion Turkish liras in 1984. Although domestic debt leads to higher taxes or more inflationary money to finance interest and amortization, it seems to be less painful than foreign debt. This is so because servicing the external debt requires payments in foreign currencies and it drains the economy with the outflow of funds that could be used domestically.

EFFECTS OF INFLATION

Controlled wages and prices by the governments of Greece and Turkey eliminate the self-corrective tendencies of the market economy and make it possible for misallocations to continue. Government spending to keep demand high, according to the prescription of the Keynesian theory, holds unemployment at lower levels than otherwise, but it stimulates inflation and turns the instability in an upward direction. The resistance of the employers to union claims diminishes and managers concede easily to labor claims because they raise prices even more than wages, perpetuating the wage-price spiral.

With no change in money wages, labor unions will respond to price increases with strikes and other forceful means as they see their real wages being reduced. As long as the unorganized masses of consumers are not expected to react, employers easily agree to increase wages, given that they can increase prices immediately. Depending on their power, labor unions may demand wages higher than the increase in prices, forcing further increase in prices and initiating inflationary spirals. This is cost-push inflation, which perpetuates itself through the interaction of both employers and workers. Such repeated processes, common in Greece and Turkey, undermine the confidence of the public in the economy, inflict inequities, and inhibit long-term growth.

Increase in money wages and profits may be beneficial to growth, especially in the case of money illusion on the part of wage earners and entrepreneurs. Money illusion of both workers and profit makers supports the argument of using inflation as an effective means of financing growth (Pigou effect). Workers will spend more if they think that they are getting more when their money wages rise, even if their purchasing power does not increase. Also, entrepreneurs, subject to money illusion, will tend to invest more if they think that their businesses are improving when money profits rise, even if the purchasing power of those profits remains the same. It is questionable, however, if educated workers and entrepreneurs in the present societies of Turkey and more so of Greece are subject to money illusions to any extent. The widespread publicity of price indices in our day may reduce or even eliminate such illusions in any social group.

In both countries, there are powerful structural factors that create inflation. Conventional monetary and fiscal measures are unable to restrain such structural inflation. The failure of some sectors to supply what the demand requires is causing increase in prices. Inflation, therefore, can be corrected by structural changes in production, imports, and income distribution, and not by changes in money income and demand. Even though inflation may be initiated by demand-pull or cost-push forces, other factors, which are chronically structured into each economy, may also cause increase in prices. The deterioration of trade in primary and other products, for example, results in reduction of the rates of exports and increase in the rates of imports. Such a trade gap usually generates cost-push inflation.

More specifically, the main structural factors affecting price increases can be classified as follows:

1. Due to pattern of land ownership and cultivation in Greece and Turkey the response to economic incentive is weak and agricultural productivity is low. As a result, urbanization and industrialization tend to lead to rising food prices.

2. The demand for imports increases more than for exports, terms of trade are not improving in both countries, and the prices of imports tend to increase more relative to the prices of exports.

3. The pattern of the income distribution is such that the demand for luxurious goods, primarily for demonstration effect purposes, increases the demand for foreign exchange

and creates large deficits in the balance of payments, while the rates of savings and investment do not increase but either remain constant or decline.

In both nations, the inefficient administrative apparatus and the structure of the economy are such that production does not respond easily to price changes. Also, sociopolitical conditions do not allow for the implementation of a hard-work ethic, rapid factor mobility, and changes in income distribution, especially in Turkey. The lack of equipment and certain raw materials may be additional reasons for structural rigidities that inhibit rapid growth and development. In such cases, capital imports are needed to break the bottlenecks. To pay for such imports, additional exports of goods and services or more external loans are required.

Measures that then must be taken to curb inflation in the long run could include gradual stabilization programs and anti-inflationary reforms dealing with monopolistic conditions, taxation, manpower utilization, urbanization, reduction in luxurious spending and public sector expenditures, and proper coordination of price changes and balance of payments arrangements.

When inflation continues, people realize that it is foolish to hold money and other liquid assets, like saving deposits and government securities. Buying stable foreign currencies, or real estate and other nonliquid assets, which are expected to rise in price, secures the purchasing power of their money.[7] In Greece and to a lesser extent in Turkey, people with money available prefer to buy lots, houses, and apartments in the large cities even though rents may be low and sanitary and other facilities unsatisfactory. This trend intensifies price increases and creates an inflationary psychology that is difficult to stop. A better alternative is the buying of stocks, issued by private or semi-public firms. Behind the stocks stand the real assets of each firm which are likely to rise in price as inflation goes on. Given that both countries have stock markets, although not so efficient, the available money can be channeled into private investment, creating additional employment and reducing the rate of inflation through the supply of additional commodities and services.

An unpleasant result of inflation is the outflow of private capital from Turkey and primarily from Greece to countries where there is monetary stability. Wealthy individuals transfer their capital to Switzerland, Britain, the United States, and other stable countries, while foreigners hesitate to invest in the inflation-plagued economies of Turkey and Greece because of the risk of losses from deterioration in exchange rates and sociopolitical instability. Also, businessmen and consumers frequently resort to accumulation and hoarding of goods, because they expect higher prices for these goods in the immediate future and higher production cost. All these elements intensify inflation, increase instability and uncertainty, and stimulate the operation of black markets. On the other hand, if there is not adjustment of exchange rates, inflation encourages imports and discourages exports, as foreign commodities and services become cheaper, while the domestic ones grow more expensive. The outcome is a worsening position of the balance of payments and accumulation of foreign debts.

There is an important question about deficit financing in these countries in which monetary policy is exercised by the central government and in which serious price inflation exists. This is so because there is a basic connection between deficit financing and inflation. It seems that in such cases monetary expansion is primarily a consequence of printing money to cover the difference between governmental expenditures and tax revenue. This is particularly so for Greece and Turkey where domestic borrowing from the public at large, to finance budget deficits, is not as extensive as it is in other countries, notably the United States. Levying taxes, on the other hand, is an unpopular practice, in addition to the distorting effects upon incentives that taxes always have. Therefore, what remains is to have the central bank make up the excess difference in expenditures over tax receipts by printing money. This is an easy practice in these countries where the central banks are under the direct control of the government and do not enjoy much independence on matters of managing money and formulating monetary policy.

INCOME POLICY TO REDUCE INFLATION

To reduce the impact of inflation on wages, the governments of Greece and Turkey introduce, from time to time, adjustment measures. Such measures have been taken by Greece, through the Automatic Wage Indexation (ATA), in 1982 and later. The wage indexation provides for increases in wages that are at least equiproportional to the increases in inflation, so that the real purchasing power of employees and workers can be maintained. It is fair for the wage earners, though, to get annual increments in their remuneration equal to the average increase in productivity plus the increase in inflation.

However, as it has been proven in many cases, wage indexation perpetuates inflation. Increases in wages now would be included in the cost of production of the near future and eventually would push prices up. Assuming a competitive market with not much possibility for profit reduction, a policy of gradual reduction of the rates of wage raises to percentages less than the rate of inflation of the previous equivalent period could reduce cost-push inflation, without discouraging work incentives.

To associate wage indexation with a better distribution of income, lower percentages in wage raises may be introduced for people with high income, and higher raises for people with low income—a measure that Greece used recently. Although this measure seems to be fair, its repetitive regressiveness may substantially reduce wage differentials to a point of weakening work incentives and improvement in specialization and productivity.

After World War II, Greece and Turkey introduced price controls to correct black marketeering. However, the controls grew in complexity and turned against the consumers they were meant to benefit. Negotiations between the ministries of commerce and the producers for reasonable profits through related mark-ups on costs frequently act as incentives to producers and sellers to increase costs. Also, they tend to increase imports of intermediate products so that price detection can be avoided.

There seems to be some lack of understanding of the serious problems of these economies by the policymakers who care mostly for holding power regardless of what happens to the economy. It might be said, allegorically, that it looks like an individual whose house is burning and he says that "it does not matter, I have the key." For the power-holders, what matters is their political benefit, regardless if the economy of their country deteriorates and is sunk into heavy debts.

The wage indexation policy, together with other government regultions that aim at ensuring employment, in practice may discourage the creation of new jobs. To confront structural imbalances in the economy, to strengthen production incentives, and to encourage new investment, wage and price controls, profit margins, and other rigidities should be reduced or eliminated. Instead, controls should be diverted to monopolistic and oligopolistic practices in the market so that a healthy competition could be encouraged.

The generous income policy and the expansionary fiscal policy in 1979–1985 in Greece were two significant causes of high demand for domestic and foreign products. During that time, average wages in the nonagricultural sector increased by 17 to 26 percent, while labor productivity did not increase. The budget deficit increased from 5.9 percent of GNP in 1979 to 17.8 percent in 1985, which is among the highest in the world. These policies increased demand more than domestic production and led to foreign borrowing to finance ever-growing imports. Labor costs higher than the rates of producitivity, in turn, undermined exports, while the devaluations of the drachma were lower than they should have been. Such devaluations of the drachma reduced the competitiveness of the Greek exports and encouraged capital outflow from the country.

In order to stabilize the economy and to reduce inflation, austerity measures are implemented by the governments of both countries from time to time. Such measures affect primarily the salaried workers and employees by prohibiting wage increases meant to catch up with inflation. However, they have not been very effective mainly because many people, as self-employed entrepreneurs, derive their income from their own businesses and related activities, not from wages and salaries. Moreover, due to the demonstration effect and the custom of living at higher consumption levels, workers and employees continue their high level of spending by drying out their savings or through borrowing. Therefore, demand is largely unaffected and demand-pull inflation continues.

INFLATION AND TAXATION

With inflation and progressive rates of taxation, the governments of Turkey and Greece collect more revenue, while people's real incomes may decline. With every rise in income that merely keeps pace with inflation, taxpayers are forced to pay higher taxes as they are propelled into higher brackets. Inflation then is a practical way of transferring command over resources from the private to the public sector.

These additional tax revenues finance additional government expenditures that stimulate inflation (as long as they are not directed toward productive investment), and the public sector keeps on expanding. From that point of view, inflationary financing for the governments of Greece, Turkey, and, to a lesser extent, the EEC seems to have all the attractions of an invisible tax. It is a form of taxation that can easily be enforced and that the public finds hard to evade. But, from the point of view of investment and growth, inflation poisons incentives, devalues the currency, and undermines the confidence of the economy.

To neutralize the impact of inflation on taxation, tax indexing is considered by the respective countries. If the income tax were indexed to the inflation rate, tax rates would not rise unless real income also rose. However, although indexing can be expected to eliminate the tax bracket creep induced by inflation, it would reduce government revenue. With the adjustment of the tax system for inflation, as consumer prices rise, so do the standard deduction, the personal exemption, and both ends of each tax bracket. Indexing, then, would end increases in tax revenues due to inflation and might limit governmental spending.[8] However, it might lead to bigger deficits in the budgets of these countries if spending is not held in check.

Inflation has increased the effective rate of taxation on income in both countries. As a result, investment in income-bearing ventures, as in the case of manufacturing, for example, has been discouraged in favor of investment in owner-occupied housing, where limited or no property taxes are paid. The nonneutral effects of inflation on the Greek and Turkish tax systems then have misdirected capital investment toward owner-occupied homes in urban areas at the expense of rapid industrialization of these countries. The inflation-tax interactions were partially responsible for high investment concentration in housing in Athens, Salonika, Patras, Herakleion, and other urban centers in Greece, as well as in Ankara, Istanbul, Izmir, Bursa, Trabzon, Konya (Iconium), and Erzurum in Turkey. This is one of the main reasons for the high prices of houses and apartments in these cities despite the extensive capital formation in housing and the low expected rate of return on investment in this sector.

Although interest income is exempt from taxation and interest rates paid by thrift institutions are relatively high, the almost nonexistent property taxes, together with inflation, increase incentives for channeling accumulated savings into housing and real estate speculation. This trend reduces investment in productive ventures that provide permanent jobs and higher incomes. From that point of view, greater emphasis on the reduction in income taxes may increase productivity, encourage exports, and combat inflation.

As Greece and Turkey are bedeviled simultaneously by inflation and unemployment, policymakers in these countries are hard put to implement proper tax measures to correct undesirable trends. Indirect taxes, which are levied against goods and services, and especially direct (income) taxes, are largely affected by inflation. Indirect taxes, which include customs duties, turnover taxes, and value added taxes, are more or less proportional to the value of goods and services on which they are levied. Therefore, an increase in prices would bring about an increase in indirect taxes. However, the real value of ad valorem excises, tariffs, and other indirect taxes will be largely unaffected by inflation, or affected less than that of direct progressive taxes. In order to lighten the punitive tax burden resulting from inflation, the governments of Greece and Turkey contemplate measures to change the tax structure and stimulate economic efficiency. Their main fiscal dilemma is how to provide sufficient tax revenue without discouraging production incentives.

The fact that the private sector might not be able to marshal enough savings to finance capital formation might necessitate utilization of government savings, that is, surplus revenue over expenditures, to fill the gap. Because surplus budget revenue is difficult for Greece and Turkey, investment is mainly financed by inflationary money or public sector borrowing.

In order not to discourage productive private investment and to suppress inflation, taxation should be directed against luxurious and wasteful consumption, unnecessary imports, and hoarding. For an anti-inflationary policy, progressive taxation, as well as real estate taxes, may be considered desirable, as long as they divert resources from conspicuous consumption and luxurious housing to productive assets.[9] Business income taxes will have the same beneficial effects if they are passed forward or backward on the consumers by monopolistic or oligopolistic firms. But they may have detrimental effects on the overall economy of Greece or Turkey if they discourage productive business investments that are expected to increase supply and reduce inflation.

In order to examine the relationship between inflation and taxation, related elasticities were used. For the measurement of inflation elasticity of taxation, the percentage changes in tax revenue over the percentage changes in inflation were used. During the last decade, the inflation elasticity of taxation was 2.5 percent for Greece and 12.2 percent for Turkey, compared to 2.3 percent for the EEC, 2.7 percent for Japan, and 2 percent for the United States. Thus each 1 percent change in inflation was related to a 2.5 percent change in total taxes in Greece, 12.2 percent in Turkey, and so on. Tax revenue in Turkey seems to be more sensitive to inflation than that of Greece and that of the United States, while a little less sensitive compared to that of the EEC. Such findings may be useful for proper policymaking in these two countries as well as in other countries with similar problems. Although it is difficult to slay the ogre of inflation with tax measures alone, proper tax policies can have significant effects upon its behavior.

An effective tax policy, which would reduce inflation, could help reduce budget deficits and capital outflow. Incentives to taxpayers would encourage them to pay their fair share and help reduce inflation and internal and external borrowing. Also, the value added tax (VAT), as a consumption tax, could discourage spending and help reduce demand-pull inflation. For countries like Greece and Turkey with high rates of inflation the VAT seems to be beneficial.[10] Investment tax credit is another tool to encourage spending for plant and equipment. If enterprises can subtract part of their expenditures for productive investment from their taxable income, more production would take place, unemployment and inflation would be reduced, and consumers could satisfy their demand with mainly domestic instead of foreign products.

NOTES

1. International Monetary Fund (IMF), *International Financial Statistics* (IFS), various issues.

2. "Ozal Outlines Turkey's Problems and Aspirations," *Wall Street Journal,* May 26, 1987.

3. Evanthia Allen, "Turkey in Transition," *Weekly Review,* New York, May 17, 1985.

4. For similar problems in other countries, see Nicholas V. Gianaris, *Economic Development: Thought and Problems* (West Hanover, Mass.: Christopher Publishing House, 1978), 174–77.

5. IMF, *IFS,* various issues.

6. For problems of deficit financing in Yugoslavia, Nicholas V. Gianaris, *Greece and Yugoslavia: An Economic Comparison* (New York: Praeger, 1984), 69–72.

7. For the effects of inflationary psychology, Xenophon Zolotas, *International Monetary Issues and Development Policies* (Athens: Bank of Greece, 1977), 348–51. Also Dimitris Halikias, *Money and Credit in a Developing Economy: The Case of Greece* (New York: New York University Press, 1978).

8. Tax indexing has been introduced in at least 15 countries, including Canada and France. A similar indexing of social security benefits was introduced in the United States in 1972. In Brazil and other Latin American countries, indexing seems to be responsible for high rates of inflation. Elio Gaspari, "Origins of the Debt Crisis," *New York Times,* November 7, 1983.

9. The elasticity of the tax system plays an important role in the use of taxation to reduce inflation. Further comments in Stephen R. Lewis, Jr., *Taxation and Development* (New York: Oxford University Press, 1984), 38.

10. For the effects of VAT in Turkey, OECD, *Economic Survey: Turkey* (September 1986), 47–49. For expected inflation and taxation in Greece see *TO VIMA,* August 30, 1987, 17.

III

INTERNATIONAL ECONOMIC RELATIONS AND COOPERATION

The following chapters of Part III deal with foreign trade and investment in Greece and Turkey and their relationship with the European Common Market and other trading nations. The possibilities and the difficulties of closer cooperation and integration with the EEC are also examined.

The continuing occupation of northern Cyprus and the purported violations of sea and airspace in the Aegean by Turkey prevent Greece's assent to Turkey's membership in the EEC. Moreover, the lack of fundamental democratic freedoms in Turkey and the significant economic and cultural differences between Turkey and the member states of the Community prevent EEC members from accepting Turkey's application for membership.

Both countries have large external debts and are obliged to pay sizeable amounts of money every year to creditor banks for interest and amortization. Large amounts of foreign exchange are used to pay for armaments as a result of their mutual mistrust and conflicts. Revenue from tourism, immigrant remittances and deposits in both nations, as well as shipping in Greece, cover part of the huge trade deficits. However, they are not substantial enough and foreign borrowing continues to be a serious problem. That is why severe austerity measures have been imposed recently according to the IMF and the creditors' prescriptions.

Although both economies produce, to a large extent, competitive products that are exported mainly to the EEC, the Arab countries, and the United States, a closer cooperation between them and the eventual access of Turkey to the EEC could stimulate their trade and development. Subsidies and other benefits offered to foreign investment have not produced satisfactory results as yet. American aid is flowing every year into Greece and more so into Turkey, primarily as a remuneration for the numerous U.S. bases in both strategic countries. Despite their mistrust and hostility, expectations are that, under the umbrella of the EEC, these two countries will move from the stage of isolation and hatred to that of cooperation and possibly to common business ventures that will tend to submerge territorial and other differences.

8

Foreign Trade and Investment

INTERNATIONAL AND INTERREGIONAL TRADE

From the point of view of international transactions, both countries, Greece and Turkey, face large trade deficits and huge foreign debts. As a result, their international financial position is weak and the Greek drachma and the Turkish lira are under constant pressure for devaluation. The main reason is their long-term specialization in mainly primary production and the need for large amounts of imports, not only in capital goods but in consumer durables and other industrial products. This is a phenomenon familiar in developing and semi-developed nations. The terms of trade, that is, the price index of exports over the price index of imports, declined for Turkey, but remained constant or increased slightly for Greece, in recent years.

Structural problems and sectoral disequilibria, inflation, unemployment, lack of confidence in the national currency, capital flight, and budgetary deficits are some additional reasons for the trade deficits and external debts of Greece and Turkey.

Increases in oil prices in the 1970s added to the trade deficits and the accumulation of their debts. Thus, due to the oil price increases, at that time, additional net expenditures for oil led to the reduction of reserves in foreign exchanges, while new loans were received from abroad to cover current account deficits. However, the decrease in oil prices in the 1980s was a comfort for their balance of payments, which would present larger deficits if it were not for the extensive fall of oil prices from 35 dollars to 18 dollars per barrel.

International recessions significantly reduce revenue from "invisible" sources, that is, tourism, shipping, and immigrant remittances. In addition, the constant decline of such revenue is due also to the lack of confidence in the Greek drachma and in the Turkish lira. As a result, a portion of foreign exchange from tourism and shipping is collected by individuals in the black market and is flown out of these countries secretly without being detected by the financial authorities and the banks.

The large deficits in the balance of current accounts and the increase in the external debt in the early 1980s were due primarily to internal factors. External conditions for Greece and Turkey were, however, mostly favorable during that period. Such favorable conditions include:

1. Decrease in oil prices
2. Decrease in foreign interest rates
3. Subsidies and other support given by the EEC, especially to Greece
4. International economic improvement, especially in 1983–1987
5. Revaluation of the dollar

Domestically, excessive increases in spending by the public sector and the low productivity of the economy led to large budgetary deficits. It seems that economic policymakers adhered to the Keynesian prescription of demand stimulation with the hope of boosting the domestic economy. However, with a high income elasticity of demand, imports were increased far higher than exports in both countries, resulting in large trade deficits. And this, in spite of the fact that imports were expected to slow down somewhat because of the relatively low real economic growth. As a consequence, the deficits in the balance of payments led to external borrowing.

Imports can be controlled and manipulated more than exports by the debtor countries. Exports depend primarily on policies of the creditor countries to boost growth. Also, other policy strategies, such as fighting inflation, should be emphasized for balance of payment improvement. Protectionist measures may make it more difficult for debtor countries to penetrate the markets of creditor developed countries. However, exemptions ought to be allowed, mainly by the EEC, to Greece and Turkey, because of their lower levels of industrialization.

Total Greek imports are about $12 billion and exports $6 billion annually, leaving a foreign trade deficit of around $6 billion. Revenue from invisibles, about $4 billion annually, declined slightly in recent years, while payments for invisibles (tourism, shipping, immigrant remittances) is about $2 billion, leaving a surplus of $2 billion. The inflow of private funds declined to about $800 million annually, while foreign borrowing is between $1 and 3 billion. Foreign exchange reserves remain the same (about $1 billion). In 1987, imports were $12.5 billion and exports $5.6 billion, leaving a trade deficit of $6.9 billion. However, invisible earnings improved and the current account deficit was $1.3 billion.

The austerity measures introduced in Greece in 1985, among other things, devaluated the drachma against the U.S. dollar by 15 percent. As it turned out, though, this devaluation proved to be ineffective, because the drachma was revalued (from 156 drachmas per dollar in October 1985 to less than 138 drachmas per dollar in 1987). Another unwise devaluation of the drachma by 15.5 percent in January 1983 also proved to be ineffective and detrimental to the Greek balance of trade. Instead of being allowed to fluctuate according to

Table 8.1
Exports (fob), Imports (fob), Current Account Balances (in millions of U.S. dollars), and Exchange Rates (drachmas per U.S. dollar, end of year) in Greece

Year	Exports	Imports	Current Account Balance	Exchange Rate
1950	90	43	—	15.00
1960	210	460	− 55	30.00
1970	612	1,509	− 422	30.00
1971	627	1,727	− 344	30.00
1972	835	2,161	− 400	30.00
1973	1,230	3,582	− 1,189	29.70
1974	1,774	4,125	− 1,143	30.00
1975	1,960	4,320	− 877	35.65
1976	2,228	4,922	− 929	37.03
1977	2,523	5,686	− 1,075	35.51
1978	2,999	6,498	− 955	36.00
1979	3,932	8,947	− 1,886	38.28
1980	4,093	9,650	− 2,209	46.53
1981	4,772	10,149	− 2,408	57.63
1982	4,141	8,910	− 1,892	70.57
1983	4,106	8,400	− 1,878	98.57
1984	4,394	8,624	− 2,132	128.48
1985	4,293	9,346	− 3,276	147.76
1986	4,513	8,936	− 1,676	138.76

Source: IMF, *International Financial Statistics,* various issues.

the rates of inflation, the exchange rate of the drachma in terms of dollars was kept constant for some eight months, making Greek exports more expensive and imports cheaper.

Large trade deficits in Turkey are covered, for the most part, by remittances from immigrant workers in Germany and by tourism. However, such invisibles are not sufficient to cover the difference and foreign borrowing is needed. In the past, especially in the 1970s, Turkey came under major multilateral restructuring and rescheduling (stretching maturities and grace periods) of official and commercial debts, because export revenue and invisibles were not sufficient to service the debt. Then sizeable loans were extended by NATO and OECD countries to make the country survive economically. Sporadic austerity measures, including controls on public sector spending, high interest rates (up to 50 percent), reduction of subsidies to state enterprises, and devaluations of the Turkish lira, were all imposed as a result of the suggestions of the International Monetary Fund (IMF) to put the economy in order.

Tables 8.1 and 8.2 show foreign trade, current account balances, and exchange rates for Greece and Turkey, respectively. For almost all years considered, imports were higher than exports, leaving huge trade deficits. Net revenues from invisibles (tourism, shipping, immigrant remittances) were not sufficient to cover

Table 8.2
Exports (fob), Imports (fob), Current Account Balances (in millions of U.S. dollars), and Exchange Rates (liras per U.S. dollar, end of year) in Turkey

Years	Exports	Imports	Current Account Bal.	Exchange Rate
1955	313	497	—	2.81
1960	320	468	– 26	9.02
1970	588	830	– 44	14.93
1971	677	1,030	43	14.15
1972	885	1,367	212	14.15
1973	1,320	1,829	660	14.15
1974	1,532	3,589	– 561	13.99
1975	1,401	4,502	–1,648	15.15
1976	1,960	9,872	–2,029	16.67
1977	1,753	5,506	–3,138	19.44
1978	2,288	4,369	–1,266	25.25
1979	2,261	4,815	–1,413	35.35
1980	2,910	7,513	–3,409	90.15
1981	4,703	8,567	–1,916	133.62
1982	5,890	8,518	– 935	186.75
1983	5,905	8,895	–1,898	282.80
1984	7,389	10,331	–1,407	444.79
1985	8,255	11,230	–1,032	576.86
1986	7,583	10,664	–1,528	757.79

Source: International Financial Statistics, various issues.

the difference. The results were large current account deficits and external borrowing. On the other hand, the price of the dollar increased from 30 drachmas in 1955 to 138 drachmas in 1987 for Greece and from 2.8 liras to 944 liras for Turkey, respectively. This shows the enormous devaluations (official or slipping) of the Greek drachma and, more so, the Turkish lira.

In order to mitigate the problem of trade deficits, efforts to connect imports with exports should also be encouraged. Even exchanges in kind with Middle Eastern and east European countries for certain products may be beneficial for Greece and Turkey because of their enormous foreign debts, especially when commercial credit has dried up and import restraints have been imposed. This would help the self-financing of the long-term development effort. Bartering would then enable these debtor countries to maintain imports and expand exports, thereby contributing to economic stability and job preservation.

One way in which the public sector can play a vital role in the economies of Greece and Turkey is to exert a protective or "inward looking" policy or, conversely, to display the lack of it. In such countries, there may be a need for protecting certain "infant" industries in order for them to survive foreign competition from more advanced countries. Greece and Turkey are rich in mining resources, such as bauxite, aluminum, iron, tin, nickel, and other primary products. Instead of exporting such products in the form of raw materials and then importing them back as finished metal products, it would be more logical to encourage their manufacture into final goods by domestic industries. This may require protection for a period of time, until the infant industries are capable of standing on their own feet and surviving competition. However, the period of protection should not be extended too long. Otherwise, such protection, which is in effect taxing consumers on imported goods or subsidizing domestic producers for substitutes, would perpetuate inefficiencies in these industries at the expense of the rest of the economy. Furthermore, protection, to the degree permitted by the EEC for Greece, may also work against saving foreign exchange because exporters may be forced, through protective tariffs, to pay more for their imported inputs and thereby become less competitive.

An important obstacle to saving and improving the trade balance is the demonstration effect. With the expansion of foreign trade, people in both nations use a large part of their savings to buy imported goods. The zeal to imitate the foreigners (xenomania) is so strong that certain people spend more than their income for consumption of foreign goods. Also, rich people spend a good part of their income or profit for mainly foreign luxury goods, instead of using it for productive investment. As a result, a high proportion of national income is spent for consumption and a small proportion is left for saving and capital formation.

Moreover, the governments of Greece and Turkey tend to formulate policies and programs in which they seek to emulate advanced countries with high technical, educational, and social standards, although such standards may be inappropriate for their economies. The demonstration effect may thus lead to deficits in balance of payments, less capital investment, and the introduction of inflationary spirals. In such cases, then, taxes on luxury consumption seem to be the sine qua non for capital formation and an improvement in the balance of payments. On the other hand, to use progressive income taxes to reduce luxury consumption may reduce private saving and discourage productive investment and exportation.

About half of the merchandise exports is in primary products for both countries, one-fourth in textiles and clothing, and the rest in other manufactured products. As a result, the terms of trade (price index of exports over price index of imports) are mostly deteriorating, as they are for other countries exporting large proportions of primary products. Compared to 1980, these terms of trade declined to 97 for Greece and 90 for Turkey.

For both countries one-fourth of imports is in machinery. Fuel imports account for about half of the total imports for Turkey and one-third for Greece. About

60 percent of the energy needs of Greece are covered by oil imports. Industrial market economies absorb about 70 percent of merchandise exports of Greece and 50 percent of Turkey's; developing countries absorb about 20 and 35 percent, respectively; oil-producing nations about 10 percent; and east European nations only 4 to 6 percent of the total exports of both Greece and Turkey.

The depreciation of the Greek drachma and the Turkish lira, periodically or gradually, stopped somewhat the loss of international reserves, but their depleted levels were hardly adequate to support the current accounts deficit and the increasing external debt-servicing payments. The entrenched government practice of subsidizing inefficient public and private enterprises resulted in inflationary pressures, low productivity, and low level of international competitiveness. Large shares of investments of these countries have indeed gone into public enterprises whose services are heavily subsidized while the prices of their goods and services are often not sufficiently high to cover the cost of production. Such subsidies increase budget and trade deficits that lead to the rise of internal and external borrowing as a means of financing them.

Interregional Trade

Figure 8.1 shows the trend of foreign trade between Greece and Turkey during the postwar years. In all these years and up to 1974, Greece imported more than it exported to Turkey. The same thing can be observed even before World War II. Thus, in 1938 Greek imports from Turkey were 270 million drachmas, compared to only 70 million drachmas in exports for that year. In the very recent past, though, Turkey buys more from Greece than it sells to it.

Although trade between these two countries is limited, compared to total foreign trade, the geographical location and the gradual specialization in different products and industries suggest that transactions between them can be largely improved. Therefore, if political disputes over Cyprus are settled, trade and investment expectations can be promising for the betterment of the standards of living of the people in the area. Moreover, the fact that Greece is a full member and Turkey an associated member of the European Common Market makes trade cooperation beneficial for both of them. Moreover, Turkey, with a population of about 54 million, may be regarded as a large potential market for neighboring Greece, while Greece may be considered as a stepping stone for Turkish products to infiltrate the large market of the European Economic Community (EEC).

Although both countries produce primarily competitive agricultural commodities, improvement in trade between them would generate more diversification and specialization in complementary goods. It would seem then that Greece could concentrate on the production of industrial and technology-intensive goods and exchange them for primary or semi-manufactured Turkish products. Furthermore, development in transportation and tourism could lead to more cooperation in the area and the improvement in the balance of payments, mostly in favor of Turkey.

Figure 8.1
Foreign Trade of Greece with Turkey, 1948–1985 (in millions of dollars)

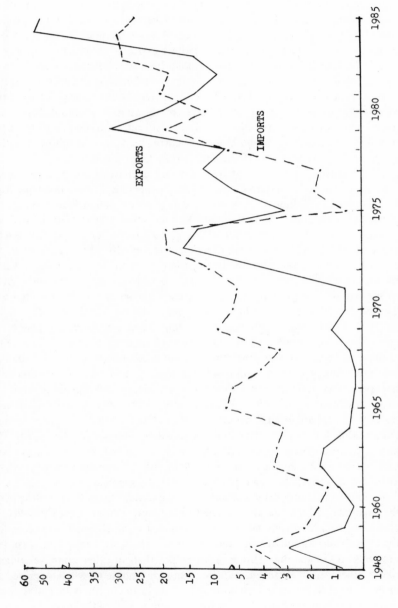

Source: United Nations, *Yearbook of International Trade Statistics*, various issues.

EXCHANGE RATES AND CAPITAL OUTFLOW

Comparatively speaking, Greece and Turkey have the largest amount of foreign trade with Germany. Therefore, their currencies are largely related to the German mark, even more than to the dollar. Fluctuations in the mark and in the economic conditions in Germany are affecting and are expected to affect even more in the future the Greek drachma and the Turkish lira. An additional reason for this is the fact that Germany has sizeable numbers of Greek and Turkish immigrants. The exchange rates of Greek and Turkish currencies and their purchasing power, versus the mark, affect not only trade among them but capital flows as well. Thus, when there are official or nominal, not real, revaluations of the drachma or the lira, in terms of the mark or other currencies, capital outflow from Greece (as happened in 1980 and 1984) and Turkey takes place.

Under present conditions, if free currency exchanges and free movement of capital are permitted in Greece and Turkey, financing of new investment would be problematic. Initially, people would rush to exchange their money in hard currencies, notably U.S. dollars and German marks, and then deposit it with foreign banks. From that point of view, two stages could be followed until complete freedom in currency transactions and deposits is permitted. First, people could be free to deposit and withdraw foreign currencies in the domestic banks for unlimited time. Second, depending on monetary stability and the confidence of the public, complete freedom in currency exchanges of the drachma and the Turkish lira vis-à-vis other hard currencies could be permitted.

There is the danger, though, that during the first stage many people would aggressively try to buy dollars and other hard currencies from tourists and other financiers. But as long as they deposit them with interest in domestic banks, the foreign currencies will remain inside the country, instead of flying abroad. This is expected to stop the flight of money from Turkey and especially from Greece to other countries and even attract return of previous deposits from abroad, notably from Switzerland, back to these countries. Also, foreigners, especially from Middle Eastern countries, may deposit their money in the Greek and Turkish banks. Such deposits are expected not only to stabilize the monetary conditions of these countries and increase their credibility abroad, but to be used for investment financing, so much needed in both economies.

As long as inflation in Greece and Turkey exceeds that of their trading partners, the drachma and the lira are expected to be depreciated to cover the difference. However, the depreciation of these currencies is, at times, inadequate and the result is deterioration in the trade balance. Thus, you may find that foreign products in Greece and Turkey are cheaper than in other countries when you pay for them in local currencies. For example, a bottle of whiskey priced at $10 in the United States or in Ireland may be bought in Greece with 1,400 drachmas and in Turkey with 10,100 liras, while it ought to have a higher price, depending on the rate of their improper appreciation. In such cases, the balance of current accounts of these countries would be deteriorating. Moreover, investors would hesitate to exchange undervalued foreign currencies into drachmas and liras until the restoration of their real purchasing power through proper devaluation. Perhaps a predetermined monthly currency devaluation according to the expected rate of inflation and the conditions in the balance of payments would restore external respectability and stimulate foreign investment.

Presently, the Greek drachma is allied with a basket of EEC currencies. Although the elements and weights of the official currency basket, against which the drachma's value is measured, have never been published, the German mark plays the most important role in such a measurement. This is so because West Germany is the most important foreign trade partner for Greece, as it is for Turkey. Therefore, fluctuations of the mark versus the dollar affect the exchange rates of the drachma and, to a lesser extent, the lira versus the dollar as well as other related currencies.

In order to minimize the extent of exchange rate fluctuations against all currencies, both countries, directly or indirectly, attach or peg their currencies largely to the main EEC currencies, which are related to the European Currency Unit (ECU). The determination of a weighted basket of currencies, practiced mainly in Greece, may be based primarily on the real exchange rate or on the balance of payments. The measurement of the exact weight seems to be a complex exercise and it is difficult to predict precisely. Under a basket peg method, which resembles a managed float system, the home currency is automatically determined by specified rules, with limited discretionary action by the authorities. This is a useful exchange rate regime for small economies, such as those of Greece and Turkey, and it can be determined by a geometric or an arithmetic average.[1]

Capital Flight Hinders Growth

Unwise policies on credit, interest and exchange rates, as well as high rates of inflation and large deficits in the balance of payments, result in capital outflow from Turkey and especially from Greece. It was estimated, by the International Monetary Fund (IMF), that such a capital outflow raised deposits to foreign banks to $1.84 billion from Turkey and $5.23 billion from Greece at the end of 1985.[2] Such a capital outflow is a major hemorrhage for these economies and has serious drawbacks for their socioeconomic stability and development. As a result, these countries have to borrow the needed funds from foreign banks and pay for the growing amounts of annual interests and amortizations. Similar massive capital outflows can be observed in other countries such as Mexico, Venezuela, Brazil, and Argentina, which also have huge foreign debts.

Overpricing of imports and underpricing of exports are the major reasons for illegal money outflows and deposits abroad. Moreover, exporters of goods and services delay, on purpose, inflows and deposits of foreign currencies with the domestic central banks. On some occasions, interest is paid abroad for loans not received (interest on inactive loans). Also, large amounts of foreign currencies collected by individuals and companies from tourism and other transactions may illegally flow out of the country to Swiss and other banks.

Capital flows should be distinguished from capital flight, which often involves accumulation of wealth by individuals in other countries to avoid taxation or other controls by their native governments.[3] Ultimately, money fleeing the country is put to work where it is safe and where it can earn more in real terms. However, stability in the economies of Greece and Turkey would lead to better expectations and eventually a drop in capital flight.

As a result of the capital flight, the chronic balance of payments deficit is exacerbated and the ability of these debtor countries to pay their debts and receive new loans is seriously threatened, unless they can recover some of the capital transferred abroad. Such a reversal is difficult and the capital flight, which has become a symptom and a source of the debt problem of Greece and Turkey, continues.

Multinational corporations and domestic enterprises may use accounting techniques and, by juggling their books, may export capital from Greece and Turkey. Normally, foreign companies can export legally a certain percentage of capital in the form of profit and capital repatriation. Over and above these permitted percentages of capital outflows, funds are exported illegally and deposited with foreign banks, mainly through overpricing imports and underpricing exports.

For Turkey, however, recent capital outflow, recorded by the IMF, is limited. It declined from $2 billion in 1981 to $1.8 billion at the end of 1985, while for neighboring Cyprus it increased from $0.36 billion to $0.65 billion and for Yugoslavia from $0.32 billion to $0.42 billion, respectively.

Expected devaluations of the local currencies, either through official government decisions or through a gradual slipping to lower values, compared to other currencies, are major causes of capital outflow.[4] When devaluations are expected, people try to buy foreign currencies that will have a higher value later. Because there are controls on foreign exchange, people resort to the black market transactions, secretly buying foreign currencies with higher prices than the official ones. To reduce demand for foreign currencies and the outflow of capital, strict monetary and especially credit policies are, from time to time, implemented in Greece and Turkey.

Developed countries with stable economies and financial security, such as Switzerland, the United States, and to some extent Britain and West Germany, accept foreign deposits with favorable terms. The United States, in particular, provides a safe haven for foreign deposits and offers favorable terms that are better than those in Switzerland. For example, foreign depositors enjoy the same interest rate with American depositors, without paying taxes on the income from interest, as Americans do.

THE RELATIONSHIP OF BUDGET AND TRADE DEFICITS

There seems to be a close relationship between budget deficits and foreign trade deficits. High government expenditures not matched by tax revenue generate budget deficits that in turn generate foreign trade deficits. They both grow and move closer to each other.

Historically Greece and Turkey always had foreign trade deficits, because exports were not sufficient to cover large imports of needed commodities. Recently, however, the gap increased dramatically. Even the current accounts, which include tourist, shipping, and other services, in addition to imported and exported commodities, present large deficits. Such deficits, which are not covered by net inflows of capital, lead to the accumulation of foreign debt. Figure 8.2 shows the trends of budget and current account deficits for Greece. Figure 8.3 demonstrates, more or less, the same trends for Turkey.

Large deficits in the public sector create an aggregate demand higher than the supply of goods and services. Such excessive demand is satisfied by more imports. With a high income elasticity of imports, which can be observed in Greece and Turkey, extra incomes are channeled primarily to foreign goods and services. If there are not enough reserves to pay for such extra imports, the way out is borrowing from foreign banks. Therefore, chronic budget deficits are largely responsible for high trade and current account deficits. This became obvious in the 1970s and more so in the 1980s.

Large budget deficits are mainly responsible for similar foreign trade deficits in both countries. Efforts to cut the trade deficit without cutting the budget deficit pose a serious threat of increasing inflation. A trade deficit represents an excess of domestic spending over domestic production, according to the principle of absorption. This can be cured by producing more exports and import subsidies, or by reducing spending. In both cases, a reduction in private and government consumption is required so that resources would be free to be devoted to production, while nonproductive or wasteful spending would be discouraged. Therefore, to close the trade gap, the budget deficit should be slashed. This is the only way for the Greek and Turkish governments to save their economies from themselves.

For some years to come, the Turkish and Greek economies will face problems of economic hemorrhage and austerity. The huge foreign debt and the annual payments for interest and principal to foreign banks will continue to drain the economy. In addition to the external public debt, there are foreign exchange deposits primarily by immigrants and other obligations which make for a higher total foreign debt. On a per capita basis, both countries are among the largest debtors in the world. The debt service (interest and amortization), as percentage of exports of goods and services (more than 20 percent), is also very high.

According to a report of the International Monetary Fund (IMF), Greece must pay for interest and amortization from 1986 to 1990 about $16 billion. In other words, both nations should achieve surplus in the balance of payments in order to meet their future obligations. Both governments, however, expect further deficits in the near future. As a result, more severe austerity measures are to be suggested by the creditor banks and the IMF.

A recent loan of $1.6 billion received by Greece, through the EEC, half of

Figure 8.2
Budget Deficits and Current Account Deficits in Greece

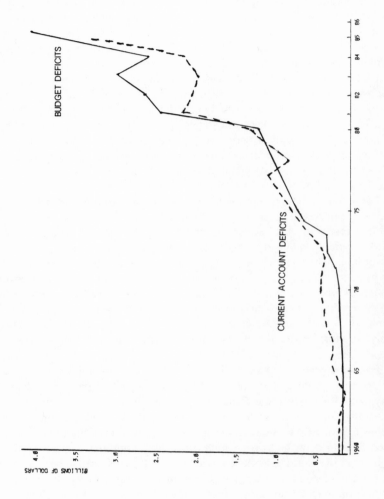

Source: IMF, *International Financial Statistics*, various issues.

Figure 8.3
Budget Deficits and Current Account Deficits in Turkey

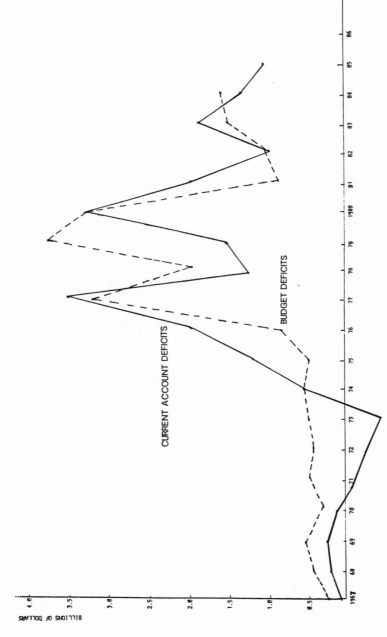

Source: IMF, *International Financial Statistics*, various issues.

137

which was given in 1986 and half in 1987, was approximately equal to the interest due from the country's debt. From that point of view, the foreign banks pay themselves for interest due. With such loans, the debts of the debtor countries increase, while they are not receiving anything. It seems then that Greece and Turkey are, more or less, in the same boat with other debtor nations, regarding interest and principal payment or servicing foreign debt.

For an improvement in foreign trade and the economy as a whole, serious efforts should be made to step up exports and especially revenues from invisibles and to put inflation back in its cage. More serious measures are needed to reduce demand for imports, and more austerity measures are expected to decrease public sector deficits. However, the relative declines in oil prices and in interest rates are anticipated to provide some comfort regarding external deficits.

Greece and Turkey, with the beautiful Mediterranean climate and attractive seashores, are expected to keep and improve their traditional sources of revenue from tourism, shipping, and trade services. However, structural changes are needed to stabilize the economies and to improve productivity. In addition to the investment incentives provided, tax reforms, reduction in budget deficits, a better economic management, and public confidence are needed for improvement in foreign trade. Policymakers should stop pursuing short-run political gains at severe long-run costs and hardships for their countries caused by wasteful spending and large public sector deficits.

National economic policies, and fiscal policies in particular, effect not only changes in domestic deficits and debts but they also have repercussions on foreign transactions. Measures on multinational corporations and mergers, rules and regulations to minimize government distortions of capital and technology transfers, and controls on foreign exchange rates practiced in Greece and Turkey influence and are influenced by fiscal and monetary policies, respectively. Technical and financial assistance, government guarantees for bank loans, absence of tax discrimination, and international agreements for business protection and economic cooperation affect world trade and economic and social conditions in both countries.

The need for international fiscal cooperation requires that the tax equity and tax neutrality principles of public finance be respected by the governments of the countries involved. Government aid and capital transfers should consider the principles of efficient allocation and income distribution as a way of raising economic growth, in the long run, without debt accumulations. Along these lines, investments in sectors and regions with low capital-output ratios are expected to receive priorities in capital formation, subsidies, and other incentive policies.[5]

In the low-income regions of Greece and Turkey, where the private sector hesitates or is unable to undertake the construction of needed infrastructural facilities, the public sector, along with the foreign sector, has an important role to play in allocating resources and training people, especially in areas with high unemployment. However, state enterprises and the public sector in general are responsible for large budget and trade deficits, which generate big foreign debts, and cautious steps are needed in the process of coordinating the domestic with the foreign sector in both nations.

FOREIGN TRADE AND JOINT VENTURES

An important question for the market economies of Greece and Turkey is how to adopt and conform to a new financial system based upon domestic and foreign cooperative ventures that would enhance people's motives and expectations toward more efficiency and a better livelihood through productive investments.

In the past, both governments have pressed for greater control over multinational corporation (MNC) activities, although it is generally recognized that they contribute to trade and capital flows and facilitate economic growth and development. For purposes of mutually beneficial relations and a better international allocation of resources, however, they have shifted their focus to active encouragement of direct investment by MNCs and minimizing government distortions of capital and technology transfers.

In order to attract foreign investment, efforts have been made to develop appropriate guidelines and standards of good practice for governments and enterprises alike, so that unilateral government interventions and conflicts can be limited or avoided. Such guidelines and good conduct are intended mainly to reduce restraints of trade and investment by private, state-owned, and mixed-ownership enterprises, to contribute to a freer, fairer, and more competitive international economic environment, and to advance the common interests of MNCs and the economies of Greece and Turkey.

For the uninterrupted flow of foreign investment and know-how onto their soil, the governments of these countries try to create favorable conditions, including protection of life and property, guarantees for interest and profit remittances, free immigration of foreign personnel, and absence of discrimination in taxes. On the other hand, they try to be selective with regard to foreign investment, asking for provisions to gradually train local personnel for skilled technical and administrative positions and directing investment to certain sectors and regions of their countries. Moreover, sometimes it is required that the financing of investment be made primarily by foreign imported sources and not by draining limited domestic sources, thereby depriving local entrepreneurs of the opportunity to borrow capital for investment.

Emphasis on primary production by fiscal and other measures in these nations proved not so helpful in rapid development, mainly because of the declining terms of trade in international markets. On the other hand, emphasis on the production of certain industrial products may lead to duplication among the EEC nations, including Greece and associated members such as Turkey. Probably, the EEC can offer selective support for certain industries and regions by providing technical and financial assistance for both nations.

Although import substitution and inward-looking policies are needed in these two nations for the protection of some infant or weak industries, outward-oriented policies proved to be more successful quantitatively.[6] Producers and entrepreneurs in export-oriented industries, under competitive conditions, have a more powerful incentive to innovate and cut costs compared to those under a more sheltered economic environment. From that point of view, policymakers in both countries should work to adjust their policies to more practical and new international conditions.

Although foreign enterprises may crowd out local entrepreneurs in these countries, there seem to be potential gains from foreign trade and investment.[7] In that sense, a feasible scheme of income taxes-cum-subsidies can be used to have those who benefit from trade and investment compensate those who lose (entrepreneurs). Also, other measures, such as taxes on profits of foreign firms, to the degree permitted by the EEC, can be used to augment the size of the local entrepreneurial class and support infant industries.[8] But care should be taken to avoid possible deleterious welfare consequences from such measures. With such policies, the degree of dependence, that is, the situation in which a country is conditioned by the development and expansion of others, can be mitigated.

Foreign investments are frequently offered incentives and tax holidays in both countries. They include reduced tax rates in the early years of operation, cash grants, and subsidized loans. Also, the EEC provides regional incentive programs, such as capital grants, interest rate subsidies, tax concessions, and labor-related subsidies. The maximum of grants permitted by the EEC is 60 percent of the cost of the project. Both nations give guarantees in transferring profits, fees, royalties, and personnel.

As Greece did in 1953 (Basic Law 2687), Turkey also introduced legislation (Basic Law 6224) to encourage foreign investment. But only $228 million was invested into the country from 1954 to 1980. In recent years, however, a more favorable climate prevailed as xenophobia and bureaucracy were reduced. Regarding regional investment, there are plans to build a second oil pipeline from Iraq through Turkey, as well as from Iran, across Turkey, to Black Sea ports. (More details on new pipelines are presented later.)

Similar plans for investment in transportation are implemented or formulated in Greece. They include a large highway from Igoumenista to Volos to facilitate transportation, through ferry boats, to Syria and other east Mediterranean countries. This project is partially financed by the EEC. Also, a long canal connecting the Danube and Axios rivers from Belgrade to Salonika is under consideration.

In cooperation with foreign firms, Greece has under construction or is planning a subway (Metro) in Athens, a new airport in Spata (near Athens), a big irrigation project in the Acheloos River, and a tunnel connecting Rio and Antirio (near Patras). There are two Free Trade Zones in Turkey (one in Mersin and a new one in Antalya) and one in Greece (in Salonika, for Yugoslavian trade activities). To attract foreign investment, Turkey introduced the system of B.O.T. (Build, Operate, and Transfer), according to which contractors can raise funds to build and operate particular projects for 10 to 15 years and then transfer ownership to the Turkish state.

Among foreign firms that entered Turkey recently is the Anglo-American Corporation, a South African mining conglomerate, for possible mining operations. Turkey spends large amounts of foreign exchange ($170 million in 1986 alone) to buy clean-burning coal from South Africa to reduce air pollution in Ankara and other cities.

There are about 600 foreign companies operating in Greece, 113 of which are American. Total foreign business investments in Greece from 1980 to 1985 amounted to $2 billion and that in land and buildings $3.3 billion, about a 50 percent increase over the previous five-year period. In Turkey, foreign direct investment has been relatively modest so far, about $100 billion per annum, despite the open-door policy since 1980.

As pipeline of 850 kilometers from Siberia to Ankara, through the Turkish-Bulgarian borders, Istanbul, Bursa, and Eski-Sechir, would provide 750 million cubic meters of natural gas to Turkey worth $60 million per year. Some 60 percent of the imported gas would be paid for with Turkish exported products. The establishment of the pipeline would be completed in 1988. A similar gas pipeline for the transfer of gas from the Soviet Union to Greece is expected to be completed in the near future. Also, a big factory for the manufacturing of bauxite to alumina, worth about $585 million, is to be established in Greece jointly with the Soviet Union.

EXTERNAL DEBT

From an accounting point of view, external debt, in a narrow sense, includes all medium- and long-term debt (of one year or more) owed by the public sector to nonresidents. A broader definition adds short-term public sector debt, private sector debt (both short and long term), and direct investment.[9] Debts of public corporations and organizations are normally included in the public sector debt. Records of trade credits, private sector capital flows, and the reserves in foreign currencies should be kept as precisely as possible for an effective economic policy and debt management.

If there is net capital inflow, from deposits of nonresidents or others, incoming funds can be used for payments of foreign debt servicing. However, the obligation to pay back such deposits and the related interest remains.

It seems that present policies of extending loans by the creditor banks and international institutions would keep the financial systems of Greece and Turkey afloat for some time. But because of compound interest and the inability of these countries to pay back the debt, endless rounds of new loans would be necessary. As long as the principal is not paid, the obligation for interest payments would last forever, unless different arrangements are made.

External public debt includes the accumulated outstanding loans of the central banks and those of the central government and the public or state enterprises and organizations. For some time now, a sort of chorus of the central banks of Greece and Turkey, as chief performers, and foreign banks has been singing of foreign debt moratoriums, reschedulings, or other arrangements. Such a chorus is expected to continue with more intensity in the years to come.

In spite of the measures taken by Greece and Turkey to restrict imports and promote exports, the current account deficits continue.[10] This indicates that the austerity measures introduced recently had limited effects on foreign transactions of goods and services. Part of the problem is that payments due for principal and interest are growing year after year becuse of previous loans. Moreover, large budget deficits continue, and external financing is required so that economic development can continue without fueling higher inflation.

After the difficulties of additional loans to finance external deficits, the direction of borrowing was somewhat shifted. Instead of using the traditional sources of debt financing, mainly through U.S. and European banks, borrowing from Japanese and Middle Eastern banks became important. This is primarily the result of the Japanese policy to offer credit and facilitate its own exports. In order to keep and expand its foreign markets, the Japanese credit system has to provide needed loans to debtor nations, such as Greece and Turkey, so that imports from Japan can continue. For example, Greece imports from Japan about $650 million and exports only around $50 million, annually. Therefore, the large trade deficit of some $600 million has to be financed primarily by Japan, in order for the Japanese exports to continue. Thus, the National Bank of Industrial Development (ETVA) borrowed $100 million from Japanese banks recently with a swap agreement from yens to dollars and with a rate 0.5 percent above the London InterBank Offered Rate (LIBOR). Also, Turkey's imports from Japan (about $400 million annually) are far higher than exports ($37 million) and point to the need for trade deficit financing by Japan so that trade between these countries can continue.

However, part of the debt may be the result of credit extended to foreign firms operating in Greece and Turkey, for which the respective governments accepted responsibility of payment. Moreover, payments for dividends and profits in foreign currencies intensify the accumulation of debt.

Obligations for principal and interest payments are expected to be higher in the future for both countries. Previous loans would start paying interest later, because of the four- to five-year grace period usually allowed. Therefore, borrowing for servicing previous loans is expected to continue.

To cover the deficits in current accounts both countries borrow from abroad. Thus, public borrowing commitments for Greece increased from $242 million in 1970 to $1,442 million in 1982, $2,169 million in 1983, and $3,068 million in 1985. For Turkey, they increased from $487 million in 1970 to $1,577 million in 1982, and $2,450 million in 1983.

EXTERNAL DEBT OF GREECE

After liberation from the Ottomans, Greece faced a number of financial crises, the most severe of which were those of 1830 and 1893. Accumulated loans up to 1893 led the country to bankruptcy. On October 30, 1893, Charilaos Tri- koupes, the prime minister and minister of finance, declared in the Greek Par- liament: "Unfortunately, Gentlemen, we are bankrupt."[11] The government then posponed payments to foreign creditors. The creditor countries, that is, the big powers of the time, mainly Germany, in order to take revenge and to reassure all their claims, pushed Turkey and, directly or indirectly, encouraged Greece to go to war over Thessaly. As a result of the defeat of June-July 1897, Greece was penalized, under the international rules, four million pounds as indemnity to Turkey and also to accept an International Financial Commission of Control. The main income sources of the public sector (revenue from the government monopolies on salt, petroleum, matches, and other items, as well as custom duties, stamps, and tobacco consumption), some 39.6 million drachmas annually, were absorbed by the creditor countries to service the debt. The economy of Greece was largely crippled for decades. At the end of World War II, the foreign public debt amounted to $500 million.

In 1980, the total external debt of Greece was $9.4 billion and in 1985 it reached $18.6 billion (14.1 long-term and 4.5 short-term). From the long-term debt, $12.4 billion was public and publicly guaranteed debt and the rest, $1.7 billion, was private guaranteed debt. Table 8.3 shows the long-term public and publicly guaranteed external debt of Greece from 1970 to 1985.

Interest payments on the external public debt alone were $1,072 million in 1985, compared with only $408 million in 1980, $136 million in 1975, and $41 million in 1970. Debt service, as percentage of GNP, was 5.4 percent in 1985, 2.1 percent in 1980, and 1.0 percent in 1970, while as percentage of exports of goods and services it was 24.7 percent in 1985, compared to 9.4 percent in 1980 and 9.3 percent in 1970.

In addition to the external gross debt, there is a sizeable amount of foreign deposits, primarily by Greek seamen and immigrants. Such deposits were esti- mated to be $6.4 billion in 1985. This is an additional obligation that should be added, along with the accumulated interest, to the total debt of the country, raising that to more than $25 billion in 1985.

Rising oil prices in 1973 and especially in 1979, from $2 per barrel to as high as $34 per barrel, may be considered as a major cause of rapid debt increases. It is estimated that the cumulative additional oil cost for 1973 to 1983 was about $7 billion. Moreover, high interest rates, varying from 10.1 percent to 13.2 percent in 1980–1985, added more burden to debt servicing, from the external high-interest loans taken during that period.

Annual borrowings for servicing external debts add more problems to the Greek economy. Thus, the Bank of Greece borrowed $370 million in the first

Table 8.3

Long-Term Public External Debt, Debt Services, and Nongold Reserves of Greece (million U.S. current dollars)

Year	Long-Term Public Debt	% of GNP	Interest On Public Debt	Total Interest & Principal Payment	Debt Service Percentage of: GNP	Exports	Nongold Reserves
1970	905	8.9	41	101.5	1.0	9.3	194
1975	2,633	13.4	136	530.6	2.7	10.5	964
1976	2,377	10.4	177	530.1	2.2	11.2	881
1977	2,635	9.9	169	574.5	2.0	9.6	1,048
1978	3,123	9.7	206	596.0	1.7	8.5	1,305
1979	3,531	8.9	301	769.2	1.9	8.4	1,343
1980	4,541	10.9	408	936.8	2.1	9.4	1,346
1981	5,817	15.4	715	1,440.7	3.5	12.9	1,022
1982	6,783	17.3	588	1,479.2	3.0	13.3	861
1983	8,193	23.5	755	1,539.3	3.8	18.3	900
1984	9,456	28.3	742	1,856.3	4.0	18.3	954
1985	12,452	40.2	1,072	2,700.0	5.4	24.7	868

Source: United Nations, *Statistical Yearbook;* World Bank, *World Development Report*; and IMF, *International Financial Statistics,* all various issues.

half of 1986 with an interest rate 0.75 percent above that of the LIBOR. Also, in February 1987, it announced the floating of a 200 million deutsche mark bond loan on the West German market with a 6.75 percent fixed interest rate and seven years' duration.

EXTERNAL DEBT OF TURKEY

The external debt of Turkey increased slowly over the postwar years, particularly in the 1970s. The Turkish government, in many cases, resorted to high public expenditures to support import substitution industrialization.[12] This policy, together with the oil price rises, led to large budget and foreign trade deficits. Each government in power thought that the next government would make the adjustments needed. Borrowing from abroad continued and external debts increased. Things became worse with the invasion of Cyprus and the restrictions in Europe regarding the absorption of Turkish workers.

These events and the overvaluation of the Turkish lira led to the debt crisis of the 1970s. Then Turkey moved from the problem of solvency to a serious lack of liquidity and to international intervention, mainly through the Interna-

Table 8.4
Long-Term External Public Debt, Debt Services, and Nongold Reserves of Turkey
(million U.S. current dollars)

Year	Long Term Public Debt	Percent of GNP	Interest On External Debt	Debt Service Ratio % of GNP	% of Exports	Interest %	Non-gold Reserves
1970	1,854	14.4	42	1.4	22.0	5.5	304
1975	3,165	8.5	106	0.7	14.5	8.7	944
1976	3,590	8.8	114	0.7	14.6	8.0	990
1977	4,305	9.5	169	0.8	18.3	10.3	638
1978	6,354	12.2	182	0.9	18.8	12.0	801
1979	10,980	19.0	253	1.1	22.6	14.4	658
1980	15,195	22.4	589	1.7	29.3	12.0	1,077
1981	15,542	23.4	658	2.0	23.1	9.1	928
1982	15,976	29.7	932	3.4	23.3	10.8	1,080
1983	15,444	30.2	1,169	4.6	28.6	14.0	1,288
1984	15,774	31.5	1,048	4.4	22.8	12.6	1,271
1985	17,821	34.7	1,253	6.8	30.8	11.6	1,056

Note: Average grace period 4–5 years. Oil trade deficit was $3,196 million in 1985.
Source: United Nations, *Statistical Yearbook;* IMF, *International Financial Statistics
           Supplementary,* 1985, 123; World Bank, *World Development Report,* various issues;
           and William Cline, *International Debt and the Stability of the World Economy*
           (Washington, D.C.: Institute for International Economics, 1983), 55, 61.

tional Monetary Fund. However, the increase in barter transactions with neighboring oil countries mitigated the debt problem in recent years.

Regarding the size of foreign debt, Turkey seems to be in the same boat with Greece. External gross debt for Turkey was $26.1 billion in 1985. This is the summation of public and publicly guaranteed long-term debt ($17.8 billion), the private nonguaranteed debt ($359 million), the IMF credit ($1.3 billion), and the short-term debt ($6.6 billion).

Interest payments on the external public debt were $1.3 billion in 1985, compared to $658 million in 1980, and $42 million in 1970. Debt service, as percentage of GNP, was 6.8 percent in 1985, 1.7 percent in 1980, and 1.4 percent in 1970, while as percentage of exports of goods and services it was 30.8 percent in 1985, 29.3 percent in 1980, and 22.0 percent in 1970 (table 8.4).

If the deposits of Turkish immigrants in West Germany and elsewhere were added ($5.7 billion), the total debt of Turkey in 1985 can be estimated to be about $32 billion. Such deposits can be withdrawn any time and the Turkish

Table 8.5

Comparison of External Debt with Other Debtor Countries in 1985

Countries	Total External Debt			Per Capita
	U.S. Million $	% of GNP	% of Exports	
Greece	18, 639	57.5	262.8	1,884
Turkey	26,123	49.2	230.3	524
Algeria	15,526	28.0	112.9	715
Argentina	48,444	79.9	467.8	1,585
Bolivia	3,972	152.0	538.5	618
Brazil	106,730	51.3	365.1	787
Chile	20,221	142.2	430.4	1,675
Colombia	14,044	42.6	291.1	491
Egypt	24,342	77.3	366.9	502
Hungary	12,989	65.5	125.8	1,221
Indonesia	35,761	44.9	187.7	219
Israel	23,873	124.1	223.4	5,644
Kenya	4,219	75.6	278.7	208
Korea	47,996	57.7	145.2	1,169
Mexico	97,429	58.3	327.6	1,241
Nigeria	18,348	25.7	141.2	193
Pakistan	12,695	37.6	349.6	132
Peru	13,688	88.2	361.2	695
Philippines	26,184	80.6	330.1	471
Portugal	14,560	73.6	183.4	1,423
Romania	6,977	53.6	184.3	303
Sudan	6,332	77.9	759.7	294
Tanzania	3,609	63.0	103.4	166
Thailand	17,488	46.7	171.4	341
Tunisia	5,250	64.4	193.0	742
Venezuela	32,079	66.0	191.8	1,852
Yugoslavia	19,382	43.6	152.9	838
Zambia	4,482	210.3	529.3	672

Source: *World Bank Debt Tables,* 1986–1987 (Washington, D.C.: *World Bank Publications* 1987); and IMF, *International Financial Statistics,* June 1987.

central and other banks have the obligation to pay the money back, including accumulated interest.

Comparison with Other Countries

Table 8.5 shows the total and per capita debts of Greece and Turkey, as compared to other countries with heavy debts. Greece has the highest per capita debt after Israel, followed by Venezuela, Chile, Argentina, Portugal, and Mexico. As a percentage of GNP, as well as a percentage of exports, external debt is high in both countries. It is about half of the GNP and more than double the exports for Turkey. For Greece, it is more than half of the GNP and close to three times the exports. However, this ratio of the external debt to GNP and/or exports is higher for a number of other nations, especially those of Latin America (which accounted for $384 billion in 1985, compared to $892.4 billion for all developing nations).

PROBLEMS OF DEBT SERVICING

Floating interest rates make debt servicing policies vulnerable to changes in the monetary policies of creditor countries, notably those of the United States and to a lesser extent the large EEC countries and Japan. The decline of the interest rates in recent years has eased the pressure on debtor nations, including Greece and Turkey, as they have to borrow less in order to pay for comparatively lower interests.

Nevertheless, real interest rates, that is nominal rates minus the rates of inflation in the creditor countries, traditionally those of the United States, are high because of the rapid decline in the inflation rates (from 13 percent in 1980 to 1.1 percent in 1986 for the United States). Thus, for the debtor countries, including Greece and Turkey, the real interest rate on external debt was $+7=(11-4)$ percent in 1984 and $+9.4=(10.5-1.1)$ percent in 1986, considering the U.S. inflation and nominal interest rates. Therefore, even though nominal interest rates may be coming down, real interest rates may be going up.

In such cases more exports are required to pay for interest. This, in turn, may lead to lower export prices because of fierce competition in foreign markets for similar Greek and Turkish products. The fact that the relative export prices of these countries are not increasing, but rather declining, makes things worse.

The huge capital outflows to service the external debt drain resources that could be used for investment financing and economic growth. Annual payments for interest and principal stagnate the economy and hinder improvement in living standards or even reduce them to lower levels. Such economic stagnations, or only marginal improvements, reduce total production and increase unemployment, especially in industry and housing.

Inordinate amounts of export earnings are consumed by interest payments. In a way, the annual payment of interest is forcing Greece and Turkey to regress. From that point of view, it is difficult for them to shift from reverse to forward position and turn around the economy, toward low unemployment and high rates of growth.

Part of current income is being used to pay interest on previous borrowing, and the financial hemorrhage continues. Therefore, present and future spending for consumption must drop to make room for higher savings for debt payments. However, more reduction in consumption and living standards may force the governments of these two nations to ask for reduced interest payments, thereby facing the wrath of the creditor banks rather than the wrath of their people.

The gloomy prognosis of these economies does not change much through borrowing to pay interest. Instead, the problem of the debt is intensified, because the new borrowing increases the debt, and the draining of the available resources is postponed to appear again more forcefully in the future. Every dollar or other currency borrowed may be kept by the creditor banks in the form of interest. The debt piles up, while the country does not receive anything.

Comparatively speaking, the public debt of Greece increased from $4.54 billion in 1980 to $12.45 billion in 1985, that is, by $7.91 billion. Interest payment during the same period was $3.87 billion, that is, 50 percent of the borrowing was used to pay interest. In 1985 one-third of the additional public sector borrowing was used to pay interest.

For Turkey, the amount of interest as a proportion of the additional public debt in 1979–1985 was 82 percent. While the external public debt increased from $10.98 billion in 1979 to $17.82 billion in 1985, that is, $6.84 billion, the interest paid during that period amounted to $5.65 billion. This means that Turkey is approaching the stage of borrowing an annual amount equal to the interest payment. If interest rates fall, as they did after 1982, annual interest payments are reduced. For each percentage lower, interest rate payment reduction for the public debt would be about $150 million annually for Greece and around $200 million for Turkey.

Borrowing to pay interest eases the pain in the short run, but it increases it in the long run. It is not used for income-producing assets that increase economic growth, so to pay for itself. On the contrary, it drains the country of potential investment resources, thereby intensifying the problems of inflation and unemployment. Moreover, if the creditors stop lending money or ask for more severe austerity measures, higher unemployment and a further decline in real income, with possible social unrest, would be the result.

Debt for Equity Swaps

To mitigate the problem of debt servicing, debt for equity swaps can be used. This financial measure was successfully used in Latin American and other debtor countries. Investment banks may buy Greek or Turkish government debt from commercial banks at a discount, say at 90 percent, or at par, and present the debt to the central banks of these countries for redemption in local currencies. The investment banks may invest the drachmas or the liras directly in Greece or Turkey, buy shares of local companies, or sell them to other firms planning to invest in these countries. Also, the money can be used for investment in government bonds or other forms of investment agreed upon in advance by the parties involved.

These can be considered as new ways of financing that can be used by Greece and Turkey or other debtor countries in cooperation with foreign bankers to whittle their mountains of debt while, at the same time, fostering investment in their domestic industries. It seems that both countries are willing to pay off some of their debt, provided the funds are then reinvested in local enterprises. They seem to be ready to facilitate swaps of their public debt for equity in problematic private or public enterprises. In such cases, foreign banks themselves may be willing to take and retain shares of Greek and Turkish enterprises or may search for third parties, primarily multinational corporations looking to expand their operations in these countries. With such swaps, both countries can gain because this is a way to attract new and badly needed investment, while at the same time avoid the hemorrhage of their economy from the payment of interest and amortization.

However, the idea of swapping may be attacked by local economists, politicians, and nationalistic factions on the ground that this is a new form of colonialism and imperialism. The fear may be that the transfer of the debt into ownership (equity) may lead to the economic domination of these debtor nations by the creditors for decades, as it has happened in the past. Moreover, the stock markets of Greece and Turkey, which are small and weak to begin with, may be disrupted if the swapping gets heavy. In any case, as long as there are no surpluses in the current accounts of these countries and large payments for debt services continue, debt for equity swaps seem to be a good and viable alternative. Moreover, Greece and, to a lesser extent, Turkey have largely open economies, especially in relation to the EEC. Foreign investment should therefore be guided by economic justifications and not by political inertia and narrow nationalistic concepts.

Moreover, the government of Greece or Turkey may buy back loans from the banks or the investors at negotiated prices, paying money in domestic currency that can be kept in the country for long-term investment. Such a program would reduce the foreign debt and the debt service without generating new inflation. Foreign corporations or banks that want to invest in these countries might be interested in such financial schemes. But these proposals are based primarily on the assumptions that banks and governments would have the political will and economic power to implement them.

New rounds of austerity measures in Greece and Turkey may prove to be counterproductive as such measures undermine political and economic stability and growth. Also, they may depress economic growth in creditor countries as well, as their exports to debtor countries are expected to decline. This, in turn, would reduce imports by creditor countries and decrease export revenues in debtor nations, such as Greece and Turkey. Then, pressures for moratoriums or bankruptcies may prove irresistible. It is a vicious circle from which debtors and creditors are in trouble and nobody is immune. In some cases, competition can be so stiff that debtors may realize that the more they produce for exports, the less they earn. Due to competition from other nations and the paradox of austerity, Greece and Turkey may discover that the faster they run to avoid losing ground, the further they fall behind.

Moreover, greater emphasis on policies to attract equity and other forms of EEC and other countries' investment could mitigate or alleviate the problem of debt servicing. However, potential investors are not likely to favor countries facing foreign exchange shortages, such as Greece and Turkey, and the problem of investment and debt servicing will most probably remain unsolved for some time to come.

Other measures to resolve the debt problem include multi-year rescheduling agreements, clauses linking debt payments to the level of export growth, interest rate caps, or having creditor countries buy up part or all of the outstanding debt. In any case, a realistic alternative would be that all the major players in the debt scenario (commercial banks, the governments concerned, and the International Monetary Fund) devise a long-term solution to the problem. Long-term moratoriums and major rescheduling agreements should reduce present levels of interest payments, probably relating them to a certain percentage of export revenues. In the last case, creditors may act as advertisement agents to stimulate Greek and Turkish exports. Guarantees from creditor countries or groups of countries, such as the EEC, might be needed at some points.

NOTES

1. For example, suppose the basket consists of the deutsche mark (with a share of 50 percent), the British pound (25 percent), and the French franc (25 percent), while the exchange rates in the base period in terms of 1 deutsche mark are: 0.50 British pounds, 4 French francs, and 80 drachmas. If the British pound depreciates to 0.60 and the French franc to 5 francs per mark, then the new exchange rates, in index numbers, will be: 100 for the deutsche mark, 120 for the British pound, and 125 for the French franc. Using the arithmetic average method, we find:

$$(100 \times 0.5) + (120 \times 0.25) + (125 \times 0.25) = 50 + 30 + 31.25 = 111.25.$$

Thus, the depreciation is 11.25 percent for the drachma.

2. International Monetary Fund, *International Financial Statistics* (March 1986), 63. Other unofficial estimates raise total deposits by Greeks to foreign banks to $20 milliion. *TO VIMA* (weekly newspaper), Athens, June 1, 1986, 1, 27.

3. In the past decade, net capital flight from 18 nations with $451 billion in foreign debts totaled $198 billion, according to estimates of the Morgan Guaranty Trust Company. Barnaby Feber, "Capital Flight Adds to Burden of Debtor Nations," *New York Times*, June 9, 1986.

4. For empirical results on the importance of devaluation-cum-liberalization for deficit reduction and economic growth, see Patrick Conway, "Decomposing the Determinants of Trade Deficits: Turkey in the 1970s," *Journal of Development Economics* 21, no. 2 (May 1986): 235–58.

5. The expected rate of economic growth (g) may be determined by the average propensity to save (s), the expected difference in foreign trade (exports − imports) as a percentage of national income (f), and the capital/output or income ratio (v).

$$g = \frac{s + f}{v}$$

Assuming $s = 0.15, f = -0.03$, and $v = 3$, the rate of economic growth would be 4 percent of the national income.

$$g = \frac{0.15 - 0.03}{3} = \frac{0.12}{3} = 0.04$$

6. Hollis Chenery presents data on semi-industrial countries, in which Turkey is included, supporting the argument that emphasis on import substitution slows growth. See his "Interactions between Industrialization and Exports," *American Economic Review*, Proceedings (May 1980): 381–92.

7. For arguments pro and con, see Raymond Vernon, *Sovereignty at Bay: The Multinational Spread of U.S. Enterprises* (New York: Basic Books, 1971).

8. Profits from joint ventures are taxed at rates reaching up to 46 percent in Turkey and Greece (compared with 40 percent in the United Kingdom, 34 percent in the United States, and 50 percent in France and Canada).

9. Hassanali Mehran, "External Debt Management," *Finance and Development* 23, no. 2 (June 1986): 40–41.

10. To keep and increase exports, both nations provide subsidies. Thus Turkey's subsidization of exports amounts to about 15 percent of their value. Branko Milanovic, *Export Incentives and Turkish Manufacturing Exports: 1980–1984*, (Washington, D.C.: World Bank Publications, 1986), 49.

11. By 1893, Greece's foreign indebtedness was consuming 33 percent of its budgetary receipts. Per capita debt increased from 15 drachmas in 1875 to 363 drachmas in 1893. Lefteris S. Stavrianos, *The Balkans since 1453* (New York: Holt, Rinehart and Winston, 1958), 472. Also, John Lampe and Martin Jackson, *Balkan Economic History, 1550–1950* (Bloomington: Indiana University Press, 1982), 381–87; J. A. Levantis, *The Greek Foreign Debt and the Great Powers 1821–1898* (New York: Columbia University Press, 1944), 72–75; and A. F. Freris, *The Greek Economy in the Twentieth Century* (London: Croom Helm, 1986), 26–28.

12. For the Turkish debt problem during its economic crisis, see World Bank, *World Development Report, 1979* (New York: Oxford University Press, 1979), 151 and 155; 1980, 139; Andrew Borowiec, "Turkey Looks to U.S. to Help Resolve Economic Crisis," *New York Times*, January 6, 1979. Also, "At Last the Foreign Investor Is Welcome," *Euromoney*, February 1982 (spec. suppl.), 31; and Chris Carvounis, *The Debt Dilemma of Developing Nations: Issues and Cases* (Westport, Conn.: Quorum Books, 1984), 85–97.

9

Relations with the European Economic Community

INTRODUCTION

The European Economic Community (EEC) was established in 1957 at Rome with six members: Belgium, Luxembourg, the Netherlands, France, West Germany, and Italy, commonly known as the "Inner Six." It was formed to gradually reduce internal tariffs. Because the group was successful, the United Kingdom and Denmark, as well as Ireland, joined the EEC in 1973. Greece and Turkey became associate members of the EEC in 1962 and 1964, respectively, and were allowed to export many of their products to the Community free of duty, while retaining tariffs during a transition period. Special arrangements and association agreements have been negotiated or signed with a number of countries in Africa, the Middle East, Asia, and Latin America, as well as Spain and Portugal.[1] Greece became the tenth member of the EEC in 1981 and Spain and Portugal the eleventh and twelfth members, respectively, in 1986. Turkey is expected to be a member in the near future.

For Spain and Portugal a ten-year transitional period (1986–1995) was provided for agricultural products and a seven-year period for fish, for which tariffs would be gradually reduced by the EEC. For industrial products the transitional period was three years for Spain and seven years for Portugal. No time interval was provided for the introduction of the value added tax for Spain and only three years for Portugal, compared to five years for Greece (extended for another two years later). Also, a seven-year period was provided for the free movement of the Spanish and Portugese workers in the EEC, as was initially provided for Greece.

In spite of the skepticism, the increasing integration of Western Europe, moving toward a United States of Europe, proves that the argument of the inevitability of war among the capitalist powers is weak. The parallel integration process in COMECON (the East European socialist countries),[2] on the other hand, and the increasing cooperation between the two groups indicate that some form of transition, and probably the genesis of a new economic system with elements of both capitalism and socialism, is in progress.

The EEC, through the Competition Directorate, began to enforce ceilings on the value of regional incentives in order to prevent distortions in trade among members and to emphasize continent-wide priorities. However, its actions supplant rather than supplement national efforts. The EEC policies seem to favor imports of labor-intensive goods from less-developed countries and tend to defend older industries by recruiting temporarily migrant workers from less-developed parts of Europe such as Yugoslavia, Greece, and Turkey.[3]

Before Spain and Portugal joined the Common Market, France seemed to have strong objections to Spain's early entry because of the pressures of the producers of competitive Mediterranean products and claimed that Spain should implement the value added tax before it entered the community.[4] Similar objections are presented to Turkey's early entry into the EEC.

To promote a better monetary system, the EEC put into operation, on March 13, 1979, the European Currency Unit (ECU), as Article 107 of the Treaty of Rome enunciated. This new monetary unit is defined as weighted average of member currencies. It was also agreed that in case of fluctuations of member currencies beyond a certain margin (2.25 percent, with some exceptions) the EEC would intervene to preserve monetary stability.

Perhaps the most important and difficult problem of the EEC is that of the agricultural policy regarding subsidy payments from the northern to the southern (Mediterranean) member nations.[5] This is one of the main functions of the Common Agricultural Policy (CAP), which deals with the determination of price-support of Mediterranean agricultural products, including those of Greece, southern Italy, and France as well as those of the new members, Spain and Portugal, and eventually Turkey. The southern European regions press for better prices while northern countries, particularly Germany and Britain, press for low prices of these products. Northern countries producing large amounts of meat and dairy products, such as Denmark, Belgium, and the Netherlands, collect sizeable subsidies. For milk only, subsidies amount to about 30 percent of the total agricultural subsidies. Italy, Spain, Ireland, Greece, and Portugal also receive substantial subsidies for their agricultural products. Germany and Britain are the major contributors to such subsidy payments.

Nevertheless, Britain wants to reduce its net cost on EEC membership from about $2 billion presently to about $500 million a year. Also, West Germany, paying currently about $2 billion a year more than it gets, wants its share on Common Market expenditures to be kept under control in the future.

The main decision-making bodies of the EEC, that is, the Commission, the Council of Ministers, and the Europarliament, determine budgetary revenues and appropriations in accordance with the Treaty of Rome of 1957 and the consequent agreements and directives of the Community.

The treaty establishing the European Economic Community (EEC Treaty) guarantees free movement of persons within the member states. According to

Article 7 of this treaty, "Within the scope of application of the Treaty, and without prejudice to any special provisions contained therein, any discrimination on grounds of nationality shall be prohibited." Therefore, workers can move freely and establish themselves, while self-employed persons can set up and manage undertakings in other member nations. The main goals of this provision and the open-door policy are to facilitate a supranational labor market, to enhance an integrated economic growth, and to promote a closer sociopolitical cooperation.

From a demographic point of view, a serious problem may appear if Turkey becomes a full member of the EEC and enjoys freedom of workers' movement and settlement in other member countries. In such a case, it would be expected that Greece, with relatively higher wages, would be flooded by unemployed or underemployed Turkish workers with the possibility of changing the largely homogeneous nature of the Greek population.

However, the free movement guarantees are not absolute and Articles 48 (3) and 56 (1) permit member states to control the influx of workers on grounds of "public policy," public security, or public health. The term "public policy" is broad and its interpretation has been left largely to the national authorities. From that point of view, Greece may prohibit Turkish workers and entrepreneurs from entering freely and establishing themselves in the country. In the long run, though, such a discrimination on the basis of nationality is expected gradually to be reduced and eventually to be abolished in all EEC states, including Greece, and eventually Turkey. Presently, Greece objects to granting the right of free movement within the EEC to Turkish workers on economic and sociopolitical grounds, according to the accession agreement. Also, long-standing practices of discrimination and oppression against minority population should be stopped.

The EEC has been successful in many aspects. Capital, entrepreneurs, labor, and consumers are free to move and compete in the markets of all member nations. Common economic policies, uniform external tariffs, and coordinated monetary and fiscal measures are rapidly being advanced. Both internal and external trade have increased, primarily because of the reduction in tariffs. Even political cooperation is successfully promoted. The countries of the EEC hold elections for the European Parliament. The members of the Parliament are elected directly by the people of each member country, instead of being selected from members of national parliaments. This process is expected to strengthen the ideals of democracy and the principles of human rights among the members, and indirectly among the countries associated with the Common Market, such as Turkey.

PROBLEMS OF ADJUSTMENT

As a result of Greece's accession to and Turkey's association with the EEC, adjustments are needed, as rapidly as possible, to the economic conditions required by the large EEC market and production technology. As long as they accepted that it is advantageous to enter the EEC, these two countries must also accept that their domestic policies should change accordingly. This means that they have to operate under conditions of an open economy without any consideration of resorting to protective measures, even for infant and moribund industries. Advances in communications and transportation and the rapid diffusion of technology require that not only Greece and Turkey, but eventually all countries, including those of Western Europe, have to adjust their policies toward a global economy. The increased globalization of the world economy creates a spider's web of interdependent interest that no country can ignore without facing dire consequences. The lessons from the British economic policies, during the last quarter of the nineteenth century, suggest that protectionism and retaliation lead to marasmus and decay. As Alfred Marshall stated a century ago, such measures would eventually harm the countries involved. From that point of view, reduction in trade barriers by such groups as the EEC would enhance free trade.

Although Greece's accession to and Turkey's association with the EEC present long-term economic and political advantages, in the short run difficult conditions and even social disturbances may appear. Already, Greece, as an EEC member nation for some years now, faces mounting economic and mainly industrial problems. Likewise, Turkey is expected to face similar problems in the near future. As it was expected, more efficient large industries in the more advanced EEC nations can apply modern capital-intensive technology and produce cheaper and higher-quality products than their Greek and Turkish counterparts. The elimination of tariffs and other protective measures in Greece and Turkey may result, in many cases, in bankrupt or "problematic" industries and enterprises, in both the private and the public sectors.

Greece and Turkey spend large amounts of money for defense to protect themselves from each other. The paradox is that both nations belong to NATO. They are "presumably" allies. Also, they are related economically, because Greece is a member and Turkey an associated member of the EEC. Their needs for further economic cooperation might be so important that eventually they might be forced to reduce their mutual mistrust and look for ways and means to improve the standards of living of their people, instead of spending large amounts of foreign exchange to buy rapidly depreciating military hardware.

From that point of view, Greece, which spends 7.2 percent of GNP for defense (the highest in the NATO alliance) and keeps 2.35 percent of its population on active duty, could ask the EEC creditors to press Turkey, economically and politically, to stop its old-fashioned expansionary policies in the Aegean and withdraw its occupation troops from Cyprus. Then, Greece would be able to use a part of foreign exchange, now spent for defense, for interest and principal debt payments to the EEC banks. It would be in the interest of the creditor banks and the other EEC countries to see Greece and Turkey eliminate their fundamental imbalances between export earnings and interest payments and move to higher development plateaus.

Deep-rooted nationalistic differences between Greece and Turkey have been and still are exploited by major powers for their own interests. The European Economic Community offers a good opportunity to reduce and even eliminate such differences and possible conflicts that proved to be so destructive to the economic and political conditions of both nations. Closer economic and eventually political ties with the EEC would make them partners in a common cause, that of socioeconomic development, as happened with the other EEC member nations.

Instead of fortifying their borders and preparing for further conflicts and wars, their EEC membership could bring them together in lasting economic and technological progress. This is the way to improve the standard of living of their peoples and move forward to new cultural, political, and economic cooperative ventures. Such a cooperation would reduce payments to other countries for army supplies and save resources for domestic investment. Then, unemployment would be reduced and production and income would increase many times over the initial investment (through the domestic multipliers).

Military expenditures constitute a large part of the budget and an even greater portion of foreign trade deficits. Both countries have to buy planes, tanks, rockets, and other armaments from other countries. Their disputes over Cyprus locked them into a mutual military buildup. As the Athenian historian Thucydides observed in the fourth century B.C., "When one side's strength is comparable to another's, their mutual strength is a deterrent to war." As a result, defense spending drains their economies and deprives them of domestic investment and mutual trade. Instead of spending in domestic projects to create jobs and increase per capita income, they spend their limited resources to buy more and more weapons that depreciate and become obsolete rapidly.

To keep up with new military technology, they have to buy new and more expensive war material, squeezing their economies further and tightening the belts of their people so that new resources can be saved for more payments for armaments and so on, ad infinitum. In that way, they create jobs and stimulate the economies of other countries that may have an economic interest in fueling and perpetuating regional conflicts in this strategic area. The EEC membership, therefore, may be considered as a panacea for their mistrust and enormous military spending. Moreover, closer economic relations and eventually accession of Cyprus to the EEC would make things easier for further cooperation of the three countries involved.

Greece, as a member of the EEC, has to adhere to tariffs and restrictions of the European Common Market as a group, regarding trade with other countries, such as the United States, Japan, and Eastern European and Third World countries. The same policies are expected to be applied eventually to Turkey, as well. Thus, although the EEC trade ministers are in favor of free trade, according to the guidelines of the General Agreement on Tariffs and Trade (GATT), they suggested restrictions in imports from the United States, regarding wheat, rice and corn, and gluten cattle feed, if the American government imposes restrictions on European exports of gin, brandy, cordials, and white wine. In order not to impose restrictions, the Europeans want the United States to cut subsidies and protectionist measures that benefit American farmers, and they want Japan to take further steps to open its markets to foreign goods. This is consistent with the agreement of the Tokyo summit of 1986 regarding agricultural products. Although such trade transactions between the EEC, COMECON, the United States, Japan, and other countries do not affect, to a large extent, present foreign trade conditions in Greece and Turkey, expected imports and exports may be influenced significantly in the foreseeable future.

In our nuclear age closer cooperation between neighbor nations becomes imperative. As a result of the fallout from Chernobyl, near Kiev, Russia, in April 1986, large areas of the EEC, along with Greece, Turkey, and other European nations, have been contaminated. Grass, grain, and fruits have been affected and the demand for agricultural and dairy products has largely declined, particularly in West Germany, Greece, and Turkey. This event indicates that ideological and political differences between the EEC and COMECON or other countries should be subordinated to the common efforts of avoiding nuclear or other similar dangers. It shows that nations such as Greece and Turkey must look for the best in each other, not the worst. National and ideological conflicts should give way to common human causes. Economic and political convergence should be emphasized, on regional as well as international levels. Although we cannot undo technology, cooperation to improve it for the protection of humanity becomes urgent, even in nations with a history of mistrust and conflict such as Greece and Turkey.

EEC Competition

Many economists argue that Greece and Turkey would enjoy significant advantages from the EEC. Others feel that they would become a "provincial backwater" and may face serious hardships, at least with respect to some sensitive and protected industries. It can be argued that the accession of Greece and eventually Turkey to the EEC would not entail a catastrophe for their economies, nor would it provide a panacea for all their problems. From an economic, and especially from a sociopolitical point of view, there would seem to be no better alternatives in the future. Even if Greece and Turkey remained outside the EEC, most of the economic results, particularly in foreign trade, would occur anyway.

For protected small-scale and old-fashioned industries producing such goods as footwear, cloth, leather, and metal products, there is heavy pressure. Complete elimination of tariffs on imports from the EEC and tariff reduction on imports from non-EEC countries (in harmony with those of the EEC) force a number of large and small industries and handicrafts operations to close. Given that a large number of the Greek and Turkish firms employ fewer than ten persons, it is obvious that EEC competition will wipe out many of these small enterprises. Moreover, the high elasticity of imports for their products or close substitutes would make things worse. In order to survive EEC competition, such small enterprises should merge with larger ones that are able to apply modern technology of mass production. However, the fact that labor cost is lower (about half in Greece and even less in Turkey) compared with that of the EEC gives an advantage to these labor-intensive industries over their EEC counterparts.

Nevertheless, the intensive competition from the EEC firms may have forced Greek and Turkish entrepreneurs and middlemen earning high profits to reduce their luxurious and conspicuous consumption in favor of productive investment. But in the near future such EEC competition may prove detrimental to these economies; unemployment may be expected to increase, emigration of skilled persons may intensify, and the balance of trade could deteriorate. From that point of view, there may be good opportunities for Greece and Turkey to increase exports to Balkan neighbors and the Middle East. EEC duties for Greek industrial products have been eliminated since 1974, and somewhat reduced for Turkey, and a large market thrust for these products is not expected. Also, tax advantages and government subsidies to exporters, amounting to about 20 percent of their value for Greece, are to be eliminated.

A serious cause of high trade deficits and the huge debts of Greece and Turkey is the low level of investment, especially in the 1980s. The low level of private investment, in turn, is due primarily to the lack of confidence, bureaucratic inertia, lack of innovative entrepreneurship and modern management, and strong competition from well-established firms in the EEC and other advanced countries. Capital owners prefer short-run financial investment in stocks, bonds, and other instruments, or deposits with financial institutions, with quick returns, at the neglect of long-term real investment in plant and equipment. Thus, for Greece, investment in plant and equipment continues to decline (from 18 billion drachmas in 1974 to 16 billion drachmas in 1985, at 1970 prices).

As to the relationship with the other member nations of the EEC, Greece seems to behave like "a newly married lady dreaming about the good things expected from marriage but ignoring the difficult and painful problems she has to face." Greece enjoys agricultural subsidies, loans, and support for regional investment projects, but ignores or neglects the harmful results to the domestic industry from the EEC's stiff competition. Given that Greece has been a member of the EEC for some time now, rapid and full adjustment must be pursued. The same is true for Turkey as an associate member of the EEC. This means that entrepreneurs and investors should not consider regional or national levels of production and limited markets but, instead, huge EEC markets and large production units with advanced industry and technology. They have to produce cheaper and better products. Otherwise, existing firms might not be able to survive and new, infant firms might be unable to stand on their own feet.

It can be argued that Greece's accession to and Turkey's association with the EEC would be beneficial in the long run from both an economic and political point of view. However, for some years to come, severe problems of unemployment, high trade deficits, and reduction in the real per capita income may be the result. Traditional manufacturing industries, such as textiles, food processing, and similar industries, may not be able to survive competition. Already a number of them have become problematic and operate uneconomically, based on government support and loans that are not expected to be paid back.

As mentioned earlier, a major reason for the debts of Greece and Turkey is their trade deficits. Imports are always higher than exports. The gap is so large that the earnings from tourism, shipping, and immigrant remittances (invisibles) are not sufficient to cover the difference. As a result, deficits appear in current accounts, particularly with the EEC. These deficits, in turn, usually lead to foreign borrowing.

Efforts to reduce imports of consumer or semi-luxurious products are expected to have better results in the short run than aggressive strategies to increase exports. Exported products of both countries, such as fruit, vegetables, and other agricultural or semi-manufacturing products, face strong competition in the EEC and other markets, primarily from Spain, Portugal, Italy, and, to some extent, France. For some products, there is severe competition even between Greece and Turkey. For example, you may see small packages of Greek figs sold for $1.50 in foreign supermarkets, while almost the same Turkish figs are sold for only $1.10. Similar differences can be observed in honey, other fruits, and so on.

On the other hand, industrial exports amount to only about 20 percent of the total production in both countries. Although exports are increasing, year after year, the rise in imports is so high, especially in Greece, that it is difficult to reduce the huge trade deficits.

As long as the world and particularly the EEC economies are growing, austerity measures in one country, say Greece or Turkey, would not have a noticeable impact on the EEC economic growth rates. One country's slower growth would not reduce the growth rates of more advanced participants in the EEC trading system. Similarly, additional exports of Greece or Turkey or any other small member or associated member of the EEC would not generate deterioration in everyone else's terms of trade. Therefore, additional exports of these two deficit countries could be absorbed by the other growing economies without much pain and dislocation in the more developed member nations, such as Germany, France, Britain, Italy, and the Netherlands.

GREECE'S MEMBERSHIP IN THE EEC

The association agreement of Greece with the EEC was signed on July 9, 1961, and became effective November 1, 1962. A transitional period of 22 years was allowed for gradual tariff reduction and preparation for full membership. With the agreement of May 28, 1979, Greece became the tenth member of the EEC, effective January 1, 1981. Despite the country's full membership there were provisions for a five-year transitional period (1981–1985) for agricultural products in general and a seven-year period for tomatoes and peaches, for which tariffs would be gradually reduced by the EEC. A similar five-year period was provided between the EEC and Denmark, Ireland, and the United Kingdom. Another seven-year transitional period was provided for the free movement of Greek workers into EEC countries.

Total Greek exports to the EEC (about $3 billion annually) are less than half of imports. This means that the EEC should be equally or more interested in keeping Greece in its economic sphere of influence because it sells far more to Greece than it buys. Moreover, with the incorporation of the sizeable Greek merchant fleet, the EEC would enhance its maritime power. At the same time, Greece needs the market of the EEC, where it sells about half of its exports. Now, trade policy is basically dictated by Articles 110–116 of the Treaty of Rome and by Articles 115–117 of Greece's EEC Accession Act.

The value of future business transactions of Greece with the EEC is expected to widen the gap in the balance of trade, since imports are expected to increase more than exports.[6] There would be some improvement in the balance of payments as a result of incoming investment capital introduced by foreign multinationals, mainly from the EEC. However, the inflow would not be great, because foreign firms generally use host-country sources of financing, making it difficult for local enterprises to use domestic savings for investment. Nevertheless, the inflow of capital for speculation and for the purchase of land will be intensified, driving real estate prices still higher.

Greece's membership in the EEC would mean more specialization and expansion in such agricultural lines as peaches, raisins, grapes, lemons, oranges, olives, and tobacco. In general, agriculture would be expected to be in an advantageous position when the EEC subsidies for it are considered.

In addition, many Greek farmers will be forced to modernize their production through mechanization, and probably will have to form larger farm units for cheaper production and distribution of their products. This is particularly important for Greek agriculture because of the fragmentation of land into small, inefficient lots (stamps). Similar favorable effects are expected in mining products, particularly bauxite, lignite, and aluminum. Another sector expected to benefit from the accession is transportation, especially shipping, mainly because of the country's geographical position and its large commercial fleet. The EEC uses oil to cover about 50 percent of its energy needs, and 90 percent of it is imported, mainly from the Middle East. Greek ships can transport oil, as well as other products, to and/or from the EEC. The Greeks, then, can continue to make their fortunes from Homer's "wine-dark sea."

From a demographic point of view, long-run expectations suggest that large numbers of Greeks would emigrate to western Europe and a number of other Europeans would establish themselves in Greece. As an outpost on the European frontier, Greece would become the eastern Mediterranean balcony of the EEC. As long as free movement of population and unrestricted property acquisition are allowed, rich Europeans, primarily Germans who exhibit a strong fondness for Greek touristic and archaeological centers, would settle permanently in the country, a process that has already begun, primarily in the islands. Such an economic "invasion" will be intensified when another EEC candidate, Turkey, with many unemployed or underemployed workers, becomes a full member of the EEC and enjoys the same freedom of movement and settlement in other member countries. *Mutatis mutandis*, similar results would be expected for the new EEC members, that is, Spain and Portugal.

However, since 1981, the EEC imposed, at times, variable import levies upon the main agricultural products imported from Greece and did not subsidize transportation costs for exports as expected. On the contrary, it offered better preferential treatment for the Turkish products that competed with similar Greek products. Moreover, Greece expected the EEC to absorb surplus agricultural products but the EEC failed to do so. In addition, it obliged Greece to cover a portion of its needs in sugar by imports from third countries, to abolish clearings with East European countries, and to modify trade policy with third countries. As a result, the main exported agricultural products, primarily peaches, oranges, lemons, tomatoes, and other fruits and vegetables, suffered extensive losses. During the initial stages of Greece's full membership in the EEC there was an upsurge in the value of Greek imports from the other countries of the EEC, whereas the value of exports remained relatively stable or declined, thereby raising the trade deficit with the EEC. To avoid further deterioration of trade, Greece asked for certain deviations from the initial agreement of accession.

Greece, though, continues to face severe hardship in agricultural exports, particularly peaches, large amounts of which remained unsold and were finally buried in large ditches all over Greece.[7] Moreover, certain protected industries producing such goods as metal products, cloth, leather, and footwear have been under heavy pressure because of the serious competition they encounter from similar EEC products.

As a result of tariff reduction, total tax revenue may not be sufficient to cover budget deficits and therefore inflation may continue to undermine the Greek economy. To protect domestic industry and to continue collecting tax revenue, Greece was permitted to reduce taxes gradually (regulative taxes), so that by 1989, tax rates on domestic products and those imported from the EEC would be the same.

As a result of accession, Greek tariffs were cut by 20 percent and quota restrictions were abolished in the first stage. Tariffs are gradually to be eliminated by 1989. However, Greece's trade deficit with the EEC continues to grow at an alarming pace. It increased to about $3 billion annually, adding to the already high overall trade deficits of the country, which amount to some $6 billion annually.

As expected, protected sleepy Greek firms have been caught unprepared by the imported European products that flooded the Greek markets. To everyone's surprise, not only manufactures but also food products, where Greece was expected to perform well, came under heavy competitive pressure from the EEC. Efficient production and distribution methods by other European partners manage to outsell Greek food products even in Greece. Thus, the food trade surpluses of previous years turned into deficits. Moreover, Greece cannot buy cheaper food from other nonmember countries because of the EEC farm policy, which asks for high import levies.

To reverse this unfavorable trend, the Greek government announced the devaluation of the drachma by 15.5 percent at the beginning of 1983. At the same time, it invoked a clause in the accession agreement to restrict imports from the EEC to the 1980 levels. Such a devaluation was expected also to stimulate tourism, shipping, and immigrant remittances. However, this and a similar devaluation of the drachma of 15 percent in 1985 did not prove to be of much help for the improvement of the balance of payments.

It is expected that Greek exports to the other EEC countries (around $3 billion annually) will rise, but not as much as imports, which are about double of exports. The increase in exports will take place primarily in agricultural products, for which EEC tariffs were eliminated after the assigned transitional period. However, exports of industrial products, for which EEC duties have already been eliminated, are not expected to increase as much. Another reason for low expectations for increases in industrial exports is the elimination of government subsidies and other tax privileges for such products as a result of Greece's accession to the EEC. Therefore, the gap in the balance of trade would, most probably, continue to be large for some years to come. Perhaps Greece has greater opportunities to increase exports to other neighboring Balkan and Middle Eastern countries than to other EEC member nations. From that point of view, EEC membership should not frustrate efforts for further economic cooperation with other Balkan and Mediterranean countries.

Transportation is a sector in which the accession to the EEC should have beneficial effects. It should continue to play its traditional favorable role in the economy in general and in the country's balance of payments, in particular. The large Greek merchant fleet would continue to play its traditional transportation role in international shipping.[8] However, earnings from shipping depend primarily on changes in world trade. Empirical research indicates that Greek shipping earnings are affected by changes in the value of world exports and, to a lesser extent, by the number of seamen.

Greece receives support payments from the EEC (Fond Europeen d'Orientation et de Garantie Agricole, or FEOGA), as a result of the implementation of Regulation 355/77, for investment in storage facilities for wheat and corn and the processing of fruits and vegetables, as well as for standardization of olives and olive oil. Moreover, there are annual payments for the price support of olive oil, sugar, tobacco, wheat, wine, peaches, tomatoes, and other fruits and vegetables, as well as for the support of the fishing industry.

Greece used to be opposed to Spain's early entrance to the EEC because of expected strong competition from such agricultural products as olive oil, wine, tomatoes, and fruits. However, Greece changed its position and supported the entry of Spain and Portugal. The conclusion was that the accession of these two countries would strengthen the bargaining position of the Mediterranean group of nations in the EEC for policies favorable to their products.

Regarding the free movement of EEC persons among the member nations, no visa issuance or other similar written statement is required, except for the showing of a passport or identification card. However, Greece continues to require that all persons entering the country fill out a special entrance card. The responsible EEC authority protested such incidents and asked Greece to stop this police-type practice that is a violation of the Treaty of Rome.

For developmental purposes, Greece receives, at times, additional aid from the Regional Fund of the EEC, mainly for infrastructural projects, such as power plants, railway improvements, and other facilities. With a recent agreement, the Community would finance regional investment in Western Greece and the Peloponnesus worth 363 million European Currency Units (ECUs). Moreover, in the context of the Integrated Mediterranean Programs (IMPs), the Council of Ministers of the EEC allocated $222 million to the Aegean Islands and $252 million to the region of Attica.

The EEC objects to subsidization of the moribund or problematic enterprises by member nations, on the ground that it violates its charter (Article 92 G1). However, Greece argues that its legislation (Greek Law 1386/1983), which supports such problematic firms, does not affect trade transactions among EEC member nations. It simply aims at the satisfaction of the claims of the creditors and provisos of such firms, while avoiding eventual bankruptcies and higher unemployment. In any case, it seems that more time and more investigation are needed to conclude if such a practice of subsidies to the Greek and eventually Turkish moribund enterprises violates EEC regulations.

TURKEY'S RELATIONSHIP WITH THE EEC

In July 1959, Turkey applied for association with the EEC. However, both parties were hesitant. Turkey's industry was weak to face free competition and the EEC feared that Turkey would require significant economic assistance and that its cheap agricultural exports would present problems in the Community. Nevertheless, Turkey became an associated member of the EEC in September 1963. By the end of the summer of 1970, the EEC concurred in Turkey's entry into the second stage of the development plan. In September 1980, the EEC imposed a protocol freezing the association agreement with Turkey because of the abolishment of democracy and human rights by the then established military dictatorship.

In order to prepare the ground for unfreezing the protocol that the EEC imposed, Turkey promised a number of investments and trade opportunities to the EEC member nations. To revitalize the traditional relations with West Germany, Turkey offered investment advantages for energy, tourism, and other projects, while negotiating the purchase of Tornado-type aircraft produced by Germany, Britain, and Italy together, as well as Mirage from France.

In order to have the support of the other EEC nations, Turkey offers advantages for the establishment of large industrial projects, hotels and other tourist resorts, banks and other financial companies, and transportation and trade facilities, so that the EEC can expand to the markets of Islamic nations. To the new EEC Iberian nations, Spain and Portugal, Turkey offers eventual support for favorable treatment of their agricultural and other Mediterranean products by the other EEC nations.

However, objections to the entrance of Turkey into the EEC are advanced by Greece, mainly because of the bad treatment of the Greek populations in Istanbul (Constantinople) and the islands of Tenedos and Imvros in the Aegean. The confiscation of the properties of the Greeks in Turkey, illegal occupation of part of Cyprus by Turkish troops, and the harassment in the Aegean Sea are all additional reasons for such Greek objections. As a result, Greece is prepared even to exercise veto, according to the Treaty of Rome, to block Turkey's accession to the EEC. In 1986, Greece refused to sign the related EEC-Turkey protocol if Turkey does not lift the discriminatory decree that affects Greeks in Istanbul.

More than one-third (38 percent) of Turkish exports are absorbed by the EEC (a slight increase from 1960), 3 percent by the United States (a decline from 24 percent in 1960 and 10 percent in 1970), and only 3 percent by the COMECON countries (a decline from 9 percent in 1960 and 1970). The largest part (45 percent) is absorbed by the Middle East and North Africa (an increase from 22 percent in 1980).

In addition to the stable and growing trade between Turkey and the Common Market, Greece, as a member of the EEC, can play a role regarding economic aid to Turkey by Athens' membership in the European Community. Because of the disputes between the two countries, primarily over Cyprus, Greece threatens not to approve future applications of Turkey to enter the EEC. Also, Greece opposed the release (unfreezing) of about $560 million appropriated to Turkey by the EEC (fourth financial protocol).

During the first five years after the association, concessions were given by the EEC to four basic agricultural exports, while the Protocol of 1970 provided for free access of all Turkish industrial products to the EEC, except textiles and petroleum. In addition, a loan of $175 million was given by the EEC over the first five years of the association and another one of the same amount in 1970–1975.

As a result of the Turkish invasion of Cyprus in 1974, relations with the EEC came to a low point and trade deteriorated. Thus, the trade deficit of Turkey with the EEC increased to $1.7 billion in 1974 compared to only $500 million in 1973. The decline of trade relations with the EEC continued up to the recent past, but trade with the Middle Eastern countries increased substantially. However, Europe is gradually again becoming Turkey's major market—a trend that is expected to continue until 1995, when Turkey is scheduled to become a full member of the EEC.

After the military coup on September 12, 1980, the EEC governments became critical of the loss of human rights and freedoms in Turkey. Particularly, the European Parliament and the Council of Europe expressed concern about the dissolution of trade unions and political parties and the imprisonment of their leaders and other people who disagreed with the regime. Although Britain, West Germany, and Belgium have been sympathetic to the military regime of Turkey, following the U.S. foreign policy, other EEC members are reluctant to admit Turkey to the EEC until democracy has been fully restored.

The 1970 Protocol envisaged the abolishment of all tariffs and other barriers between Turkey and the EEC over a period of 12 to 22 years, beginning in 1973, as well as the harmonization of Turkish external tariffs until full membership by 1995. However, because of the weak Turkish industry and the expected economic burden on other members from Turkey's cheap agricultural products, mainly cotton, and related EEC subsidies, full membership is not predicted to take place until the year 2000.

Another serious problem is that of free movement of labor provided by the above protocol. It would seem that it is impossible for the Community and especially for Germany to absorb the large and growing numbers of unemployed Turks. Germany with 1.6 million Turks, out of 2 million in the EEC, faces problems of integration and possible repatriation of the Turkish workers. This is a sensitive issue for Ankara because of the substantial remittances received every year that are so valuable for closing the gap in the trade balance.

The "invisible" sources, especially tourism and emigrant remittances, will continue to cover part of trade deficits. But these sources and, even more, deposits from abroad, especially from emigrants, are subject to international and domestic political and economic changes—and therefore are unstable and unpredictable.

However, there is nothing wrong with Turkey, Greece, or any other country searching simultaneously for trade expansion and, possibly, other regional associations to the south, the east, or elsewhere. Such trade expansion would make the country a more independent and less subservient partner in the EEC or any other group. This policy would raise its prestige and improve its bargaining position in the future, instead of its remaining a poor satellite of the EEC or an underdeveloped nation. Therefore, Turkey should explore the possibility of entering other economic groups or signing trade agreements with other nations, mainly other Mediterranean nations that import large amounts of Turkish products. Also, accession to the EEC might be instrumental and helpful toward closer cooperation between the EEC and COMECON.

Most difficulties would occur in the industrial sector, mainly manufacturing. Depending on the degree of tariff protection and subsidization, certain industries may expand, but most of them will be suppressed or wiped out. More important, the establishment of new ones would be difficult.[9] It is not only that most European industries are already more advanced and can produce cheaper and better products, but also that they will continue innovating and modernizing, making it difficult for old or new Turkish industries to compete or even to survive.

From a sociopolitical point of view, as an integral part of the EEC, Turkey can expect to enjoy more protection and more respect from other countries. Moreover, the social structure of the country may improve, and its democratic institutions may be strengthened, as recent events in other EEC countries indicate.

As an associated member, Turkey was allowed to export many products to the EEC countries duty free, while gradually reducing tariffs on imports from the EEC during the transition period of association. Turkish agricultural products would enjoy preferential treatment compared to those of other third countries. The EEC would be expected to absorb surpluses at guaranteed prices, subsidize agricultural exports, and support regional development and structural adjustment in the Turkish economy.

The complete elimination of Turkish tariffs on imports from the EEC leads not only to the reduction of customs revenue, but also to losses of income and employment. This is so because of the replacement of domestically produced industrial as well as agricultural goods (for which productivity is less of that in the EEC) with imported goods. Special treatment of the Turkish products, along with similar Mediterranean products, seems to be needed for some time to come. In that case, the negative effects of the accession could be reduced through redistribution of taxes and EEC grants for regional and social development, especially for the poor areas.

Turkish agriculture is inferior to that of the other EEC countries. The average size of each farm in Turkey is smaller, compared with the EEC nations, farms are scattered over large distances, and the level of agricultural equipment is very low. Furthermore, agricultural population is more than 50 percent, compared to less than 10 percent, on the average, for the EEC. As a result, farm productivity in Turkey is far lower than that in the EEC countries, and average income is even lower. The policy of the EEC, which favors large agricultural units with modern equipment, leads to higher productivity in the long run, but to more unemployment and misery for the small and medium-size farmers in the short run. Turkish farmers, with limited or no proper training, may try in vain to find jobs in the industrial sector, which is already under heavy pressure from EEC competition. Therefore, pressure for migration of young farmers to European industries will continue.

Close relations of Turkey with the EEC mean that the economy is more open to international or Common Market competition. This means that if Turkey is unable to achieve the desired structural changes and improve its industrial position, it might be forced to specialize even more in the primary sector. Competition is expected to be more intensive after the reduction of tariffs on imports from the EEC for such protected products as clothing, footwear, and metals. Moreover, the reduction of Turkish tariffs on similar imports from third countries to the levels of the EEC would make things worse.

Consequently, the government and the financial institutions, in exercising their fiscal and credit policies, should emphasize productive investment, mainly in the manufacturing and the exporting sectors. The fact that labor is relatively cheaper in Turkey than in the other EEC countries should make such investment successful in reducing inflation and improving the balance of trade. Perhaps investment in entrepreneurial and technical training is the most promising endeavor to be pursued by public policy, both for long-term employment and higher productivity.

Turkey wants full EEC membership, but serious obstacles lie in its path that may delay actual membership until the end of the century. In addition to the Greek objections for economic reasons and the conflict over Cyprus, doubts are expressed about Turkey's fitness for membership by other EEC members as well. As mentioned previously, there are fears that Western Europe would be flooded with Turkish emigrant workers, while large subsidies would be paid by the EEC to the agricultural sector, which absorbs about half of the workforce and accounts for only 16 percent of gross domestic product. Also, there is an ambiguity in Turkey's claim to be considered European at all, despite its recognition in the Treaty of Paris in 1856 and its associate membership in the EEC since 1964. Moreover, there are fears that EEC membership could provoke an Iran-style Islamic fundamentalist backlash among the poor classes, although most Turks adhere to Sunni rather than Shia Islam.

Regarding reduction and eventual elimination of protective measures, by agreement with the EEC, Turkey was to dismantle its tariff barriers to EEC products between 1973 and 1995. However, little has been done so far to prepare for this eventuality, mainly because of fears of severe competition from European goods when the tariff walls come down.

Improvements in the Democratic System

Because Greece wants to remain a member of, and Turkey wants to join, the EEC, they both have to respect the majoritarian political system and implement the Western European-style democracy with political and economic liberty. For material growth to coexist with such a democratic system, socioeconomic liberty should be preserved as a primary virtue for all EEC nations and Turkey. It should be noted though that economic liberty or free market capitalism has positive and negative sides. It promotes individual incentives and ambitions but it may also produce greed, monopoly, and diverse disparities in individual wealth. It seems that, for the common good, a careful balance, a compromise between majoritarian democracy and laissez-faire economics, should be pursued by the countries considered.

Accepting the reasoning of coexistence of a majoritarian political system and economic liberty, as well as that of the private and the public sectors, transfer of inefficient public enterprises to the general public, the investors, and the employees (with perhaps more favorable terms) should be pursued. This policy, which is practiced presently in Britain, France, and other EEC countries, is particularly important for Greece and Turkey, because of the enormous deficits in many of such public enterprises and economic organizations. However, to avoid concentration of economic power and monopolization, no shareholder should be allowed to own more than, say, 15 percent, as happened with British Airways and other enterprises.

From a political point of view, EEC member states should respect and implement democracy and the civil rights of their citizens and harmonize their foreign policies with those of the European community. For Turkey to achieve a favorable consideration of its application for accession to the EEC it should abolish the martial law prevailing in five major provinces and the state of emergency that still applies to some eleven other provinces.

Moreover, free elections, with all political parties participating, and human freedoms must be restored in Turkey, while the holding of political detainees and torture reported by Amnesty International should stop. If genuine democracy and political freedoms are restored, then the Budget Committee of the European Parliament would release a sum of 19 million ECUs from the third financing protocol destined for Turkey.

On the other hand, some EEC members oppose Turkey's accession to the EEC on the grounds of human rights violations, lack of democratic protection, and continuation of notorious torture. Relentless interrogations, beatings, and electric shock torture continue, according to recent reports. Thus a 5-year-old boy was given electric shocks in front of his parents in order to force them to "confess." A young woman and mother of a child who was tortured for twenty days in the Gayrettepe Police Station in Istanbul said, "It's not the electricity that hurts, it's the convulsions and hitting yourself during them."[10]

The restoration of trade union freedoms and the respect of human rights and cultural identities of minorities such as Kurds and Armenians are also to be implemented for the Turkish accession to the EEC. From that point of view, it would seem that a long time would be needed for Turkey to be ready for a full EEC membership, no matter how strategically important it is locationwise.

TAX HARMONIZATION AND OUTLAYS

Tax harmonization with the EEC standards, as articles 95–99 of the initial EEC Treaty of Rome provide, means that Greek and eventually Turkish tax policy must consider a relative increase in direct taxes and a decrease or no increase in indirect taxes. Since direct taxes are paid primarily by high-income people and indirect taxes by low-income people, such a policy would not increasingly damage the welfare of low-income classes. The gradual reduction of tariffs on imports from third countries to the same level as those levied by the EEC, and on imports from the EEC, is expected to decrease the relative share of excises and other indirect taxes. Then Greece and Turkey will be forced to increase other taxes to provide needed governmental revenue or to decrease public sector spending.

The Greek and Turkish economies need structural changes toward industrialization and improvement in the public sector, particularly in their tax system. Close relations with the EEC are expected to speed up such structural changes and bring some limitations on matters of policy making, not only on tariffs and foreign trade in general, but also on a number of domestic economic policies, such as adjustment of taxes, elimination of export subsidies, budgetary appropriations, exchange rate fluctuations, and the like. The newly introduced value added tax (VAT) in Greece and Turkey, in place of the turnover tax, is a case in point. Given that the laws and regulations of the Community must be observed by member nations, Greek and eventually Turkish laws on taxation and related matters will have to be adjusted to those of the EEC.

The value added tax, or consumption tax, as it may be called, was first introduced by France in 1954. It was adopted by the First and Second Directives of the EEC in 1967 and was implemented by the member nations. Also, the Sixth Directive of 1977, as modified by the Ninth Directive of 1978 and later directives, aims at the improvement and simplification of the VAT throughout the European Economic Community.

The member nations, however, are permitted enough flexibility to apply their own policies on matters of incentives for investment and the development of a tax system that would stimulate productivity and reduce inflation. In the case of Greece a transitional period was provided initially for the review and application of the value added tax and other reforms that were badly needed, independent of EEC membership. Turkey, though, has plenty of time to implement tax reforms that are expected to reduce bureaucracy and increase the productivity of the public sector. Moreover, there will be less confusion over tax legislation, which has resulted in the expansion of the legal profession in Greece and Turkey.

About 50 percent of total EEC revenue comes from the value added tax (VAT) which is 1 percent of those collected by the member countries, 33 percent from custom duties, and 13 percent from levies on certain agricultural products, such as sugar. For member nations that have not introduced the VAT as yet, GNP is used as the basis of VAT calculation.

Net budgetary allotments from the EEC are received primarily by Italy, Greece, Ireland, and the Netherlands, while West Germany and Britain usually have net payments. As a result of their demand for budget cuts in farm spending, EEC meetings end, at times, in deadlocks, leaving the twelve-nation common market on the brink of bankruptcy. On the other hand, it is argued that, in terms of investment and new technology, Japan and the United States are leaving Europe behind.

The EEC increased economic cooperation with neighboring countries, particularly Yugoslavia. Thus, in 1976 the European Investment Bank was authorized by its board of governors to grant loans of $68.5 million to Yugoslavia for such projects of mutual interest as the extension of the high tension electricity network and its connection with Greece, Italy, and other European countries, as well as the construction and widening of the trans-Yugoslavian motorway, which provides a direct link between the Community on the one hand and Greece, Turkey, and the Middle East on the other. This last project is particularly important for Greece and Turkey to facilitate transit traffic and foreign trade.

The Treaty of Rome, establishing the EEC, required that benefits of Community membership be evenly spread among its members. In reality, however, inequalities among the regions and countries of the Community are growing larger instead of diminishing, especially between the northern regions and the southern or Mediterranean regions. This trend endangers the Community's cohesion and forces the EEC budgetary authorities to change policies toward export subsidy payments for various agricultural products.

A serious problem of the Common Agricultural Policy (CAP) of the EEC is the establishment of upper limits on the production of dairy and other products and the determination of common agricultural prices, including price support of Mediterranean products. About 60 percent of total EEC revenue is spent annually for price support of agricultural products.

REALIGNMENT OF CURRENCIES

On the international financial sector, the rapid development of the EEC and world money markets cannot leave the monetary policies of Greece and Turkey unaffected. The recent divergence of a rapidly growing "symbolic" economy of money, credit, and capital and a slowly growing "real" economy of goods and services has repercussions upon the determination of exchange rates, interest rates, and related policy measures in both countries. They both borrow large amounts of money from the international capital market, which accounts for more than $300 billion in total transactions annually, and both are affected by interests and amortizations they have to pay, respectively. The epidemic of too much trading of money, bonds, and stocks, representing commercial assets, and not operation of the real assets in the production process, presents dangers not only for the more-developed EEC and other countries but for the less-developed economies of Greece and Turkey as well.

The new trend of creating homogeneous money market services in the EEC and expanding the role of the financial institutions on a worldwide basis requires significant reforms and innovations in the Greek and Turkish, largely stagnating, banking systems. Also, international competition in banking and money markets will, sooner or later, force deregulation, more efficient operations, and aggressive marketing in Western Europe and in Greece and Turkey in particular. With the gradual shift of more financial activities to the money markets of the EEC, innovative reforms in Greek and Turkish banks, with perhaps less emphasis on their intermediate role and more on financial investment activities, become imperative.

Although the Greek drachma (GD) and the Turkish lira (TL) are not fully convertible into other European hard currencies, primarily the German mark, realignments of the currencies of the EEC nations (except Britain in 1979), linked under the European Monetary System (EMS), and currency speculations affect exchange rates and monetary policies in Greece and Turkey. Interest rate differentials, trade performance, differences in productivities, strikes and other disturbances force down the values of weak currencies, notably the GD and the TL, and may drain the reserves of the respective central banks. All these events put pressure on the EMS, where currencies are permitted to fluctuate (by $+2.25$ percent against one another and $+6$ percent for the Italian lira), and are expected to affect more and more future monetary decisions in Greece and Turkey.

Greece, along with the other EEC members (except Britain, West Germany, Luxembourg, and the Netherlands), retains curbs on capital movements. However, according to the proposal of the Executive Commission of the EEC, all the trade and capital barriers within the twelve EEC states would be eliminated by the end of 1992. In addition to free movement of commodities and investments, current and deposit account operations, short-term securities, and financial loans and credit would be covered. Also, the European Parliament endorsed a proposal by the EEC Commission to abolish taxes on stock market transactions, varying from 10 percent in Ireland and Denmark to 5 percent in Britain, 3 percent for France, 2.5 percent for Germany, and 1.2 percent for the Netherlands. Greece, Luxembourg, and Portugal have no such taxes, while Spain has proportional excise stamps. These measures are expected to promote trade in securities and to improve the competitiveness of the EEC as an international financial center. The less-developed Turkish economy, however, needs far more time to introduce free movement of capital and to adjust itself to related EEC rules.

Exchange Rates and the ECU

Economic development and closer cooperation of the EEC nations lead to their gradual currency unification. The introduction of the European Currency Unit (ECU), although weak at the beginning, slowly and steadily gains ground among the member nations and eventually in international financial markets.[11] Because of low inflation and the growing, stable economies of West Germany, Britain, and France, their currencies, especially the German mark, are among the soundest currencies in the world, making the ECU also an important monetary unit.

The European Currency Unit is based on a currency basket that includes the currencies of the EEC member nations, but with different weights. The German mark carries the most weight (32 percent), followed by the French franc (19 percent), the British pound (15 percent), and the Italian lira (10.2 percent). Less weight has been assigned to the currencies of smaller member nations, such as the Netherlands (10.1 percent), Belgium (8.2 percent), Denmark (2.7 percent), Greece (1.3 percent), Ireland (1.2 percent), and Luxembourg (0.3 percent). The two new members, Spain and Portugal, are not expected to have much influence on the value of the ECU because of their relatively weak economies. Although the influence of the Greek drachma compared to that of the ECU is very small and that of Turkish lira nil, they are both largely affected by changes in the value of the ECU.

Both Greece and Turkey present daily prices of their currencies in terms of the U.S. dollar. But exchange rates are complicated because the Greek drachma and the Turkish lira (to a limited extent) have been aligned with a bundle of the currencies of the main EEC member nations, predominantly the German mark. For example, at the end of 1986, the exchange rates were 138 GDs and 750 TLs to the dollar. However, at the end of 1985 the rates were 148 GDs and 557 TLs per dollar. This means that during 1986, there was an appreciation of the GD, versus the dollar, by 7.2 percent, while the TL was devalued by 30 percent. The appreciation of the GD, though, was not justified, affecting the balance of payment unfavorably.

The inflation rates in Greece and Turkey in 1986 were 17 percent and 34 percent, respectively. On the other hand, real economic growth was less than 2 percent for Greece and about 6 percent for Turkey.[12] Assuming other things the same, the Greek drachma was supposed to depreciate, with respect to the dollar, in 1986 by 14 percent (17 percent inflation for Greece minus 3 percent inflation for the United States). Instead, the drachma was appreciated by 7.2 percent, making Greek exports more expensive, and imports cheaper, by 21.2 percent (14 percent plus 7.2 percent), affecting negatively the balance of trade for the country. For Turkey, though, the rate of depreciation (30 percent) was consistent with the difference between the rates of inflation of Turkey and that of the United States (34 percent minus 3 percent), having little effect on relative prices of exports and imports. Table 9.1 shows the rates of inflation for Greece, Turkey, and the EEC from 1960 to 1986. A comparison of these inflationary rates would show the expected rates of devaluation of the Greek and Turkish currencies vis-à-vis the ECU of the EEC.

The alignment of the Greek drachma to mainly the German mark seems to be responsible for its recent unjustified revaluation. However, the German mark is strong because of the good trade performance and the large surpluses in the balance of current accounts with respect to the United States. But Greece has large current account deficits and its currency is to be devalued, not only in relation to the mark but to other currencies, including the dollar. This seems to be the proper policy to improve the balance of payments of the country and to stimulate growth in the economy.

In cases of serious problems with the balance of payments of an EEC member nation, articles 108 and 109 of the Rome Treaty of 1957 provide for a special committee that suggests measures of mutual support and possible deviations from certain obligations of the member states in question. Greece used these articles to preserve certain import restrictions and to postpone free capital movement. Previously, Greece invoked the same articles to postpone implementation of the VAT, elimination of export subsidies, and prohibition of state monopoly in

Table 9.1
Inflation Rates in Greece, Turkey, and the EEC (percentage increase in the Consumer Price Index)

YEARS	GREECE	TURKEY	EEC
1960–1970	2.1	5.3	3.8
1970	2.9	6.6	7.8
1971	3.0	15.7	7.8
1972	4.3	11.7	6.8
1973	15.5	15.4	7.8
1974	26.9	15.8	10.8
1975	13.4	19.2	11.3
1976	13.3	17.4	9.6
1977	12.1	27.1	9.1
1978	12.6	45.3	8.13
1979	19.0	58.7	9.4
1980	24.9	110.2	11.7
1981	24.5	36.6	9.7
1982	21.0	30.8	10.2
1983	20.2	32.9	7.9
1984	18.4	48.4	6.7
1985	19.3	45.0	6.4
1986	17.0	34.1	3.1

Note: For the EEC, the GDP deflator was used.
Source: IMF, *International Financial Statistics,* various issues. For the EEC, GDP Price Index
1971–82, OECD, *National Accounts,* various issues.

matches, salt, cards, and other products. As long as inflationary rates remain high, both the Greek drachma and the Turkish lira are expected to deviate widely from the ECU.

NOTES

1. For growth limits of the EEC, see John Paxton, *The Developing Common Market,* 3d ed. (London: Macmillan, 1976); Paul Taylor, *The Limits of European Integration* (New York: Columbia University Press, 1983); and Dubley Seers and Constantine Vaitsos, eds., *Integration and Unequal Development: The Experience of the EEC* (New York: St. Martin's Press, 1980).

2. Peter Wiles and Alan Smith, "The Convergence of the CMEA on the EEC," in *The EEC and Eastern Europe,* eds. Avi Shlaim and George N. Yannopoulos (London: Cambridge University Press, 1978), chap. 3.

3. Sociopolitical and environmental aspects of the EEC are in C. Pinkele and Adamantia Polis, eds., *The Contemporary Mediterranean World* (New York: Praeger, 1983), chap. 5.

4. More discussion on the enlargement of the EEC in Loukas Tsoukalis, *The European Community and Its Mediterranean Enlargement* (London: Allen and Unwin, 1981), chap. 1.

5. Richard Pomfret, *Mediterranean Policy of the European Community* (New York: Macmillan, 1986).

6. Theodore Georgakopoulos, "Greece in the EEC: Intercountry Income Transfer,"

Journal of Common Market Studies 25, no. 2 (December 1986). For previous trade effects, see Theodore Hitiris, *Trade Effects of Economic Association with the Common Market: The Case of Greece* (New York: Praeger, 1972).

7. To counter higher food costs, Greece receives about $600 million a year from the EEC. See "Greece: European Tragedy," *Economist* 286, no. 7272, January 15–21, 1983, 74.

8. In 1960–1980 the world share of the EEC merchant fleet fell from 34 to 18 percent, while the Greek-flag fleet grew tenfold, numbering some 3,800 ships (600 more than the nearest competitor, Britain), John Carr, "New Trade Horizons: Greece Could Strengthen Ties between East and West," *Europe*, January-February 1981, 10–13.

9. For the relationship between industrialization and foreign trade, see World Bank, *Turkey: Industrialization and Trade Strategy* (Washington, D.C.: World Bank, 1982). Also, Anne Krueger and Baran Tuncer, "An Empirical Test of the Infant Industry Argument," *American Economic Review* 72, no. 5 (December 1982): 1146.

10. Jeri Lader and Lois Whitman, "Turkish Hypocrisy on Ending Torture," *New York Times,* July 13, 1987. Recent developments in "Ozal Prepares to Reconquer Turkey," *Economist* 305, no. 7519, London, October 10–16, 1987, 47. For previous trends, see C. H. Dobb, *Democracy and Development in Turkey* (London: Euthen, 1979).

11. More information on related EEC policies in Peter Coffey, ed., *The Economic Policies of the Common Market* (London: Macmillan, 1979).

12. For statistical data, see OECD, *Economic Surveys: Greece*; and *Economic Surveys: Turkey*, various issues.

10

Geopolitical Considerations

DIFFICULTIES FROM LOCAL CONFLICTS

Throughout history, Greek-Turkish economic relations were and still are at low levels, mainly because of conflicts in the region and the production of competitive products such as tobacco, wine, fruits, and other primary products. After the Turks, coming from the plateaus of Asia, occupied Anatolia and during the Ottoman period, economic conditions were those of a master to the slave or at least the serf. Large and rich estates were confiscated by the Turks, while heavy taxes were imposed on the Greek and other Balkan subjects. Foreign trade was conducted primarily with Western Europe and the ports of the Black Sea.

With the departure of the Ottoman rulers and the independence of Greece, the Greek Orthodox Church became the largest landowner. At present, the Church, second to the Greek government in property ownership, is holding about 370,000 acres of forest, agricultural, and urban land (estimated at $192 million). The government is in the process of redistributing this property, except that of the Monastery at Mount Athos and a few other monasteries, among public sector enterprises, local authorities, and agricultural cooperatives. However, these public enterprises and cooperatives have not proved to be efficient, compared to private ventures.

After World War I and the Greco-Turkish War (1919–1922), the 1.5 million Greek refugees from Asia Minor and 400,000 Turks from Greece proved to be beneficial to handicrafts and industry. However, severe problems of housing shortages and unemployment appeared for the uprooted refugees. Under the politicians Eleutherios Venizelos and Alexander Papanastassiou of Greece and Kemal Ataturk of Turkey economic cooperation and trade between the two nations were enhanced in the 1930s.

In the post–World War II years, the crises over Cyprus and the expansionary desires of Ankara in the Aegean Sea kept economic relations at very low levels. However, Greece's membership and Turkey's association with the European Economic Community provide hopes that relations between these two countries would be improved. Then the dreams of the refugees of both sides to go back, under different conditions, to their roots as entrepreneurs or residents may be materialized, and "the dreams of today might be the reality of tomorrow."

Recently, Greece and Turkey have faced each other across the Aegean Sea with suspicion and bitterness. They edged toward war on March 27, 1987 over sea boundaries and drilling rights. According to international law, Greece, while claiming a six-nautical-mile territory around its islands, reserves the right to extend this claim to twelve miles. In addition to the dispute over the continental shelf (up to 200 meters below the sea surface), Turkey refuses to recognize Greece's ten-mile airspace limit, which Turkish warplanes regularly violate.

The fact that some 35,000 Turkish troops have continued to occupy almost 40 percent of Cyprus since 1974 makes the Greeks suspicious regarding long-term expansionary policies of Turkey against their independence, national sovereignty, territorial integrity, and freedom. Moreover, 120,000 Turkish troops, supported by 120 landing craft, are pointing in the direction of the Greek Islands. This army is not integrated in the North Atlantic Treaty Organization (NATO) defensive plans. The Turkish side proposes to negotiate, but the Greek side asks: "To negotiate what, our territorial rights?"

The two countries, which are partners in NATO but are mutually hostile, agreed to take the matter to the International Court in The Hague. Greece, which left NATO's military wing between 1974 and 1980 because of NATO's failure to discipline Turkey for its invasion of Cyprus, wants a return to the pre–1976 command arrangements, under which it had total oversight of the Aegean. To avoid other crises over the Aegean, Greece and Turkey could adapt the 1972 United States–Soviet Union "Incidents at Sea" agreement, stipulating "Rules of the Road" for their navies operating in the vicinity of one another, to avoid acts of harassment.[1]

As a result of the Turkish invasion of Cyprus in July-August 1974, the U.S. Congress decided in July 1975 to stop all military aid to Turkey pending withdrawal of Turkish troops from Cyprus. Turkey then was forced to increase military budget expenditures, which in 1977–1978 were estimated at $2.63 billion or about 30 percent of the budget. Also, Turkey borrowed heavily from abroad to pay some $500 million annually for arms, in addition to the amounts needed to cover other current account deficits. In the meantime, West Germany provided Turkey with about $100 million a year in military aid.

Mainly because of the stoppage of American aid (embargo) and high budget expenditures, the Turkish economy was in a serious crisis in the second half of the 1970s. However, in September 1978, the U.S. embargo was lifted, without the withdrawal of the Turkish troops from Cyprus, and thereafter the United States continued to provide about $500–700 million annually in aid to Turkey.[2]

Closer relations and sincere talks between the governments of Greece and Turkey could begin, according to the Greek representatives, when the Turkish troops depart from occupied northern Cyprus and when Turkey abandons threats against the Greek islands in the Aegean Sea. On the other hand, Greece consistently contends that it has the right to extend its territorial waters according to the international rules. Turkey, though, contends that such an extension of territorial waters and the Greek claims to the continental shelf would be unacceptable.

Greece raises objections to Turkey's accession to the EEC, on the ground that Turkish troops occupy about 40 percent of Cyprus and that Turkey creates problems in the Aegean with expansionary objectives in the area. Moreover, Greece argues that Turkey is violating human rights, keeping political prisoners, after the military dictatorship of 1980, which still keeps power, despite the allowance of some form of pseudodemocracy in recent years.

Because Turkey is considered an important member of NATO's southern flank, the United States, West Germany, and other EEC nations helped it to build up the largest NATO force after the United States. Thus, Turkey's army has increased to 500,000 men and its air force and navy to 102,000, while it has about 3,600 medium and heavy tanks and some 280 fighter bombers. After the Cyprus invasion in 1974, Turkish field forces deployed along the Soviet frontier and the Black Sea coast have substantially diminished in numbers and transferred primarily to the western Anatolian coast, opposite the Greek Aegean islands, and as an occupation force in Cyprus. The Fourth Army, with approximately 150 assault and transport naval crafts and 80 transport aircraft, is concentrated in Izmir and the surrounding area, while the Second Army's principal attention has shifted to the direct or indirect control of Cyprus.[3] The unusual Turkish army concentration against the eastern frontiers of Greece, another NATO ally, and the frequent air and naval violations in the Aegean Sea force Greece to appropriate large amounts of spending for defense against another "ally," Turkey.

RELATIONS WITH THE UNITED STATES

Both nations are members of the North Atlantic Treaty Organization (NATO) and receive military and nonmilitary aid from the United States, which has a number of military bases in both Greece and Turkey. There are four major and twenty smaller U.S. bases in Greece. The most important of them are those in Souda Bay, Crete (for navy and submarine installations), in Nea Makri near Athens (mainly for electronic surveillance and communications), at the Hellenikon National Airport, and the one near Kavala in northern Greece. Of the 16 bases in Turkey, the most important are those of Korlou and Izmit on both sides of the Dardanelles straits, of Balikeshir (near Izmir), Eskisehir and Mourtent (near Ankara), Ortakoy and Insirlik (near Syria and Cyprus), Erzurum (close to the Soviet Union), and Erhak-Malatya (in southeastern Turkey). Two bases (Mous and Batman) are under consideration in eastern Turkey; one (Merzifon) near the Black Sea; and another two (Genisechir and Sigli) near the Aegean Sea. A number of the bases have nuclear weapons, and U.S. AWACS (planes of early warning) have been stationed in both countries.

In October 1986, Greece and the United States signed the Defense and Industrial Cooperation Agreement (DICA), which is part of a broader Defense and Economic Cooperation Agreement (DECA). Although it does not list specific projects, it refers to future participation in technological research and know-how, so that the Greek armed forces can become self-sufficient in hardware development and eventually be able to sell spare parts and defense equipment to the United States. A similar agreement (DECA) was made between Turkey and the United States in February 1987.

Nevertheless, Turkey has a heightened sense of conventional vulnerability regarding defense against the Soviet Union. Recently, Turkey asked for greater U.S. aid to modernize its 600,000-member army to match reduction and, eventually, elimination of medium- and long-range nuclear missiles in Europe, as a result of the agreement between the United States and the Soviet Union. The Turkish argument is that a nuclear reduction would expose the country to far superior Soviet conventional forces.

On the other hand, Greece is in favor of eliminating nuclear weapons in Europe and strongly supports a Balkan nuclear-free zone. Regarding transfer of military technology, there are presently trials in Athens on charges of providing secret information on shoulder-fired portable antiaircraft (Stinger) missiles to the Soviet Union by some responsible communications and navy officials. This enabled the Russians to incorporate the related technology into their SA–14 missiles.[4]

Both countries receive some form of aid, mainly from the United States, and Turkey also from the Soviet Union. U.S. postwar aid (1946–1977) amounted to $5.1 billion for Greece ($1.5 billion under the Marshall Plan in 1947–1951) and $3.7 billion (1954–1982) for Turkey. Also, Turkey received $4.2 billion in aid from the Soviet Union and the Eastern Bloc. Technical assistance to Greece was terminated in 1962, and major economic aid ended in 1964; only military assistance under the auspices of NATO continued thereafter.[5]

To enjoy continuing use of bases and sites for listening posts in Turkey, the United States supplies Ankara with additional weapons from surplus stocks. Washington may also reduce Turkey's payments on the $1.6 billion it owes in military debt.[6] This may take place through a buy-down feature, that is, by transferring Turkish military debt to the private banking sector with U.S. government guarantees. Similar supply measures and transfers may be considered between Greece and the United States as well.

In addition to the annual financial and military assistance for the American base rights ($590 million in fiscal year 1987), Turkey, along with Egypt, Israel, and other military debtors, is offered debt relief worth an estimated $800 million over the next ten years. Also, Turkey will be able to purchase secondhand U.S. military equipment at bargain prices ($300 million).

There are arguments, though, that the United States is using Greece and Turkey, along with Spain and Portugal, not as respected NATO allies but as military real estate, supporting sometimes the authoritarians. U.S. aid is provided for rights to military bases that often have little to do with the interests of these countries.[7] Greece threatens to close American bases unless the United States guarantees to protect her against Turkish attacks and to end the Turkish occupation of Cyprus.

Because of complaints of Greece against Turkey over the occupation of northern Cyprus, the U.S. Congress has imposed a seven-to-ten ratio of aid to Greece versus Turkey since 1975.[8] Presently, in U.S. aid, Greece receives about $350 million and Turkey receives about $500 million annually.

In a number of European and non-European countries, including Greece and Turkey, the United States maintains the Voice of America (VOA) facilities. Such facilities on the island of Rhodes and outside Kavala (in northern Greece), as well as in eastern Turkey, are important for broadcasting American viewpoints to Eastern Europe, North Africa, and the Middle East to counter similar Soviet propaganda techniques. Washington intends to invest large amounts of money to improve VOA facilities and prefers long-term (25-year) agreements, while Greece and Turkey want short-term (mainly 5-year) agreements, so they can have the power to negotiate and ask for larger amounts of aid more frequently. From a political point of view, they want to avoid criticism that they sell their countries' rights for a long period. On the other hand, Washington argues that such sizeable investments would not be worth their while for short-term projects.

Both nations, primarily through Greek and Turkish minorities in the United States, are making serious efforts to maintain and improve educational and other cultural activities in U.S. cities, mainly in New York and Washington, and to influence Congress and other policymakers through lobbies and other organizations. Thus, the Greek Community of New York, some 500,000 people, holds its annual Independence Day parade every year (around March 25) to commemorate the Greek struggle for freedom against the Ottoman yoke. The small Turkish minority also has been holding annual parades since 1986 every April, while the Armenians do the same every April 24 in commemoration of the Turkish massacres of some 1.5 million people in 1915–1923. Among the centers of Hellenic studies established in U.S. universities, the recent one (1987) in New York University (NYU) is the most prominent. It was created through the use of a gift of $15 million (the largest ever to NYU) by the Alexander Onassis Public Benefit Foundation for teaching and research of Greek history—from the most ancient through the Byzantine era right up to the present day. Another important center for modern Greek and Byzantine studies is and has been operating for years at Queens College of the City University of New York and smaller ones at Harvard, Columbia, and Rutgers universities. Moreover, serious efforts are made for the establishment of similar Turkish cultural centers and exhibitions, such as that of Suleiman the Magnificent (who expanded the Ottoman Empire from the gates of Vienna to North Africa and the Persian Gulf, 1520–1566) in the Museum of History in New York. Greek cultural events include the Alexander the Great Exhibition of 1982–1983 in New York, Washington, Baltimore, Chicago, and Toronto.

U.S. trade with Greece and Turkey is relatively constant or growing. Greek exports to the United States ($370 million in 1985) account for 8 to 9 percent of total exports, while imports ($320 million) account for only 3 to 4 percent of total imports. Likewise, Turkish exports to the United States ($368 million in 1984) account for 5 to 6 percent of total exports, while imports ($614 million) measure for 10 percent of total imports, leaving a deficit of about $250 million per year. However, the United States recently imposed a quota on Turkish textile imports for protective reasons. Although U.S. trade with Greece and Turkey is limited, many industries, large and small, look across the Atlantic for capital equipment and know-how for the improvement of their competitiveness against their EEC counterparts.

EXPECTED DEVELOPMENTS

Future socioeconomic and political developments between Greece and Turkey depend primarily on the settlement of the problems over Cyprus and the Aegean Sea. Although peace efforts by UN Secretary General Perez de Guellar have been frustrated so far, implementation of the UN resolutions seems to lead to a viable and lasting solution for Cyprus. Such resolutions call for the withdrawal of all foreign troops (notably the 35,000 Turkish soldiers), freedom of movement (including the return of some 200,000 Greek Cypriot refugees to their homes), and the setting up of a Federal Cypriot Republic to accommodate both the Greek Cypriot majority (80 percent) and the Turkish Cypriot minority (18 percent). This would ensure the rights of the Turkish Cypriot and the Greek Cypriot communities and reduce or eliminate hatred and conflicts between Greece and Turkey.

The Cypriot government complains that the Turkish government transfers people from eastern Turkey to Cyprus to occupy the homes of the Greek Cypriot refugees. Populating northern Cyprus with peasants from other regions of Turkey is a familiar policy even from the times of the Ottoman expansion. After the Turks conquered Anatolia (1071–1081), they slowly and surely uprooted and chased away the Greek and other peasants or converted them forcefully or persuasively to Islam. New conquered areas in the Balkan Peninsula and elsewhere were populated to a large extent by unemployed warriors and collaborators from other regions. At the same time, the diabolic policy of taking Christian baby boys violently away from their parents and converting them into Moslem soldiers (janissaries) proved to be a crude and inhuman, yet effective, measure to keep Ottoman control over Greece and other Balkan countries for more than four centuries. Perhaps such measures may be considered strange in modern societies, but the example of northern Cyprus is frightening.

From a political point of view, Greece and, more so, Turkey experienced uneasiness and disturbances during the postwar years. Although mostly under democratic regimes, Greece had a seven-year (1967–1974) military dictatorship and Turkey had more years under military than democratic rule. For the first time after the military dictatorship in 1980, the third in less than 30 years, elections were conducted in 1983 in Turkey, but politicians of the previous major parties, including former Prime Ministers Suleiman Demirel and Bulent Ecevit, were barred from election, because they were considered responsible for frequent legislative stalemates fostering political violence that claimed 5,000 lives. The present prime minister, Turgut Ozal, conducted a referendum on September 6, 1987 on whether to lift bans on his political rivals. In a narrow contest (50.26 percent) the voters favored the lifting of bans on politicians. Elections were conducted on November 29 instead of November 1, of the same year, because the courts required that nomination of candidates be approved by their constituencies, not by the party leadership alone. Although not completely free, such democratic measures create a favorable climate for the eventual accession of Turkey to the EEC.

Although the Turks are mostly Sunni Muslims, there is a sizeable minority of Shiites, about a quarter of the population. Power is held primarily by the westernized camp, but, from time to time, there appeared violent conflicts between the traditionalists or fundamentalists and power holders. The Sunni-Shiite rivalry and the struggle for independence by the Kurds are the two main internal problems of modern Turkey. The theocratic character of Islamic fundamentalism is at odds with secular western values and supports a return to religiopolitical fanaticism and the violent ethos of Islam in fulfillment of God's will.

While Greece and the rest of Europe face problems of depopulation, Turkey, a Muslim country, faces risks of demographic explosion and therefore slow or no growth in per capita income. However, Turkish leaders, boasting of population increases in their country, promise to rescue Europe from depopulation by flooding the EEC countries, including Greece, with Turkish immigrants. There are already about 5.5 million Muslims in Western Europe.

The geographical position of Greece and Turkey, between Europe and the oil-producing countries of the Middle East, gives them some economic and strategic advantages. Because of the problems in Iran after the revolution against the Shah and the long Iran-Iraq war, a substantial amount of oil is transferred to the western countries via land pipes. Only 15 percent of the non-communist oil production is transferred through the Persian Gulf now, compared to 41 percent ten years ago. Because of the insecurity of the oil pipe network going to the Red Sea (through the desert of Saudi Arabia) and the troubles in the Persian Gulf, growing amounts of oil are transferred through Turkey and the eastern Mediterranean. Also, about 50 percent of Soviet exports and imports travel through the Dardanelles straits and the Aegean Sea.

From a strategic point of view, there is the impression among U.S. and other Western policymakers that Turkey is an important country because it is located right under "the belly" of Russia. Turkey, as a NATO member, tries to keep good relations with the United States and Western Europe so that it can attract aid and increase trade. On the other hand, being an Islamic country, it tries to keep good relations with other neighboring Islamic countries. Thus, although

Iran and Iraq have been at war for years, they both feel safe to transport their oil to the west through Turkey. These events accommodate Turkey's efforts to promote the idea that it is a vital bridge between East and West.

Since the fall of the Shah and the installation of the Ayatollah Khomeini, Iran has been following policy that is not as pro-western as it used to be in the past. As a result, Turkey and Greece acquired more importance for the EEC and the other western countries.

In order to secure energy supplies from the Middle Eastern countries for the West and Japan, a number of oil pipelines have been constructed or are under construction in Turkey in recent years. Turkey's neutrality in the Iran-Iraq War, as well as the risks of the oil supply route in the Persian Gulf (through the Strait of Hormuz), make such pipelines vital to the energy interests of the West.

More than four million barrels of oil a day are now carried through pipelines. It is expected that in the near future at least 6.5 million barrels a day would be transported to the Red Sea port of Vanbu of Saudi Arabia and mainly the Mediterranean Sea port of Ceyhan in Turkey. The Petroleum Pipeline Company of Botas, an Iraqi-Turkish venture with headquarters in Ankara, completed recently a pipeline that moves 500,000 barrels a day through a 40-inch diameter from the Kirkuk oilfields in northern Iraq to the port of Ceyhan.

Not only Iraq, from which Turkey buys one-third of its estimated 300,000 barrels a day oil consumption, but also tiny Qatar started negotiations with Turkey on a project to pipe or liquefy its huge gas reserves for shipment to Europe. Similar negotiations are under way with Iran for building a natural gas pipeline to sell energy to Turkey and Europe. Turkey also buys about one-third of its oil consumption from Iran and about 20 percent from Libya. Some $450 million a year are collected by Turkey as pipeline fees and taxes for moving 1.5 million barrels of Iraqi crude and 100,000 barrels refined oil.[9]

Recently, much attention has been paid by Turkey to the ramification of the long Iran-Iraq war. There is speculation that Turkey intends to occupy the Kirkuk oil wells in case the Iranians invade Iraq. As a result of a law passed by the Turkish National Assembly, Turkish troops have pursued and bombed Kurds inside Iraq. Pretending that they are after revolutionary Kurds, and being helped probably by Iranians and Western interests, Turkish forces may occupy the rich oil regions of northern Iraq.[10]

On the economic front, both countries take measures to stabilize their economies. As other market economies do, Greece and Turkey face the dilemma of following a reasonable course between the Scylla of inflation and the Charybdis of recession without wrecking the boat of the national economy. Recent fiscal measures had some success in reducing inflation in Greece but not much in Turkey. Nevertheless, average real wages declined in both countries, thereby reducing cost of production and making Greek and Turkish products more competitive than otherwise.

Both economies gradually move from protectionism to open markets and free trade. Greece, as a member of the EEC, will further open her borders to international trade and investment. On the other hand, at one time, Turkey ranked second only to China among the world's most closed economies. However, recently the Turkish economy has become more open and more emphasis has been given to foreign trade. From the point of view of monetary policy, successive devaluations of the drachma and the lira encouraged exports of agricultural and manufacturing products, as well as foreign investments.

The huge foreign debt and its servicing would require less spending by the governments of both nations, not only on consumption, but also on investment programs, such as road building, irrigation, and other public facilities. Annual payments for interest and amortization of external loans is expected to be the most serious problem for both the Greek and the Turkish economies in the near and the remote future.

At the time of their association with the EEC, Greece was weak and Turkey was an "economic corpse." The agricultural sector was backward, capital was scarce, and industry was primitive and unable to stand competition. Although there is substantial improvement in all sectors of both economies, questions still arise: Can they survive EEC competition? Particularly for Turkey, some groups oppose accession on religious (Islamic fundamentalist) and ideological or political grounds. "The more you make yourself a European, the more you become a stranger in your own land," a Turkish editor said.[11]

As a result of trade rise with the EEC, short-run pressures from industrial competition may increase unemployment and reduce growth. However, long-run adjustments and assimilation of new technology are expected to improve economic and sociopolitical conditions in both nations, particularly in Turkey.

Turkey wants to be a memer of the EEC not only for economic reasons but for sociopolitical reasons as well. Turkey's "Europeanization" seems to have an appeal for the Turkish people and their leaders, even from the time of Kemal Ataturk. However, member nations have reservations, not only because of the great economic gap, regarding the level of development between Turkey vis-à-vis the EEC, but on political grounds as well. Reports of the Amnesty International charge that "torture is still widespread" and some "Eurocrats" feel that for Turkey to be a full member of the EEC full restoration of western-type pluralistic democracy with respect to human rights is needed and not a system of "democracy under military supervision" with a number of regions still under martial law. Moreover, Greece, an EEC member, argues that Turkey cannot belong to the same politico-economic group and at the same time threaten another member, to wit Greece, in the Aegean with anachronistic designs of expansionism.[12]

However, the prolonged war between Iraq and Iran increased the strategic importance of Turkey in the eyes of the EEC, the United States and other NATO countries. Politically and diplomatically, Turkey is using these events to push for an early full membership in the European Common Market. Turkey complains that as a member of NATO she should belong also to a united Europe, as do almost all other European countries. The argument is that Turkey should have benefits, as well, not only obligations, as a NATO member.

The major problem of both Greece and Turkey has historically been that of competing nationalism. However, the two people who have lived so close to each other and shared similar cultural traits for centuries may turn their hatred into socioeconomic cooperation for higher levels of development and the improvement of their livelihood. Closer ties with the EEC are expected to improve economic, political, and cultural relations between the Greek and the Turkish populations. Under the umbrella of the European Economic Community, suspicion between them would be reduced and common economic and investment policies might be developed.

A meeting of Prime Ministers Andreas Papandreou of Greece and Turgut Ozal of Turkey in Davos (Switzerland) in January 1988 created a favorable climate for cooperation between these two countries.[13] A "hot line" of communications was established between Athens and Ankara and friendly visits in Greece by Ozal and in Turkey by Papandreou were arranged. A number of newspapers, though, criticized Papandreou, for being a "flip-flopper," in that he gave in to Ozal on some important issues. Ozal mentioned that there are no Greek Cypriots missing (hostages) in Turkey as a result of the 1974 invasion of Cyprus by the Turkish army. The Cypriot government, though, argues that more than 1,600 Greek Cypriots were missing and possesses films (mainly from the BBC-TV station in London) showing many such persons in Turkish camps and prisons, a number of them at a stage of extermination. A solution to the Cyprus dispute and the continuation of negotiations between Greece and Turkey is further complicated by the arrival of as many as 65,000 settlers from the Turkish mainland and the return of some 200,000 Greek Cypriot refugees to their northern homes.[14] On the other hand, with the newly elected president of Cyprus, George Vassiliou, there are positive signs of a warming trend in Greek-Turkish relations, as he promised to seek direct talks with Turkey to unify the island. Prime Minister Ozal visited Athens in June 1988, with plans for Papandreou to reciprocate the visit in Ankara.

NOTES

1. For related discussion, see *Economist,* April 4–10, 1987, 38–39. Richard N. Haass, "How to Keep Greece and Turkey Apart," *New York Times,* April 13, 1987; and Alan Cowell, "Aegean Dispute Worsens Turkish-Greek Ties," *New York Times,* March 24, 1987.

2. Ron Ayres, "Turkish Foreign Relations," in *Modern Turkey: Development and Crisis,* Khamsim Collective (London: Ithaca Press, 1984), 117–27.

3. Alexander Kyrou, "Turkey's Militaristic Foreign Policy," *Greek Accent,* New York, September-October 1986, 7.

4. Paul Anastasi, "Athens Charges Greek with Giving Stinger Missile Secrets to Soviet," *New York Times,* October 29, 1987.

5. Rinn S. Shinn, ed., *Greece: A Country Study* (Washington, D.C.: U.S. Government Printing Office, 1986), 53, 216. For a historical review, see Theodore Couloumbis, John Petropoulos, and Harry Psomiades, *Interference in Greek Politics: An Historical Perspective* (New York: Pella, 1976).

6. *International Financial Report* (Weekly, U. K.), November 21, 1986, 1395.

7. Clifford P. Hackett, "How We've Corrupted Our NATO Allies," *New York Times,* October 16, 1987.

8. George Harris, *Turkey: Coping with Crisis* (Boulder, Colo.: Westview Press, 1985), 192–96. Also, Richard Clogg, "Troubled Alliance: Greece and Turkey," in *Greece in the 1980s,* ed. R. Clogg (New York: St. Martin's Press, 1983). For the postwar policy of the United States, see Theodore Couloumbis, *The United States, Greece and Turkey: The Troubled Triangle* (New York: Praeger, 1983); William McNeill, *The Metamorphosis of Greece since World War II* (Chicago: University of Chicago Press, 1978); and Harry N. Howard, *Turkey, The Straits and U.S. Policy* (Baltimore: Johns Hopkins University Press, 1974).

9. Youssef Ibrahim, "New Pipelines Are Reducing Persian Gulf's Strategic Role," *New York Times,* October 7, 1987.

10. For speculation on this scenario, see "More Problems Ahead," *Athena* 10, November 1986, 324.

11. Alan Cowell, "Turks Finally Ask, Are We Europeans or What?" *New York Times,* May 27, 1987. Also, Sevan Nisanyan, "Turkey and the EEC" (Lecture at the Center of European Studies, Graduate School of the City University of New York, April 29, 1981). The word *Turk* was considered derogatory by the Ottomans. Also, the Byzantines did not want to be called "Hellenes" because of the pagan connotation. For Turkey's support, see Dankwart Rustow, *Turkey: America's Forgotten Ally* (New York: Council on Foreign Relations, 1987).

12. Further details in William McGury, "Turkey's Challenge to the Common Market," *Wall Street Journal,* December 3, 1986; and Theodore Couloumbis, "The Question of Turkish Accession," *Athena* 10, November 1986, 343; and *Milliyet,* October 27, 1986.

13. A Bridge Across the Aegean," *Economist,* February 6–12, 1988, 45–46.

14. "Cyprus Leader Pledges Talks in Taking Office," *New York Times,* February 29, 1988.

Appendix:
Correlations of Gross Domestic Product with Investment and Exports

Statistical regressions are used to find the relationship between gross domestic product (GDP) and investment (INV), as well as between GDP and exports (EXP) (table A.1). Moreover, a multiple regression of GDP on investment and exports is presented in the same table. Greece had a lower regression coefficient of GDP on investment (3.6) compared to Turkey (4.2). This means that a 1-unit change in investment is associated with a change in GDP of 3.6 units for Greece and 4.2 units for Turkey. An even greater difference exists in the regression coefficients of GDP on exports. Thus, a 1-unit change in exports is associated with a change in GDP of 1.3 units for Greece and 3.1 units for Turkey. On the other hand, the multiple regressions show that, for both countries, "exports" is a better explanatory variable of changes in GDP than is investment, especially for Turkey. It would seem, therefore, that postwar economic growth in Greece and Turkey was based on increases in investment and more so on increases in exports.

In the simple regressions, the slope of change in output (ΔQ) over change in investment (ΔI), $\Delta Q / \Delta I$, which is a notion of the multiplier, does not show the productivity of investment, because other factors in addition to investment, primarily labor, contribute to the increase in production.

For both countries, the coefficient of determination, R^2, was more than 0.830, indicating that the regression fit was very good. Therefore policymakers can use such reliable regressions for future economic projections on economic growth based on investment and export changes.

In both Greece and Turkey, as well as in the United States and other countries, there is a close relationship between trade deficits and budget deficits. Thus, regression of trade deficit on budget deficit for Greece indicates that the regression coefficient was 0.73 for 1975–1985. This means that a unit change in budget deficit (BD) was associated with a change of 0.73 units of trade deficit (TD). Also, a similar regression shows that a unit change in inflation was related to a change of 0.21 units in trade deficit. However, the coefficient of correlation (R)

Table A.1
Simple and Multiple Regression Analysis of Gross Domestic Product (GDP) on Investment (INV) and Exports (EXP), 1958–1984 (current prices)

	a	b_1	b_2	F	R^2
FOR GREECE	68.9	3.6 INV		403	0.937
	(3.8)	(20.1)			
	27.7	1.3 EXP		135	0.833
	(4.3)	(11.6)			
	100.2	1.7 INV	2.9 EXP	1,388	0.990
	(13.4)	(9.6)	(12.0)		
FOR TURKEY	86.5	4.2 INV		597	0.960
	(8.5)	(24.4)			
	-6.8	3.1 EXP		362	0.935
	(-2.0)	(19.0)			
	60.4	1.8 INV	8.2 EXP	685	0.981
	(7.1)	(3.8)	(5.4)		

Note: In some cases, previous years' data were available.
Source: Organization for Economic Cooperation and Development (OECD), *National Accounts;* and United Nations, *Yearbook of National Accounts Statistics,* both various issues.

was higher in the case of inflation than that of budget deficit indicating a closer relationship between trade deficit and inflation. That is:

$$TD = 2.86 + 0.73\ BD \qquad R = 0.563$$
$$(0.88)$$

$$TD = 0.35 + 0.21\ INF \qquad R = 0.960$$
$$(0.09)$$

Figures in parentheses represent standard errors of estimate (SEE).

More or less, similar relationships between trade deficits and budget deficits can be observed for Turkey.

Figure A.1 shows a very close relationship between gross domestic product and trade deficit for Greece for the period 1960–1984. This leads to the unfortunate conclusion that, *ceteris paribus,* reduction in trade deficit is related to reductions in consumption spending, where the regression of trade deficit on private consumption was 0.22 (R = 0.99), and eventually reduction in GDP.

Figure A.1
The Relationship of Gross Domestic Product (GDP) and Trade Deficit (TD) for Greece, 1960–1984 (billions of U.S. current dollars)

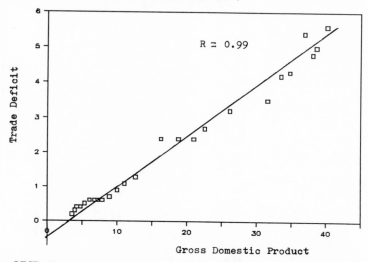

Source: OECD, *National Accounts;* and IMF, *International Financial Statistics,* both various issues.

Bibliography

"A Bridge Across the Aegean." *Economist* 306, no. 7536 (February 6–12, 1988).

Allen, Evanthia. "Turkey in Transition." *Weekly Review,* New York, May 17, 1985.

Anastasi, Paul. "Athens Charges Greek with Giving Stinger Missile Secrets to Soviet." *New York Times,* October 29, 1987.

Andreades, Andreas. *A History of Public Finance in Greece.* Cambridge: Harvard University Press, 1933.

Angell, Norman. *The Story of Money.* New York: F. A. Stokes, 1929.

"At Last the Foreign Investor Is Welcome." *Euromoney,* February 1982.

Ayres, Ron. "Turkish Foreign Relations." In *Modern Turkey: Development and Crisis.* Khamsim Collective. London: Ithaca Press, 1984.

Ayres, Ron, and T. Thomson. *Turkey, A New Era.* London: Euromoney Publications, 1984.

Bardkjian, Kevork. *Hitler and the Armenian Genocide.* Cambridge, Mass.: Zoryan Institute, 1985.

Barth, Fredirick. *Principles of Social Organization in Southern Kurdistan.* Oslo: Universitets Ethnografiske Museum, 1953.

Boeckh, Augustus. *The Public Economy of Athens.* New York: Arno Press, 1976.

Borowiec, Andrew. "Turkey Looks to U.S. to Help Resolve Economic Crisis." *New York Times,* January 6, 1979.

Botsford, George, and Charles Robinson, Jr. *Hellenic History.* 5th ed., rev. D. Kagan. London: Macmillan, 1971.

Cahen, Claude. *Pre-Ottoman Turkey.* New York: Tabbinger, 1968.

Candilis, Wray. *The Economy of Greece, 1944–66.* New York: Praeger, 1968.

Carey, Jane, and Andrew Carey. *The Web of Modern Greek Politics.* New York: Columbia University Press, 1968.

Carr, John. "New Trade Horizons: Greece Could Strengthen Ties between East and West." *Europe,* January-February 1981.

Carvounis, Chris. *The Debt Dilemma of Developing Nations: Issues and Cases.* Westport, Conn.: Quorum Books, 1984.

Ceram, C. W. (pseud. for Marek, Kurt). *The Secret of the Hittites: The Discovery of an Ancient Empire.* New York: Alfred A. Knopf, 1956.

Chaliand, Gerard. *The Armenians, From Genocide to Resistance.* Trans. Tony Berrett. London: Zed Press, 1983.

Chenery, Hollis. "Interactions between Industrialization and Exports." *American Economic Review,* Proceedings, May 1980.

Churchill, Winston. *Memoirs of the Second World War.* Boston: Houghton Mifflin, 1959.

Clogg, Richard. "Troubled Alliance: Greece and Turkey." In *Greece in the 1980s,* ed. Richard Clogg. New York: St. Martin's Press, 1983.

Coffey, Peter, ed. *The Economic Policies of the Common Market.* London: Macmillan, 1979.

Conway, Patrick. "Decomposing the Determinants of Trade Deficits: Turkey in the 1970s." *Journal of Development Economics* 21, no. 2 (May 1986).

Cook, M. J. *Greeks in Ionia and the East.* London: Thames and Hudson, 1962.

Couloumbis, Theodore. *The United States, Greece and Turkey: The Troubled Triangle.* New York: Praeger, 1983.

―――. "The Question of Turkish Accession." *Athena,* November 1986.

Couloumbis, Theodore, John Petropoulos, and Harry Psomiades. *Interference in Greek Politics: An Historical Perspective.* New York: Pella, 1976.

Cowell, Alan. "Greek Bill Would Tax Church Land." *New York Times,* March 15, 1987.

―――. "Aegean Dispute Worsens Turkish-Greek Ties." *New York Times,* March 24, 1987.

―――. "Turks Finally Ask, Are We Europeans or What?" *New York Times,* May 27, 1987.

―――. "Turkey Admits Inroads by Kurdish Guerrillas." *New York Times,* October 22, 1987.

Cross, Doris, "The Unanswered Armenian Question." *New York Times,* March 26, 1980.

"Cyprus Leader Pledges Talks in Taking Office." *New York Times,* February 29, 1988, sec. A.

Davies, David G. *United States Taxes and Tax Policy.* Cambridge, Mass.: Cambridge University Press, 1986.

Davis, William. *A Short History of the Near East.* New York: Macmillan, 1937.

Day, John. *An Economic History of Athens under Roman Domination.* New York: Arno Press, 1973.

Dobb, C. H. *Democracy and Development in Turkey.* London: Euthen, 1979.

Ermin, Kenan. *Aphrodisias.* New York: Facts on File, 1986.

Evans, Lawrence. *United States Policy and the Partition of Turkey, 1914–1924.* Baltimore: Johns Hopkins University Press, 1965.

Feber, Barnaby. "Capital Flight Adds to Burden of Debtor Nations." *New York Times,* June 9, 1986.

Fenton, Charles. *The Apprenticeship of Ernest Hemingway.* New York: Farrar, Straus and Young, 1954.

Freris, A. F. *The Greek Economy in the Twentieth Century.* London: Croom Helm, 1986.

Gaspari, Elio. "Origins of the Debt Crisis." *New York Times,* November 7, 1983.

Georgakopoulos, Theodore. "Greece in the EEC: Intercountry Income Transfer." *Journal of Common Market Studies* 25, no. 2 (December 1986).

Gianaris, Nicholas V. "The Instability of the Incremental Capital-Output Ratio." *Socio-Economic Planning Sciences* 3 (August 1969).

―――. "International Differences in Capital-Output Ratios." *American Economic Review* 60, no. 3 (June 1970).

————. *Economic Development: Thought and Problems.* West Hanover, Mass.: Christopher Publishing House, 1978.

————. "Fiscal Policy: Greece and the EEC." *Spoudai* 15 (January-March 1980).

————. "Indirect Taxes: A Comparative Study of Greece and the EEC." *European Economic Review* 15 (1981).

————. *The Economies of the Balkan Countries: Albania, Bulgaria, Greece, Romania, Turkey, Yugoslavia.* New York: Praeger, 1982.

————. *The Province of Kalavryta: A Historical and Socioeconomic Review.* New York: National Herald, 1983.

————. *Greece and Yugoslavia: An Economic Comparison.* New York: Praeger, 1984.

Gilbert, G., and M. Mouillart. "E Dynamiki Ton Forologikon Domon Stis Hores tou OOSA" (The Dynamics of the Tax Structure in the Countries of the OECD). *Oikonomia kai Koinonia,* April 1981.

Glover, Terrot. *The Challenge of the Greeks and Other Essays.* New York: Macmillan, 1942.

Goddard, John. "Kayaks down the Nile." *National Geographic Magazine* 107, no. 5 (May 1955).

"Greece: European Tragedy." *Economist,* 286, no. 7272 (January 15–21, 1983).

Greek Government. *Statistiki Epetiris Dimosion Oikonomikon* (Statistical Yearbook of Public Finance), annual.

Haass, Richard N. "How to Keep Greece and Turkey Apart." *New York Times,* April 13, 1987.

Hackett, Clifford P. "How We've Corrupted Our NATO Allies." *New York Times,* October 16, 1987.

Halikias, Dimitris. *Money and Credit in a Developing Economy: The Case of Greece.* New York: New York University Press, 1978.

Haralampidis, Heraklis. *Naftilia kai Oikonomiki Anaptyxi* (Shipping and Economic Development). Athens: Center for Economic Research and Planning, 1986.

Harris, George. *Turkey: Coping with Crisis.* Boulder, Colo.: Westview Press, 1985.

Hendy, Michael. *Studies in the Byzantine Monetary Economy, c. 300–1450.* London: Cambridge University Press, 1985.

Hitiris, Theodore. *Trade Effects of Economic Association with the Common Market: The Case of Greece.* New York: Praeger, 1972.

Hoffman, George W. *The Balkans in Transition.* New York: D. Van Nostrand Co., 1963.

Howard, Harry N. *The Partition of Turkey: A Diplomatic History, 1913–1923.* New York: Howard Fertig, 1966.

————. *Turkey, The Straits and U.S. Policy.* Baltimore: Johns Hopkins University Press, 1974.

Howe, Marvine. "Turks, Angry at 'Passivity,' Mourn Slain Diplomats" *New York Times,* March 13, 1981.

————. "Turks Imprison Former Minister Who Spoke up on Kurd's Behalf." *New York Times,* March 27, 1981.

————. "Turkey Opens Campaign Against Kurdish Rebels." *New York Times,* April 1, 1981.

Ibrahim, Youssef. "New Pipelines Are Reducing Persian Gulf's Strategic Role." *New York Times,* October 7, 1987.

International League for the Rights and Liberation of Peoples. *A Crime of Silence: The Armenian Genocide.* London: Zed Books, 1985.

International Monetary Fund (IMF). *International Financial Statistics* (IFS), monthly.

International Financial Report (weekly, U. K.), various issues.

Kaltchas, Nicholas. *Introduction to the Constitutional History of Modern Greece.* New York: Columbia University Press, 1940.

Kamm, Henry. "Bulgarian-Turkish Tensions on Minority Rise." *New York Times*, October 4, 1987.

Keles, Rusel. "The Effects of External Migration or Regional Development in Turkey." In *Uneven Development in Southern Turkey*, ed. Ray Hudson and Jim Lewis. New York: Methuen, 1985.

Khorenatsi, Moses. *History of the Armenians.* Trans. Robert Thomson. Cambridge: Harvard University Press, 1978.

Kinnane, Derk. *The Kurds and Kurdistan.* London: Oxford University Press, 1964.

Kopits, George. "Turkey's Adjustment Experience, 1980–85." *Finance and Development* 24, no. 3 (September 1987).

Kostopoulos, T. *Beyond Capitalism toward Nomocracy.* New York: Praeger, 1986.

Krane, Ronald. *International Labor Migration in Europe.* New York: Praeger, 1979.

Krueger, Anne. *Turkey.* New York: National Bureau of Economic Research, 1974.

Krueger, Anne, and Baran Tuncer. "An Empirical Test of the Infant Industry Argument." *American Economic Review* 72, no. 5 (December 1982).

Kurkjian, Vahan. *A History of Armenia.* New York: Armenian General Benevolent Union of America, 1964.

Kyriakides, Stanley. *Cyprus: Constitutionalism and Crisis in Government.* Philadelphia: University of Pennsylvania Press, 1968.

Kyrou, Alexander. "Turkey's Militaristic Foreign Policy." *Greek Accent*, New York, September-October 1986.

Lader, Jeri, and Lois Whitman. "Turkish Hypocrisy on Ending Torture." *New York Times*, July 13, 1987.

Lampe, John, and Martin Jackson. *Balkan Economic History, 1550–1950.* Bloomington: Indiana University Press, 1982.

Levantis, J. A. *The Greek Foreign Debt and the Great Powers 1821–1898.* New York: Columbia University Press, 1944.

Lewis, Geoffrey. *Modern Turkey.* New York: Praeger, 1974.

Lewis, Stephen, Jr. *Taxation and Development.* New York: Oxford University Press, 1984.

Lowry, S. Todd. "Recent Literature on Ancient Greek Economic Thought." *Journal of Economic Literature* 17 (March 1979).

Mackenzie, Kenneth, and Orkun Akpinar. "Turkey's Privatization Program Picks Up Steam." *Wall Street Journal*, May 26, 1987.

Magnarella, Paul. *Tradition and Change in a Turkish Town.* New York: John Wiley and Sons, 1974.

Makinen, Gail. "The Greek Hyperinflation and Stabilization at 1943–1946." *Journal of Economic History* 156, no. 3 (September 1986).

McCarthy, Justin. *The Arab World, Turkey, and the Balkans (1878–1914).* Boston: G. K. Hall, 1982.

McGrew, William. *Land and Revolution in Modern Greece, 1800–1881.* Kent, Ohio: Kent State University Press, 1985.

McGury, William. "Turkey's Challenge to the Common Market." *Wall Street Journal*, December 3, 1986.

McNeill, William. *The Metamorphosis of Greece since World War II*. Chicago: University of Chicago Press, 1978.

Mehran, Hassanali. "External Debt Management." *Finance and Development* 23, no. 2 (June 1986).

Milanovic, Branko. *Export Incentives and Turkish Manufacturing Exports, 1980–1984*. Washington, D.C.: World Bank Publications, 1986.

Miller, William. *The Ottoman Empire and Its Successors 1801–1927*. New York: Octagon Books, 1966.

"More Problems Ahead." *Athena* 10, November 1986.

Munkman, C. *American Aid to Greece*. New York: Praeger, 1978.

Musgrave, Richard, and Peggy Musgrave. *Public Finance in Theory and Practice*. New York: McGraw-Hill, 1980.

Negreponti-Delivani, Maria. *Analysis tis Ellinikis Oikonomias* (Analysis of the Greek Economy). Athens: Papazisis, 1981.

Nyrop, Richard F., ed. *Turkey: A Country Study*. Washington, D.C.: American University, Foreign Area Studies, 1980.

O'Ballance, Edgar. *The Kurdish Revolt: 1961–1970*. Hamden, Conn.: Archon Books, 1973.

Organization for Economic Cooperation and Development (OECD). *Economic Surveys: Greece*. Paris: OECD Publications, annual.

———. *Economic Surveys: Turkey*. Paris: OECD Publications, annual.

———. *National Accounts*. Paris: OECD Publications, annual.

———. *Revenue Statistics of the OECD Member Countries*. Paris: OECD Publications, annual.

"Ozal Outlines Turkey's Problems and Aspirations." *Wall Street Journal*, May 26, 1987.

"Ozal Prepares to Reconquer Turkey." *Economist* 305, no. 7519 (October 10–16, 1987).

Paine, Suzanne. *Exporting Workers: The Turkish Case*. London: Cambridge University Press, 1974.

Papandreou, Andreas G. *Democracy at Gunpoint: The Greek Front*. New York: Doubleday, 1970.

Paxton, John. *The Developing Common Market*. 3d ed. London: Macmillan, 1976.

Pechman, Joseph, ed. *What Should Be Taxed: Income or Expenditure?* Washington, D.C.: Brookings Institution, 1980.

Pierce, Joe. *Life in a Turkish Village*. New York: Holt, Rinehart and Winston, 1964.

Pinkele, C., and Adamantia Polis, eds. *The Contemporary Mediterranean World*. New York: Praeger, 1983.

Pomfret, Richard. *Mediterranean Policy of the European Community*. New York: Macmillan, 1986.

Prest, Alan. "The Structure and Reform of Direct Taxation." *Economic Journal* 89, (June 1979).

———. *The Taxation of Urban Land*. Manchester, England: Manchester University Press, 1981.

Price, Philip. *A History of Turkey: From Empire to Republic*. London: Allen and Unwin, 1965.

Prinz, Joachim. *The Secret Jews*. New York: Random House, 1973.

Psomiades, Harry. "The Economic and Social Transformation of Modern Greece." *Journal of International Affairs* 19 (1965).

Raphael, Frederic. "Where History's Sweep Conquers the Visitor." *New York Times*, January 18, 1987.

Richter, Heinz. *British Intervention in Greece*. London: Merlin Press, 1986.

Rostow, W. W. *The World Economy: History and Prospects*. Austin: University of Texas Press, 1978.

Rousseas, Stephen. *The Death of a Democracy: Greece and the American Conscience*. New York: Grove Press, 1967.

Rustow, Dankwart, *Turkey: America's Forgotten Ally*. New York: Council on Foreign Relations, 1987.

Schevill, Ferdinand. *The History of the Balkan Peninsula*. Rev. ed. New York: Harcourt, Brace, 1933.

Seers, Dubley, and Contantine Vaitsos, eds. *Integration and Unequal Development: The Experience of the EEC*. New York: St. Martin's Press, 1980.

Shaw, Stanford. *History of the Ottoman Empire and Modern Turkey*. London: Cambridge University Press, 1976–1977.

Shinn, Rinn S., ed. *Greece: A Country Study*. Washington, D.C.: U.S. Government Printing Office, 1986.

Shoup, Carl, ed. *Fiscal Harmonization in Common Markets*. New York: Columbia University Press, 1967.

"The Sorrows of Armenia." *New York Times*, April 26, 1985.

Stanley, C. *Roots of the Tree*. London: Oxford University Press, 1936.

Stavrianos, Leften. *The Balkans since 1453*. New York: Holt, Rinehart and Winston, 1958.

———. *The Ottoman Empire: Was It the Sick Man of Europe?* New York: Holt, Rinehart and Winston, 1959.

———. *Balkan Federation*. Hamden, Conn.: Archon Books, 1964.

Stern, Lawrence. *Wrong Horse*. New York: New York Times Publishing Co., 1980.

Strarr, C. *The Economic and Social Growth of Early Greece: 800–500 B.C.* New York: Oxford University Press, 1977.

Taylor, Paul. *The Limits of European Integration*. New York: Columbia University Press, 1983.

Thornburg, Max, Graham Spry, and George Soule. *Turkey, An Economic Appraisal*. New York: Twentieth Century Fund, 1949.

Toutain, Jules. *The Economic Life of the Ancient World*. New York: Alfred A. Knopf, 1930.

Toynbee, Arnold. *The Western Question in Greece and Turkey*. New York: Howard Fertig, 1970.

Tsoukalis, Loukas. *The European Community and Its Mediterranean Enlargement*. London: Allen and Unwin, 1981.

"Turkey Says Its Planes Raided Kurdish Guerrilla Bases in Iraq." *New York Times*, March 5, 1987.

Ulusan, Aydin. *Political Economy of Income Distribution in Turkey*. New York: Holmes and Meiers, 1980.

United Nations. *Statistical Yearbook*, annual.

Vernadakis, Nikos. *Econometric Models for the Developing Economies: A Case Study of Greece*. New York: Praeger, 1978.

Vernon, Reymond. *Sovereignty at Bay: The Multinational Spread of U.S. Enterprises*. New York: Basic Books, 1971.

Vucinich, Wayne. *The Ottoman Empire: Its Record and Legacy*. New York: D. Van Nostrand Co., 1965.

Walstedt, Bertil. *State Manufacturing Enterprise in a Mixed Economy: The Turkish Case*. Baltimore: Johns Hopkins University Press, for the World Bank, 1980.

Weiker, Walter. *The Modernization of Turkey*. New York: Holmes and Meier, 1980.

Wicker, Tom. "Travels in the Ages." *New York Times,* October 1, 1987.

Wiles, Peter, and Alan Smith. "The Convergence of the CMEA on the EEC." In *The EEC and Eastern Europe,* ed. Avi Shlaim and George Yannopoulos. London: Cambridge University Press, 1978.

Wolff, Robert. *The Balkans in Our Time*. New York: W. W. Norton, 1967.

Woodhouse, Chris M. *Karamanlis: The Restorer of Greek Democracy*. Oxford: Clarendon Press, 1982.

World Bank. *Turkey: Industrialization and Trade Strategy*. Washington, D.C.: World Bank, 1982.

————. *World Development Report*. New York: Oxford University Press, for the World Bank, annual.

Zolotas, Xenophon. *International Monetary Issues and Development Policies*. Athens: Bank of Greece, 1977.

Index

About the Author

NICHOLAS V. GIANARIS earned his B.A. at the Graduate School of Economics and Business of Athens, his LL.B. at the University of Athens, and his M.A. and Ph.D. in economics at New York University. He has taught in the United States and abroad. At present he is professor and economics program coordinator at Fordham University, Lincoln Center, New York.

Dr. Gianaris is a member of the American Economic Association, Royal Economic Society (U.K.), Economic History Association, and American Association of University Professors. Listed in *American Men of Science* and similar volumes, he has also received the NYU Founders Award for scholarly achievements.

He has contributed a number of articles to both American and international economics publications, such as *American Economic Review, European Economic Review,* and *Socioeconomic Planning Sciences,* and has presented panel papers at symposia regarding the United States, Europe, and other regions. Parts of his first book, *Economic Development: Thought and Problems* (1978), were translated into French and Spanish by the International Monetary Fund for use in the IMF Institute's courses on financial analysis and policy. His second book, *The Economies of the Balkan Countries: Albania, Bulgaria, Greece, Romania, Turkey, Yugoslavia* (1982), was published by Praeger Publishers. His most recent book, *Greece and Yugoslavia: An Economic Comparison* (1984), was also published by Praeger.